Health and Physical Education

Health and Physical Education

J. C. Aggarwal

SHIPRA

(Reprinted no. of times, First Published 2005)

Rs 1400

ISBN: 978-93-91978-79-2

2025 Imp. PoD

Health and Physical Education

Published by:
SHIPRA PUBLICATIONS
LG 18-19, Pankaj Central Market
I.P. Ext., Patparganj, Delhi 110092, India
91 11 47322068; 9650028065, 9810522367
info@shiprapublication.com
www.shiprapublication.com

Preface

The memorable words of wisdom said by Swami Vivekananda should guide us in formulating and implementing our educational policies. "Be strong, my young friends, that is my advice to you. You will be nearer to Heaven through football than through the study of the '*Gita*'. You will understand Gita better with your biceps, your musles, a little stronger. Your will under the mighty strength of Krishna better with a little strong blood in you. You will understand the Upanishads better and the glory of the 'Atman', when your body stands firm on your feet and you feel yourselves as men."

It is rather not a happy state that in our educational institutions, it is usually considered that it is the sole concern of the physical education Teacher/Director to look after the health and physical education of the students. The sooner we get rid of this notion, the better it is. Every teacher is expected to pay adequate attention to this aspect. For instance, correct postures must be formed by the students from their earliest school stage. A nursery school teacher, thus can make a substantial contribution in this regard.

The book duly takes note of the emerging problems like AIDS, Drug Abuse, Smoking and Sex Education, etc.

Recommendations of several Committees and Commissions on Health and Physical Education are incorporated in the book.

In view of the vast and deep coverage of the various topics, it should prove of much assistance to all those engaged in the field of education, especially in-service and pre-service education of teachers.

The author extends his sincere thanks to the UN and its various agencies, for providing information on several topics. I am also grateful to authors for using any needed material for the book.

Suggestions for making this publication all the more useful would be thankfully received.

J.C. AGGARWAL

Contents

1

Concept of Health Education

1.1 SIGNIFICANCE OF HEALTH

It has been widely accepted that

When health is absent
Wisdom cannot reveal itself
Art cannot manifest
Science cannot develop
Strength cannot fight
Wealth becomes useless

And intelligence cannot be applied.

"A Vedic prayer says
May all human beings be happy
May all be without disease
May all witness auspicious sights
May none have to undergo suffering."

Charak, a renowned physician of ancient India has observed that health is vital for artistic, ethical, material and spiritual development of man.

Health is not only basic to leading a happy life for an individual but also necessary for all the productive activities of life.

Locke's famous saying 'a sound mind in a sound body' is true for all ages. Regarding the importance of health, Ben Johnson has stated, "O Health! Health! The blessing of the rich! The riches of the poor! Who can buy thee at too dear a rate, since there is no enjoying this world without thee." Similarly Herbert Spencer writes, "The preservation of health is a duty and a few seem conscious that there is a thing physical morality." The Secondary Education Commission has greatly stressed the importance of physical well-being in these words, "The physical welfare of the youth of the country should be one of the main concerns of the State, and any departure from the normal standards of physical well-being at his period of life may have serious consequences." Health education should form an integral part of education.

Hall has very emphatically stated, "A ton of knowledge bought at the expense of an ounce of health which is the expense most ancient and precious form of wealth and worth costs more than its value."

Carlyle in this regards points out, "We manufacture devils by the thousands because health is not the object of party politics."

Great seer Swami Vivekanand stresses the importance of well-built bodies in these words, "What India needs today is not the 'Bhagwadgita' but the foot-ball field."

W.M. Ryburn remarked, "We need in Indian education a general philosophy of physical education—we need a conception of education in which physical education takes it rightful place in which its vital importance is recognised."

Ben Johnson has observed, "O Health! The blessings of the rich! The riches of the poor! Who can buy the at too dear a rate, since there is no enjoying this world without thee."

1.2 RELATIONSHIP BETWEEN HEALTH AND SOCIO-ECONOMIC DEVELOPMENT

The relationship between socio-economic development and progress of health is extremely important. In fact an economy has a health component which has an important bearing on the overall economic development. Health not only affects socio-economic complex but is also affected by it.

Who would deny that a soldier who is not keeping good health can be expected to defend the frontiers of his country even if he is provided with the latest sophisticated weapons! Similarly who would deny that an unhealthy farmer with the best possible technological know-how would not succeed in producing the best that can be expected of him! It is equally true in the case of the child.

Poor health results in frustration in life. Likewise emotional disturbance has an adverse impact on the health.

Poor health hinders the development of mental faculties and vice versa.

Undoubtedly intellectual efficiency, mental alertness and physical agility, good health and productivity are interrelated.

A disease stricken individual can hardly hope to make progress in life.

Health is the pivot upon which an individual's life as well as the well-being of the community depends.

Good health is an essential condition for a purposeful existence. It lends joy to living. Health is a matter that affects not only each one of us as individuals but also the community in which we live. Good health enables us to perform at our best as individuals, as families, as communities and as a nation. Aptly there is a common saying that "Healthy people make a happy community."

1.3 MEANING AND CONCEPT OF HEALTH

Now let us understand the word 'health'. Health is not only freedom from sickness and disease but also freedom from anxiety and social and psychological tension.

According to World Health Organisation (WHO) (1948) health is defined as "a state of complete physical, mental and social well-being and not merely the absence of a disease or infirmity."

This definition of health was further updated in 1978 and now it includes "The ability to lead a socially and economically, productive life."

When we combine these two definitions, health is defined as "a state of complete physical, mental and social well-being and not merely the absence of a disease or infirmity. It is the ability to lead a socially and economically productive life."

According to J.F. Williams, "Health is the quality of life that enables an individual to live most and to serve best."

The First Five Year Plan stated, "Health is a positive state of well-being in which harmonious development of mental and physical capacities of the individuals lead to the enjoyment of a rich and fuller life. It implies adjustment of the individual with his total environment—physical and so-sound in body and mind."

W.A. Yeager has stated, "One's ideal of health should be the highest realization of physical, mental and spiritual possibilities rather than the mere freedom from diseases and deformities."

'*Webster New Collegiate Dictionary*' gives the meaning of health as, "the condition of being sound in body, mind or spirit, especially freedom from physical disease or pain."

1.4 MAIN ELEMENTS OF HEALTH OR CHARACTERISTICS OF A HEALTHY PERSON

From the above mentioned definitions, a healthy person is expected to possess in general the following qualities;

One: Absence of disease.

Two: Ability to work hard, with efficiency and enthusiasm.

Three: Ability to endure strain and stress.

Four: Cheerfulness

Five: Courage

Six: Freedom from anxiety.

Seven: Self-control and self-confidence

Eight: Sense of well-being

Nine: Wholesome mental attitude

Ten: Regularity in work

Important Characteristics of a Healthy Child:

1. The child is active and never listless.
2. The child does not tire easily.
3. The child's muscular control is coordinate to age.
4. Child's movements are quick and positive.
5. Child's eyes are bright and clear, alert and interested.
6. Child's hair is glossy.

7. Child is plump and not fat.
8. Child makes regular increases in height and weight which are in proper proportion to age and body build.
9. Child's flesh is firm.
10. Child's lips are moist and pink.
11. Child's appearance is good.
12. Child loves to play.
13. Child remains happy and cheerful.
14. The child enjoys food.

1.5 COMMUNITY HEALTH AND PERSONAL HEALTH

Personal health is directly linked with the community health. Health of a person is influenced by the environment and the community one lives in. A person may have clean personal habits, may eat balanced food and has a happy atmosphere at home but if the neighbours dump the garbage in open, waste water flows in open space, water supply is not clean, mosquitoes, houseflies and germs breed in the neighbourhood, a person cannot keep good health for a long time. Unhygienic personal habits of others create health problems for the whole community. Hence, it is important to have a healthy community and to understand the means to keep it healthy.

Community health care involves the provision of clean drinking water, efficient sewage disposal systems, green open spaces, medical centres and above all education to its people so that they are able to check health problems before they are aggravated. Some of the important services to be provided to keep the community healthy are:

(i) Establishment of health care services like primary health centres, district hospitals, community health centres, Medical Institutes, Medical Colleges, Regional Hospitals etc.
(ii) Provision of safe purified drinking water.
(iii) Agencies for proper disposal of garbage.
(iv) Prevention of harmful insect breeding sites.
(v) Awareness campaigns for vaccinations against number of infectious diseases like tuberculosis, diphtheria, whooping cough, tetanus, measles, hepatitis etc.
(vi) Provision of family planning advices and services.
(vii) Provision of medical care to school going children.
(viii) Prevention of food adulteration.
(ix) Health education.
(x) Management of Central and State Pollution Control Boards to check pollution.

1.6 MEANING OF HEALTH EDUCATION

In single words, health education is a process which enables an individual-child or an adult to understand 'why' and 'how' of matters relating to health.

According to Dr. Thomas Wood, "Health education is the sum of experiences, which favourably influence habits, attitudes and knowledge, relating to individual, community and social health."

Prof. Grouts states the meaning of health education as, "Health education is the translation of what is known about health into desirable individual and community behaviour pattern, by means of educational process."

In a broad sense, health education is a process which enables people to find out their health needs leading on to programme planning, utilising the available resources, modifying their health behaviour, breaking down the barriers, misconcepts, ignorance and prejudices regarding health after intelligent thoughtful consideration of the relevant health knowledge and enabling them to attain the optimum/the highest possible standard of health, by their own efforts.

1.7 OBJECTIVES OF HEALTH EDUCATION

The World Health Organisation (WHO) has formulated the following objectives of health education:

1. To ensure that health is valued as an asset in the community.
2. To equip the people with skills, knowledge and attitudes to enable them to solve their health problems by their own actions and efforts.
3. To promote the development and proper use of health services.

1.8 SCOPE OF HEALTH EDUCATION

The scope of health education is very wide. In fact it touches all dimensions of human life, namely personal life, school life and community life.

Health education is the combined and coordinated use of medical, social and educational measures for training and retraining the individual to the highest possible level of functional activity.

S.L. Goel in his book "*Health Care Administration*" has explained the scope of health education as well as interrelationship as shown in Fig. 1.1

Health education includes the following elements;

1. Food and its significance in the development of the body.
2. Significance of air, light, water etc. in health development.
3. Physical exercises.
4. Recreation, rest and sleep, etc.
5. Various ailment and diseases.
6. Emergency and first aid.
7. Domestic and community hygiene.
8. School health education programme
9. Mental hygiene
10. Sex hygiene.

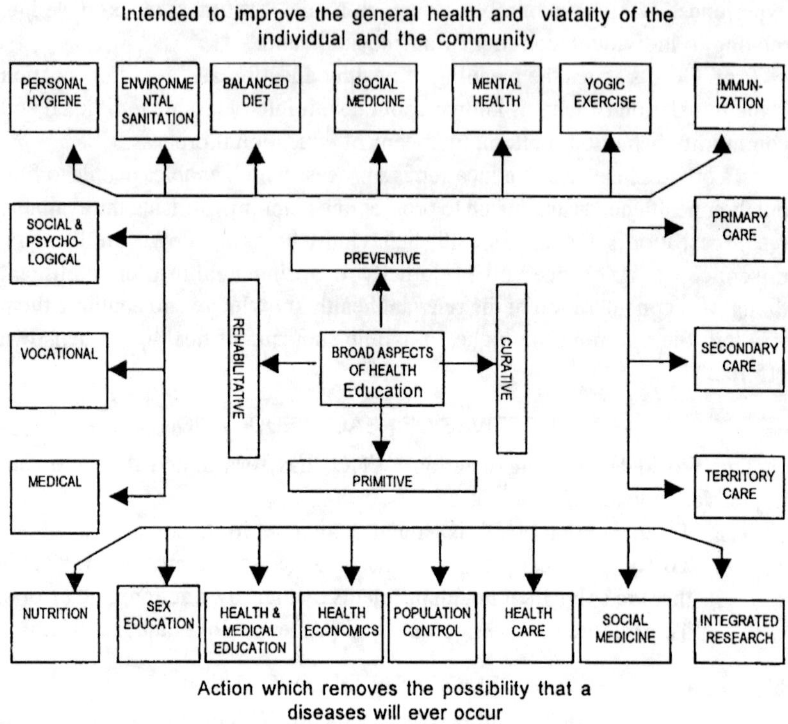

Fig. 1.1: Scope of Health Education and Interrelationship Aspects

1.9 HEALTH EDUCATION AND PHYSICAL EDUCATION

Health education and physical education are complementary forces leading to the total development of the individual, family, community and nation. Health education employs the media for acquisition of knowledge about living healthfully and the immediate participation in health practices. Physical education for these purposes employs the media of exercises, games, sports, dances etc.

Health education represents the sum of all experiences in school and elsewhere that favourably influence habits, attitudes and knowledge related to individual and community health.

Health education is a comprehensive term while physical education carries a limited scope. Physical education can be called one of the aspects of health education. Health education is the whole and physical education a part. J.B. Nash has very appropriately remarked, "Health and recreation are the results while physical education activities are the means."

Physical education is the concern of physical instructors and directors of physical education. On the other hand, health education is the work of teachers of hygiene and physiology, medical officers, physical training instructors, local bodies, municipal councils, panchayats etc.

1.10 PERSONAL AND SOCIAL ASPECTS OF HEALTH EDUCATION

Interrelatedness of Personal Aspects of Health Education: There is a very intimate relationship between personal aspects of health education and social aspects of health education. Both are complementary and supplementary. Each influences the other and is influenced in turn. Man is a social being and his individuality has little significance apart from society. Naturally therefore, personal and social aspects of health cannot altogether be separated. Nevertheless for making the subject more vivid, each aspect is dealt with separately to the extent it is possible to do so.

Personal Aspects of Health Education

Personal aspects of health education relate to issues like how to keep oneself in good health by paying attention to the following:

1. Cleanliness of the body, and of each of the organs, *viz.*, eyes, ears, hair, teeth etc.
2. Provision of necessary rest and sleep.
3. Provision of personal comfort through proper clothing, lighting, temperature, ventilation, etc.
4. Maintenance of good postures.
5. Provision of recreation and relaxation through hobbies etc.
6. Toning of various systems of the body-digestive system, nervous system, respiratory system, etc.
7. Provision of nutritious and balanced diet.
8. Provision of exercises.
9. Prevention of diseases in general and infectious diseases in particular.
10. Provision of medical examination.
11. Learning elementary rules of first aid.
12. Inculcation of habits that are beneficial and not hurtful in nature.

Social Aspects of Health Education

Broadly speaking following are the main social aspects of health education:

1. Improving Human Relations in Matters of Health.
2. Developing a Sense of Civic Responsibility.
3. Influencing and Educating Ignorant People.
4. Developing Proper Emotional Environment.
5. Rendering Health Service to the Community.

1. *Improving Human Relations in Matters of Health:* In order to become a healthy nation, we must ensure that all the agencies and individuals in the homes, schools and the community develop good human relations in matters of health.

2. *Developing a Sense of Civic Responsibility:* An appropriate programme of health education should make people conscious of unhealthy social behaviour like spitting anywhere, urinating anywhere, and every where, coughing and sneezing on other person's face, not isolating oneself when suffering from any infectious disease or throwing rubbish without any consideration for other's health.

3. *Influencing and Educating Ignorant People:* Health education programme of a school should influence the adults of the locality also. The clean, disciplined and healthful way of life imparted to children in the school and followed by them, should be helpful in influencing and educating the ignorant parents and other members of the community.

4. *Developing Proper Emotional Environment:* It should be the endeavour of the school personnel, the parents and the community to provide a suitable emotional environment so that it may have a conducive impact on child's health.

5. *Rendering Health Service to the Community:* Health camps and first aid services can be provided by the school during fairs etc.

1.11 GENERAL AIMS AND OBJECTIVES OF HEALTH EDUCATION IN SCHOOLS

Following are the aims and objectives of health education in schools:

1. To make the student realise the necessity of having good health.
2. To give information regarding health rules.
3. To develop healthy health habits among children.
4. To develop certain skills concerning health, e.g., training in first aid and etc.
5. To enable children to understand the educative value of sanitation, cleanliness and healthful living.
6. To develop a will to listen to rules relating to health.
7. To develop better human relationship in matters concerning health.
8. To acquaint children with the causes and remedies of general diseases.
9. To influence parents and other adults to better habits and attitudes through the health programme of school and to make the school an effective agency for the promotion of the social aspects of health education in the family and community as well as the school itself.
10. To take precautionary and corrective measures against contamination and spread of diseases.
11. To take curative measures like medical check up of students.
12. To develop and promote emotional and mental health of the students.

1.12 SPECIFIC OBJECTIVES OF HEALTH EDUCATION AT DIFFERENT STAGES

The guidelines and syllabi formulated by the NCERT in 2001 list the following objectives under the caption 'The Art of Healthy Living'.

I. Specific Objectives at the Primary Stage (Class I to V)

1. To develop proper regular habits and attitudes to meet the natural needs of the body.
2. To know and understand the functions of the different parts/organs of the body and develop habits to keep them clean.
3. To develop awareness and sensitivity towards the immediate environment and understand the interdependence between humans and the environment.
4. To develop physical, mental and emotional well-being through 'yoga' and games.

II. Specific Objectives of Health Education at the Upper Primary Stage (Class V to VIII)

1. To enable the students understand the meaning and importance of being healthy.
2. To enable the students identify factors and conditions influencing their own health and that of others.
3. To enable the students recognize common, personal, family and community health problems and seek help from teachers and parents to solve them.
4. To enable the students acquire healthy practices relating to personal health, environmental health, exercise, rest, recreation, relaxation, sleep, posture, safety, eating and serving food.
5. To enable the students take care of body-parts, especially, the sense organs.
6. To enable the students consult a physician.
7. To enable the students acquire healthy practices of community living and getting along with others.
8. To enable the students help parents in the case of younger brothers and sisters to protect and promote their health.
9. To enable the students learn about human body, changes that take place while growing up from a boy to a man, and from girl to woman and take measures to stay healthy.
10. To develop in the students skills in providing first-aid in athletic and other common childhood injuries that occur in the home, school and outside the home and school.
11. To enable the students know about qualified health functionaries practising in the community to seek help when needed.
12. To enable the students develop organic fitness, normal sense organs and efficient organic systems.
13. To help the students cultivate habits of engaging in appropriate exercises so that immediate and future health needs will be met.
14. To develop student's neuro – muscular skills and promote the ability to perform work with ease and grace.
15. To develop attitudes of cooperation, good sportsman and fair play

16. To prepare students for making a worthwhile use of leisure time by acquiring knowledge of sports for the purpose of participating and observing, appreciating and enjoying them.

III. Specific Objectives of Health Education at Secondary Stage (Class IX and X)

1. To bring the overall awareness of values and to inculcate among students the desired habit and attitudes towards health and to raise their health status.
2. To make the pupils physically, mentally and emotionally fit and to develop their personal and social qualities that will help them to be good human beings.
3. To identify personal, family and community health problems and acquire relevant scientific knowledge and information to prevent and control these problems to stay healthy.
4. To take action, individually and collectively to protect and promote.
   (i) their own health
   (ii) health of their family members
   (iii) health of those around them in the community seeking help when required from valuable community resources.
5. To promote improved preventive and promotive self-care behaviour in the families and in the community.
6. To develop awareness of HIV, AIDS and drugs abuse in the community.
7. To develop an awareness regarding the importance of physical fitness and organic efficiency in individual and social life.
8. To develop awareness of the importance of self-defence and self-dependence.
9. To develop awareness of good posture so that one may strive to maintain a good posture.
10. To enable an individual to lead an enthusiastic and active life.

IV. Specific Objectives of Health Education at the Senior Secondary Stage (Class XI and XII)

1. To give students desirable knowledge about the importance of 'yogic' exercises as well as their relationship with health education programme.
2. To give students sufficient knowledge and training in first aid.
3. To give students desirable knowledge about marriage and sex
4. To enable students understand the importance of clean environment, environmental pollution and the ways and means of their prevention.
5. To enable students understand the population dynamics.
6. To enable students understand the significance of small family size.
7. To enable students understand the harmful effects of smoking and drug abuse etc.
8. To enable students acquire knowledge of various communicable diseases and to be able to protect them.

9. To enable the students understand the importance of community participation in health promotion.
10. To develop among students awareness of HIV and AIDS.
11. To develop among students awareness of specific adolescence issues influencing health.
12. To make students know about the functioning of various organisations working for the maintenance and promotion of health.
13. To enable students understand how rapid changes in information and communication technology (ICT) have influenced health aspects.

Objectives of Introducing Health and Physical Education at the Elementary Teachers' Training

1. To enable the teacher trainee to plan, organise and conduct activities and practices directly relating to the life style of children in order to make them health conscious.
2. To enable the teacher-trainee acquire knowledge of various communicable diseases and to be able to protect them.
3. To enable the teacher trainee arrange health competition and inculcate sportsman spirit.
4. To enable the teacher trainee appreciate the cultural heritage of India in the area of 'Health and Physical Education' especially in relation to Yoga.

Factors Affecting Health

There are number of factors that affect the health of a person which in turn affect the community. Given below are the four important factors necessary for good health:

1. *Physical well-being:* It refers to physical fitness of an individual at every stage of life. It results from eating the right kind of food in sufficient amount along with doing exercise to keep the body fit. A person should have adequate strength and stamina to carry out daily activities. The person should feel a sense of well-being. Thus it includes the following main elements:

(i) Nutrition
(ii) Exercise and relaxation
(iii) Habits

2. *Mental and emotional well-being:* It refers to the tensions, worries, emotions such as hatred, fear, love or anxiety that affect the health. An individual should be mentally strong and able to handle the emotions. A mentally depressed person develops physical troubles also. On the other hand a healthy mind helps to overcome obstacles and becomes physically strong too.

3. *Social well-being:* A socially healthy person has many qualities like tolerance, helpfulness, caring, pleasant and affectionate attitude. The social well-being of community depends upon the broad-mindedness, thoughtfulness and social security of its members. Social life influences the physical and mental life of the persons and vice-versa.

4. *Spiritual well-being:* Due to stress and strains of modern life, it is very important to consider this aspect of health also. Moral values, ethics and meditation are some ways to attain spiritual well-being. Positive attitude and strong faith in one's capabilities along with meditation or prayers help in gaining the inner strength.

Favourable and Unfavourable Factors/Conditions Affecting Health

	Favourable	*Unfavourable*
1.	Good heredity	Poor heredity
2	Healthful and safe living conditions	Pollution and unhygienic conditions
3.	Optimal nutrition	Deficient nutrition
4.	Adequate exercise	Lack of exercise
5.	Play opportunities	Lack of play opportunities
6.	Optimism	Pessimism
7.	Recreational facilities	Lack of recreational facilities
8.	Regulated discipline	Over – protective or over – strict discipline
9.	Desirable health practices	Unhealthy behaviour
10.	Emotional maturity	Tension
11.	Friendly and cheerful environment	Choking environment
12.	Fun and humour	Boredom
13.	Adequate medical care	Inadequate medical care

2

School Health Programme

2.1 IMPORTANCE

Since health plays an important role in effective learning, development of all faculties of the child, his happiness and success in life, it is very important to have a well thought-out and skilfully implemented school health programme. The present day school is concerned with the many-sided development of the child. Like other programmes of intellectual development, school health programme must form an integral part of the school programme. It is as important as any other school programme. Its neglect as is the case of traditional educational programme, is fraught with serious consequences. Now we need a philosophy, sociology and psychology of health programme to highlight school health programmes.

With the increasing possibilities of spread of contagious and communicable diseases among children, the role and importance of school health programme would assume all the more importance. An awareness of HIV and AIDS has to be provided to them.

2.2 MEANING AND CONCEPT

According to a report of the Committee on Terminology in School Health Education in America, the school health programme is defined as "the school procedures that contribute to the maintenance and improvement of the health of pupils and school personnel including health services, healthful living and health education."

H.F. Kilander defines school health programme as, "School health programme is the composite of procedures, used in school health services, healthful school living and health education, to promote health among students and other school personnel. This programme is closely related to physical education and education of the handicapped children."

2.3 OBJECTIVES

The "*National Curriculum Framework for School Education*" formulated by the NCERT in 2000 envisages the following objectives of school health programme:

1. It should develop desirable understanding, attitudes and practices with regard to health, nutrition and sanitation.
2. It should help the learners develop an awareness about the health and sanitation at the community level.
3. It should enable the students to improve health status of the self, family and the community.
4. It should promote healthful living.
5. It should develop an awareness of the new problems like HIV/AIDS.
6. It should enable the adolescents to understand the specific problems of this stage.
7. It should enable to students the understand the nature of population dynamics and its implications for health.
8. It should determine the health status of the learner through health examination.
9. It should provide wholesome school environment.
10. It should include suitable learning activities on health matters.
11. It should provide for appropriate guidance and counselling on health matters.
12. It should enable the students to understand sex matters during adolescence.
13. It should enable the learners to study suitable self-instructional material in this regard according to age groups.

2.4 CHARACTERISTICS

E.B. Johns has mentioned the following characteristics of the school health programme:

1. Health education is an integral part of the general education of all students.
2. Health education is an integral part of the school curriculum.
3. Health needs of the learners is the starting point of providing experiences that enable them to develop their abilities for action towards improved individual and group health.
4. Health programme should give consideration to student needs as they relate to dental, medical, nutritional and psychiatric activity.
5. Health eduation programme is not confined to learners only but it also extends beyond the school and college to the home and the community and into adult life.
6. School health programme needs to be supplemented by community agencies.
7. The conduct of the total school health programme requires the talent of many health and education personnel, working together in a cooperative manner to achieve common goals.
8. The individual/learner has the responsibility for the creation and maintenance of conditions which contribute to his health and to the health of others.
9. Group action is important in motivating the learner/learners to solve his/their health problems.

10. For providing the required personnel, materials and equipment to achieve the goals of health education, adequate financial support is necessary.
11. Special methods of evaluation would be needed to find out the adequacy of health education.

2.5 SCOPE

School health programme as observed by National Curriculum Framework for School Education is concerned with the total health of the learner and the community. Its scope, therefore, is very wide. School health programme is an integral part of general education. It includes all such instruction that enlightens a student about activities and functions contributing to preservation, promotion and restoration of health. By means of a health education programme the spread of diseases in the school-going children can be checked and their eradication can also be attempted. A thorough knowledge of health rules underlines the needs of the study of anatomy and also the symptoms of common diseases of children. Practical knowledge of causes and diagnosis is equally essential. School health education also includes knowledge about the environment, equipments and routine of the schools as well.

Components/Scope of School Health Programme

(1) *Healthful Living or Health Protection*

1. This includes physical environment of the school.
   - (i) Health and sanitation of the school plant
   - (ii) Suitable light and ventilation
   - (iii) Drinking water and toilet facilities
   - (iv) Cleanliness
   - (v) Appropriate furniture
2. Suitable emotional environment
3. Suitable Social environment

(2) *Health Instruction*

1. Formal instruction on health matters.
2. Incidental instruction on health matters
3. Correlated instruction on health matters

(3) *Health Services*

- (i) Health/medical examination.
- (ii) Follow-up programme on health examination
- (iii) Provision of school clinic
- (iv) Protective measures
- (v) First Aid and emergency care
- (vi) Special care for exceptional children
- (vii) Control of communicable diseases
- (viii) Nutritional services like mid-day meals
- (ix) Guidance and counselling services
- (x) Health examination of school staff

2.6 ORGANISATION OF SCHOOL HEALTH EDUCATION PROGRAMME

Meaning

Organisation of school health education programme implies the practical measures which the school takes to ensure that the system of work or mechanism which it uses will be of the greatest possible assistance in fulfilling objectives of health education.

Organisation may be functionally defined as an organised body or system of structure or arrangement or framework which is used for ensuring unity of effort, efficiency, goodwill, harmonious relations and appropriate use of resources.

Organisation of school health programme may be compared to a lens that brings everything about the school health system into focus.

Changing Concept

In view of the rapid changes in the society in all areas of life, organisation of school health programme also needs corresponding changes. The old concepts and principles are now fading into insignificance. New challenges in health matters have emerged which demand new organisation.

Constitution of School Health Education Programme Committee

In every school a committee may be constituted with Principal as the chairman and Physical Education Teacher/Health Education Teacher as its convenor. The Committee may also include one representative of PTA, Science Teacher, School Doctor/Nurse and representative of the local Health Department. The Committee would study the needs, purposes and procedures essential to the development of health education programme and to set the necessary policy. It is also expected to play an important role in impressing upon all concerned with the education of the child to attend to the health needs of the students and maintaining accuratic records in this regard.

The Committee is expected to perform two main functions: (I) Organisation of the school health education programme (ii) Supervision of the school health education programme. Of course, both these functions are supplementary and complementary and therefore, should go side by side.

Supervision includes all the activities relating to the health education programme.

On certain occasions supervision may be done by the Principal/Head of the institution assisted by a team consisting of members not associated with the school Health Education Committee.

Components of Supervision of School Health Education Programme

1. Supervision of school complex. This comprises:
   (a) Cleanliness of school building

(b) Cleanliness of school play-ground.

(c) Timely repairs and maintenance of school classrooms, laboratories, etc.

2. Supervision of school equipment to ensure that it is in proper working order and is not prone to injuries.
3. Supervision of the school furniture to ensure that it has no adverse effect on the health of the students.
4. Supervision of the school time-table to ensure that it does not cause fatigue.
5. Supervision of the physical conditions in the library and reading material to ensure that it is not damaged by insects etc. Elements of adequate light and air also to be kept in view.
6. Supervision of the lavatories and urinals to ensure that they are always kept clean.
7. Supervision of the school canteen to ensure that eatables are of the requisite standard and are kept in hygienic conditions.
8. Supervision of the postures of the students.
9. Supervision of drinking water.
10. Supervision of the general sanitation of the school.
11. Supervision of the school dispensary.

School Health Education Programme Convener/Coordinator

The Physical Education Teacher of the school should be the convener of the school health Education Programme. He is in a very strategic position to perform the work of coordination. He comes into close contact with a large number of students in a formal as well as in an informal way. Therefore, he is in a better position to understand the health problems of the students.

Functions of the Physical Education Teacher as the Convenor of the Health Committee

(1)	(2)	(3)	(4)	(5)	(6)	(7)	(8)
Conven-ing meetings of the School Health Education Progra-mme Commi-ttee	Planning and Coordina-ting School Health Education Progra-mmes	Implemen ting School Health Education Progra-mmes	Training Students in Health Education	Guiding students in the selection of physical activities, athletics and games, suiting their aptitudes and abilities	Supervisi ng School Health Education Progra-mmes	Maintaing records	Evaluat-ing

Role of the Teachers

Teachers' role is not confined to the intellectual development of the students. They are concerned with the all round development of the students. They must appreciate that there is no element which does not involve health of the students. In their daily routine, they should attend to the postures of the students, and cleanliness of the school premises. They should render all possible cooperation to the School Health Education Programme Committee.

Role of the Head of the School

The head of the school is the key figure in all type of school work, including health education programme. His important functions relating to school health education programme are:

1. It is generally observed that the health aspect of the students is the one of the most neglected areas in the entire school programme. It is not uncommon to find that periods devoted to physical and health education in the school programme are utilised for academic work pertaining to school subjects. Physical education is considered something as 'extra'. This attitude has to be removed from the minds of all concerned. The initiative for this must come from the head of the school. He must develop the philosophy of health and physical education. Health education programme must be treated as an integral part of the school programme.
2. He should constitute the School Health Education Committee.
3. He has the responsibility of helping the members of the staff understand the importance of 'shared responsibility' for pupil's health and physical growth and development.
4. He has the responsibility of interpreting the programme of health education services to the school and the community.
5. He has the responsibility of providing in – service training facilities in health and physical education to teachers including the physical education teacher to acquire greater knowledge, attitudes and skills.
6. He must ensure that requisite resources for health education are made available.
7. He must ensure that the periods allotted for physical and health are utilised for this purpose.
8. He should establish liaison with local health education authorities.
9. He must ensure that the work of health education is not confined to physical education teachers. It is the work of all teachers.
10. Due importance must be given to the status of physical education teacher. He should not be treated as a '*danda* teacher' *i.e.* 'teacher with rod'?-*i.e.* a teacher whose sole responsibility is to maintain discipline through the use of physical force.

2.7 IMPROVEMENT OF SCHOOL HEALTH EDUCATION PROGRAMME: SUGGESTIVE GUIDELINES

Report of the School Health Committee

The School Health Committee was appointed by the Government of India in February1960 under the chairmanship of Shrimati Renuka Ray to assess the standard of health and nutrition of school children and suggest ways and means of improving them.

Terms of Reference: (a) To examine the present position of school health programme in the country in all its aspects (excluding physical education, games and sports), e.g. prevention of diseases, medical care and follow-up service, nutrition, health, education, healthy environment, etc. of the students at all stages of education and to suggest: (i) further survey of studies if required; and (ii) how the work of various agencies such as medical, social and welfare associations can be coordinated to assist in the promotion of health of school children.

(b) To examine studies and surveys so far made to assess the nutritional standard of school children and to indicate: (i) further survey of studies needed in any specific areas; (ii) to give concrete suggestions to institute appropriate measures to improve standards of nutrition among school children recommending, inter alia, ways and means for financing and organising such a programme.

(c) To examine and recommend the possibility of entrusting Primary Health Centres and other organisations for conducting a comprehensive and realistic school health programme in association with the local education administration. The recommendations should include measures to develop an effective school medical service suitable to the country.

(d) To examine the present facilities available for promoting nutritional standards of pre-school children and to suggest practical measures to improve the present position.

Major Recommendations

1. *School health services:* (i) All children should be provided with school health services.

(ii) The functions of the school health services should be the provision of health measures both preventive and curative. These should include the detection and treatment of defects and the creation and maintenance of a hygienic environment in and around the school.

(iii) All newly admitted children should have medical examination first and then again after four years, as the limited facilities available at present do not permit medical examination at frequent intervals.

(iv) Prevention and control of communicable diseases in schools should be the responsibility of public health authorities.

(v) Emphasis should be laid on compulsory primary and revaccination against smallpox immediately. Immunization against diphtheria, whooping cough and tetanus should be made compulsory in the immediate future.

(vi) With adequate training in health education and school health services, it should be possible for the teachers to undertake certain functions connected with school health services such as: (a) observation of children with a view to spot out any deviations from normal health; (b) recording of height and weight and simple testing of vision and hearing; (c) maintaining of health records of children; and (d) giving first-aid.

2. *School meal:* (i) The primary aim of the school meal programme should be to improve health and encourage sound dietary habits among children.

(ii) The school meal should be based on cheap nutritions and locally available foods. A sample menu may comprise a minimum of: cereals and millet:-2.5 oz.: pulses-1 oz.: non-leafy vegetables-1 oz.: oil-¼ : and condiments and salts.

(iii) Every school should be provided with protected water supply and facilities for drainage; sanitary environment; facilities for storage; preparation and distribution of food; adequate space for feeding of children; and sanitary disposal of garbage.

(iv) It is necessary that the Government should support the school meal programme besides the contribution of the community at the rate of 50 per cent of the total cost.

3. *Pre-school child:* (i) A comprehensive health and welfare service for pre-school children should be introduced.

(ii) Services of 'Balwadis', 'Mahila Samitis', maternity and child welfare centres, health centres, clinics and nursery schools, the pre-primary schools, paediatric centres of hospitals and social welfare and similar organisations should be utilised for the distribution of milk to pre-school children.

4. *School health education:* (i) Health education should be included as a part of general education in the primary, middle and secondary schools.

(ii) The State Administration should take immediate steps to publish text-books on health education and to have health lessons included in other appropriate text-books.

5. *Training, studies and research:* (i) In teacher training programmes, health education and school health should be a required part of training. The teacher should have the knowledge of the growth and development of children, personal health, community health, school health practices and methods of health education.

(ii) For the teachers who are already in service, special short term courses should be organised by the local school organisations with the technical assistance from the health personnel.

(iii) Future school health and school meal policies and programmes should be developed from the results obtained through scientific surveys and studies.

Studies and research are quite essential for making school health programme efficient, effective and economical.

6. *School environment:* (i) School buildings should be simple, safe, attractive and sanitary.

(ii) Every school building in urban areas, where public water supply is available, should have water supply connection and adequate number of taps. In rural areas, an independent water supply system is desirable for each school.

(iii) In urban areas wherever drainage facilities exist, these should be extended to all schools. In rural areas, drains should be constructed for the removal of waste water.

(iv) The sale of food by hawkers in and around the school should be prohibited.

7. *School health administration:* (i) At the Centre, there should be National School Health Council. Such a Council will facilitate cooperation and coordination of many individuals and groups that are concerned with the health of the children.

(ii) Each State should have a State Council of School Health. The Director of Education and the Director of Health Services should alternatively be Secretary and Joint Secretary of the Council.

(iii) At district level, School Health and School Meal Committees should be set up as sub-committees of the District Development Councils.

(iv) The district health and education organisations should be strengthened appropriately to plan, implement and supervise this additional work.

Summing Up: Adequate attention has not been accorded to these suggestions. Progress is slow. Still a large number of schools including many pubic schools do not have adequate health facilities.

3

Health Instruction

3.1 MEANING AND IMPORTANCE

Health instruction may be defined as the process of promoting understanding health and observing desirable health practices. Provision of a healthy environment and health services in a school alone cannot serve all the health needs of the students. It is, therefore, very important to understand the significance of health instruction.

Theory and practice of health instruction and practice are equally important.

In view of the important role that health instruction plays in the growth and development of child, it should be made an integral part of regular teaching programme.

For the protection, preservation and promotion of health, a well organised programme of health instruction is very important.

3.2 MAIN AIMS AND OBJECTIVES

Important aims and objectives of health instruction are:

1. *Setting up standards:* The school has to set up certain standards of health for all concerned to follow these. Appropriate health laws and principles of health must be followed.
2. *Developing scientific knowledge:* Health instruction is needed to acquaint the students with the scientific basis of health protection and promotion.
3. *Developing scientific attitude:* Health instruction promotion is intended to inform the students to conduct themselves according to recognised scientific knowledge.
4. *Acquainting the students with healthful behaviour:* The health instruction aims at informing the students of the characteristics of healthful behaviour.
5. *Acquainting the students with the harmful effects of superstition*: Health instruction informs the students that there is a cause of every disease and there is a possible scientific cause. '*Tona jadu*' and superstitions have no place in removing diseases.

6. *Inculcating healthy habits in students:* The health instruction should inform the students to what good health habits are—for instance, washing hands before taking meals.
7. *Undertaking proper exercises*: Students need to be informed of the usefulness of regular exercise.
8. *Acquainting students with diseases*: The health instruction aims at developing knowledge about the common diseases, their causes, symptoms and remedies etc.
9. *Training in different types of health and physical exercises:* The formal instruction is mostly devoted to this end.
10. *Disseminating health knowledge among parents:* The aim of health instruction is to enlighten the parents also on health matters so that they take proper care of the health of the students.

(see also chapter 1)

3.3 TYPES OF HEALTH INSTRUCTION

Types of Health Instruction

(1)	(2)	(3)
Formal Health Instruction	**Incidental Health Instruction**	**Correlated Health Instruction**
Formal health instruction implies teaching of a specified health course	During personal contact with the students, the teachers get several opportunities to give health instruction.	Correlated Health Instruction can be imparted while teaching various school subjects. This implies correlating the subject being taught with health matters.

3.4 ROLE OF THE TEACHERS

All the teachers of the school need to be made conscious of health issues. It must be accepted that the health should be the concern of all teachers. It is not the concern of the physical education teacher, school doctor or the teacher teaching Home Science or any allied subject. Teachers get several opportunities of correlating health information with their teaching subjects. They can also provide health instruction through informal ways.

The class teacher and the school health education instruction: The functions of the classroom in health instruction and health education programme are many and varied. He can also inform the students of the ways and means of creating and maintaining healthful environment in the classroom.

The role of the art teacher in health instruction: He can teach several aspects of health instruction like postures, spreading of diseases etc. by preparing posters and cartoons etc.

3.5 HEALTH NEEDS OF CHILDREN AND HEALTH INSTRUCTION

Health Needs of Children and Health Instruction

(1)	(2)	(3)
Health Needs and Health Instruction at the Primary Stage	Health Needs of the child and Health Instruction at the Middle Stage	Health Needs of the Child and Health Instruction at the Secondary Stage

3.6 HEALTH NEEDS OF THE CHILD AT THE PRIMARY STAGE HEALTH INSTRUCTION AND ITS CONTENTS

A. Health Instruction in Classes I and II should

1. inform the child how to develop regular habits and attitudes to carry out his own daily routines relating to morning natural calls, thirst and hunger, etc.
2. acquaint the child with the functions of the different parts of the body and develop habits how to keep them clean *i.e.* teaching how to keep their hands, feet, eyes, nose, ears and hair clean and also to acquaint him with the importance of developing the habit of having a bath everyday.
3. acquainting the child with the rules of the school to meet their natural needs as per the given school conditions *i.e.* taking lunch during lunch hours of school.
4. enable the child to identify the factors which influence the cleanliness of their surrounding and to keep it neat and clean.
5. acquaint the child with the necessary information of participating in activities for keeping classroom and school clean through collective efforts.
6. enable the child to understand the necessity of participating happily in games and sports.
7. acquaint the child with a few simple yoga exercises.
8. to enable the child to understand the merits of taking part in group P.T., group songs.
9. enable the child to understand the importance of taking care of different things inside and outside to school surroundings.
10. enable the child to understand the importance of avoiding spoiling public places, e.g. roads, playgrounds, libraries, historical buildings and places of prayers, etc.

B. Health Needs of the Students at the Primary Stage (Class III to V) and Health Instruction

Health instruction at this stage of primary education should:

1. inform the child how to keep his clothes, house, school and environment clean as well as in order.
2. acquaint the child how to utilise the services of the primary health centres for meeting his health needs
3. acquaint the child with the necessary precautions to be taken against diseases.
4. acquaint the child with the need and methods of taking the precautionary measures related to health and cleanliness of homes, family and society at large.
5. enable the child to understand the significance of becoming sensitive towards his immediate surrounding and keeping him neat and clean.
6. enable the child to understand the significance of loving their environment.
7. enable the child to understand the need to shed all inhibitions and take interest and enjoy participating in various group activities for keeping the school surroundings clean and beautiful.
8. enable the child to practise simple yoga exercises which he has learnt in their daily routine.

Topics of Health Instruction at the Primary Stage

R.C. Havel and E.W. Seymour have suggested the following topics at this stage. It may be remembered that health instruction at this stage is primarily the responsibility of the class teacher. Basically it will be in the form of experiences:

Class I-II-(i) Cleanliness (ii) Safety (iii) Diet (iv) Dental Hygiene (v) Clothing.

Class III-V-(i) Play and Exercise (ii) Rest and Sleep (iii) Eye Hygiene (iv) Hearing (v) Postures.

(Note: Objectives of Health Instruction: See Chapter 1)

3.7 HEALTH INSTRUCTION AT THE UPPER PRIMARY STAGE/MIDDLE STAGE AND CONTENTS (CLASSES VI TO VIII)

Considerations in Preparing the Subject Matter of Health Instruction at the Middle Stage

According to the NCERT Guidelines (2001), following are the considerations in the selection of health instructional material at this stage.

1. The term 'Health Education' includes knowledge of health, science and recreational activities.
2. All the programmes of health instruction are for all students.
3. It should be incumbent on every student to participate in all programmes of health instruction.

4. Participation in health instruction and health education programme should get preference over competitions.
5. Health instruction should cover a wide range of subject-matter and activities so that each student can participate according to his/her interest and needs.
6. Health instruction should not involve activities which can be organised by only selected schools.
7. Content in health instruction syllabus should be meaningfully related to the pupils' environment and life.
8. There can be some overlapping between topics under health instruction and science. To avoid this, the science syllabus may be studied before formulating health syllabus.
9. Community involvement should be initiated at all levels in providing various resources. For this Panchayat should be approached.

Objectives of Health Instruction at the Middle Stage (*See* Chapter 1).

Outlines of Syllabus for Class VI to VIII

- Meaning of Health: Physical, Mental, Emotional and Social
- Environmental Hygiene
- Growth and Development
- Food and Nutrition
- Family and Health
- Communicable Diseases
- Prevention of Using Harmful Products
- Safety, First Aid and Home Nursing
- Civil Defence (Class III and VIII)

Contents of Health Instruction: Syllabi at Class VI to VIII

Class VI

- Meaning and importance of health and health education.
- Nutrition and its meaning, nutrients and their functions, deficiency, diseases and their prevention by taking low-cost food items rich in specific nutrients available locally, cooking practices to prevent loss of nutrients, indigenous and modern ways to preserve food, practices related to food hygiene that preserve and promote health, beliefs and superstitions that may influence health adversely.
- Environmental condition in school, home and community, conducive to health promotion-sanitary surroundings, safe-drinking water, sunshine and fresh air to play and work in, proper drainage, adequate light and ventilation.
- Role of individual; official and non-official agencies to promote community health.
- Individual differences in the growth of boys and girls-make them aware that the body changes during growth and development are natural.

Class VII

- Practices that promote health—keeping body and surroundings clean; keeping balance between work, play, recreation, relaxation, rest and sleep; maintaining good posture; protection against weather; following regular habits of eating, sleeping and elimination; following safety rules in the home, school and community to prevent accidents, practice and good manners approved by family, school and community.
- Organs of body that help it to get rid of body waste, chemical control of body over its own functions.
- Growing up from a boy to a man and from a girl to a woman.
- Characteristics of a mentally healthy person.
- Need of family; personal rights, privileges and responsibilities of family members that are to be mutually respected; ways and means to promote healthy family relationships.
- First – aid related to common accidents met by school children and their younger brothers and sisters.

Class VIII

- Building blocks of human body, structure and functions of various types of body cells, characteristics of body cells.
- Human reproduction: care during pregnancy; low birth weight (LBW children; factors responsible for LBW; importance of mother's milk for proper growth and health of the newborn; feeding and weaning practices and their influence on a child's health; child care practices to protect the child from diseases and to ensure proper growth and development.
- Sense organs; their structure and functions; care of skin, nose, eye, ears, tongue to enable them to discharge their functions properly.
- Communicable diseases – how they travel from a sick person to a healthy person and specific measures to prevent diseases transmitted through a particular mode of transmission; individual and community measures to prevent disease: sanitary disposal of waste, use of latrines for defecation; avoiding indiscriminate spitting, prevention of contamination of food and water, timely immunization against preventable diseases, vaccination of dogs and care of pets; anti-fly, anti-mosquito and anti-rodent measures; sewage disposal; community water supply; proper drainage, construction of compost pits and soakage pits; disinfection of wells, going to a qualified medical practitioner for consultations.
- Pollution—types of pollution; influence of various types of pollution on human health; role of individual, community and Government for prevention of various types of pollution.
- Harmful effects of self-medication and misuse of drugs, alcohol and tobacco on the individual, his family and his social life.
- Primary health care set-up to achieve health for all, measures to control health problems of communities through their active participation in health programmes.

3.8 HEALTH INSTRUCTION AT THE SECONDARY STAGE AND SYLLABI (CLASS IX AND X)

Objectives of Health Instruction at the Secondary/High School Stage. (*See* Chapter 1)

Considerations in the Selection of Syllabus: Learning Outcomes

While selecting syllabus for health instruction it should be ensured that it results in the following learning outcomes:

(i) The learners develop a scientific point of view of health.
(ii) The learners identify personal, family and community health problems and are able to prevent and control these problems to stay healthy.
(iii) The learners take action individually and collectively to protect and promote their own health, health of their own family and of the people around them in the community.
(iv) The learners are always ready to promote improved preventive and promotive self-care behaviour in the family and in the community.

Topics of Health Instruction/Education

Class IX

- *Meaning and nature of health,* ecological concept of health, interdependence of physical, mental, emotional and social dimensions of health, factors and conditions influencing health, importance of health, meaning, purpose, principles and methods of health education; role of media in Health Education.
- *Environmental conditions* in villages, towns and slums in relation to the health status of people, waste disposal practices, measures to prevent pollution, compost pits, soakage pits, sanitary latrines, sources of safe drinking water, municipal water supply system, healthful housing.
- *Relationship of personal and environmental health* practices with prevention of diseases and health promotion, cultural practices and health.
- *Major accidents* which cause deaths in rural and urban areas, factors responsible for accidents, general principles for prevention of common accidents, safety rules related to lighting fires, using stoves/ cooking gas, using electricity, climbing stairs, crossing roads, boarding means of transport, cycling, swimming, playing, storing medicines and poisonous chemicals, practising crafts, working in laboratories and using electrical and mechanical gadgets and machines, measures to remove accident hazards.
- *First-aid measures for cuts*, wounds, sprains, strains, continuous bleeding, fractures, bites and stings, drowning, fainting, shock burns: principles of first-aid, home nursing and skills in dealing with specific situations.

- *Review of body structure and functions*, meaning of growth and development, factors influencing growth and development, individual differences in growth and development, growth and development of children at different ages, their special needs with emphasis on their nutritional needs. Characteristics of growth of boys and girls in adolescent stage, their needs and interests, emotional problems of adolescents and how to adjust with them, characteristics of a mature person. Role of adolescents in the welfare of the family, preparation for marriage and family responsibilities.
- *Factors and conditions affecting nutritional status of an individual*, nutritional needs of the body in terms of calories and nutrients, low-cost, locally available sources of food-rich in these nutrients, nutritive values of commonly used foodstuff, balanced diet-its importance and requirements according to age, sex, occupation, pregnancy and geographical location, principles of diet planning, deficiency diseases and their prevention.
- *Gender bias* in terms of destroying female child (foeticide) in the womb of the mother.
- Looking after persons with *special needs*.

Health Instructional Topics for Class X

- *Health hazards of modernization*-pollution, effect of population explosion on health hazards, family and community life.
- *Communicable and non-communicable diseases*; role of host agent and environment in the spread and control of communicable diseases, body defenses, immunity natural and acquired, importance of regular medical check-up in preventing the diseases, immunization schedule and importance of booster dose. Morbidity and mortality in India; National Health Programmes, importance of pupils and people's participation in the implementation of these programmes. Primary health care, meaning and scope. Health care set-up in rural and urban areas.
- *Importance of international health*, international health measures to check spread of communicable diseases from one country to another, quarantine measures, World Health Organisation—its functions and activities, UNICEF—functions and activities, significance of World Health Day.
- *Approved systems of medicine being practised in India*, specialization available, prescription and non-prescription drugs, habit-forming drugs, dangers of self medication and going to a quack-harmful effects of alcohol and tobacco. Health set up at the village, town, district, state and country levels, voluntary agencies working in the field of health and health education.
- *Awareness of HIV and AIDS*; students may also be acquainted with evils associated with promiscuity and child and drug abuse. Adolescence education and sex-education may also be provided in a suitable manner.

Health Instructional Topics for Class XI

1. Health Education

(i) Meaning and Concept of Health and Health Education
(ii) Concept and Objectives of Health Education
(iii) Importance of Health Education
(iv) Principles of Health Education
(v) Importance of Community Participation for Health Promotion and Welfare: Individual, family and community.

2. Communicable Diseases

(i) Meaning of Communicable Diseases
(ii) Essential Conditions for Communicable Diseases to occur and Disease Process.
(iii) Mode of Transmission, Common Symptoms and Prevention of AIDS, Hepatitis B and C, Rabies, Tetanus, Malaria, Tuberculosis

3. Contemporary Health Problems

(i) Health Hazards in Society
(ii) Effects of Alcohol, Tobacco and Drugs on Sports person.

Health Instructional Topics for Class XII

1. Healthful Living

(i) Concept of Environment
(ii) Scope of Environment—Living in Environment. Work Place Environment and Environment for Leisure Activities.
(ii) Essential Elements of Healthful Environment—Safe Water, Low Level of Noise Clean Air, Sanitary surroundings. Low Level of Radio Active Radiations and Absence of Hazards Responsible for accidents in (a) Home and Neighbourhood in Rural and Urban Areas (b) School and Work Places (c) During Leisure Time Activities, Recreation and Sports.

2. Family Health Education

(i) Meaning and Functions of Family and Its Importance as a Social Institution.
(ii) Needs and Problems of Adolescents and Their Management.
(iii) Human Reproduction—Menstruation, Conceptional and Prenatal care.
(iv) Problems Associated with Pre-martial Sex and Teenage Pregnancies.
(v) Preparation of Marriage.
(vi) Role of Parents in Child Care.

3. Prevention and First Aid for Common Sports injuries

(i) Soft Tissue Injuries-Sprain and Strain
(ii) Bone Injuries
(iii) Joint Injuries

3.9 METHODS OF IMPARTING HEALTH INSTRUCTION

Apart from verbal instructions, teachers can impart health and physical education to the students in an interesting manner through the methods suggested below:

1. *Health Posters:* Posters depicting correct methods of washing of bodies, about various diseases like plague, malaria, etc., and about food, sleep and exercise, etc., can be made and pasted on the school walls. Health authorities may be requested to supply these. The posters should be very simple. Each poster should illustrate one idea only. Striking headings catch our attention. Students may be asked to help in preparing simple charts and posters regarding health.

2. *Health Projects and Weeks:* Once a year, a week may be set apart for the purpose of health education. Cleanliness campaigns in the school and locality go a long way in instilling ideas about health. Various committees of the students regarding different aspects of personal cleanliness, e.g., teeth, hair, nails, etc., may be formed. One teacher may serve as an adviser to each committee. The good posture committee should arrange posture competition and the participants should be asked to show proper postures. Prizes may be awarded to the best ones. Similarly exercise competitions may be arranged. Data regarding height, weight, chest measurements etc. may be collected by respective committees. Special lectures on general hygiene may be arranged. The Panchayat, Health Department or the City Health Department, as the case may be, should be requested to help.

3. *Health Book:* Each student should be asked to maintain a health book. One important health rule should be pasted on the top of each page. Pictures illustrating certain health rules may be pasted in it. It should also contain his health records.

4. *Healthy Environment:* Attempts be made to make classroom and the school building very attractive and conducive to health. This has a direct bearing on the child. 'As is the environment so is the individual.'

5. *Film and Film Strips:* Well-made health films and film strips are valuable aids in the teaching of health education.

6. *Educational Trips:* 'Seeing is believing' is a true saying. Excursions to good dispensaries, water supply centres, etc. may be planned for health educational purposes.

7. *Health Clubs:* Like literary clubs, health clubs, should be organised in schools. A definite weekly or monthly programme may be chalked out in co-operation with the school Red Cross Society. Debartes and declamation contests on health matters may be arranged. Plays depicting health rules be staged.

8. *Radio:* Special programmes for children relating to health should be broadcasted.

9. *Television:* Television provides a good medium to telecast features on healthful living. The teachers should take interest in such programmes.

10. *Flannel-graphs:* They are good for talking with groups because we can keep on making new pictures. We should cover a square board or piece of card-board with a flannel cloth. We can place different cut-out drawings or photos on it on health matters. Strips of sandpaper on fannel glued to the backs of cutouts help them stick to the flannel-board.

11. *Models and Demonstrations:* These help get ideas across. For example, if we want to talk with mothers and midwives about care in cutting the cord of a newborn child, we can make a doll for the baby and pin a cloth cord to its belly. Experienced midwives can demonstrate to others.

12. *Story Telling:* When we have a hard time explaining something, a story, especially a true one, will help make our point clear. Stories also make learning more interesting. Story telling helps if we are good story tellers.

13. *Play Acting:* Stories that make important points clear can reach pupils and people with great effect if they are acted out. Perhaps the school teacher, or someone on the health committee can plan short plays or 'skits' with the school children. For example, to make the point clear that food should be protected from flies to prevent the spread of disease, several small children could dress up as flies and buzz around food. The students would understand that flies make dirty the food that has not been covered. Then children eat this food and get sick. But the flies cannot get at food in a box with a wire screen front. So the children who eat this food stay well.

14. *A Village Health Committee:* A group of able and interested persons can be chosen to help plan and lead activities relating to the well-being of the community, for example, digging garbage pits or latrines. The teacher and health worker can and should share much of his responsibility with other persons. This is a very effective practical way of imparting health instruction.

15. *Group Discussions:* Mothers, fathers, school children, young people, or other groups can discuss needs and problems that affect health. Their chief purpose could be to help people share ideas.

16. *Health Counselling and Follow-up:* The main aims of this service are:

1. Giving pupils the information about their health status as revealed by appraisal or medical inspection.
2. Acquainting parents with the significance of health problems and encouraging them to obtain needed care for their children.
3. Motivating pupils to seek and accept needed treatment.
4. Promoting each pupil's acceptance of responsibility for his own health in keeping with his stage of maturity.

Teachers, nurses and parents have to play an important role in the follow-up programme as actual improvement in the health of children depends more on follow-up than on any other school health activity.

Summing up: We may sum up the subject of imparting health instruction to students with the observations contained in the NCERT Guidelines (2001), "Though some topics of Health Education can be taught in the class by using traditional methods, sometimes team-teaching becomes necessary as the Health

Education Component is integrated in other subjects like Work Education, Environmental Studies, Sciences and Languages, etc." The guidelines also stress that activities of Health Education cannot be taught in isolation.

Class XII

Part A

1. Physical Fitness and Wellness

1.1 Meaning and Importance of Physical Fitness and Wellness
1.2 Components of Physical Fitness and Wellness
1.3 Factors affecting Physical Fitness and Wellness
1.4 Principles of Physical Fitness Development
1.5 Means of Fitness Development
  1.5.1 Aerobic Activities-Jogging, Cycling Calisthenics and Rhythmic exercises
  1.5.2 Participation in Games and Sports
  1.5.3 Circuit Training

2. Training Methods

2.1 Meaning and Concept of Training
2.2 Warming up, Limbering down and their Importance
2.3 Development of Leadership Qualities and Group Dynamics

Part B

1. History of the Game/Sports (Any one game/sport of student's choice).
2. Latest General Rules of the Games/Sports (Any one game/sport of student's choice)
3. Measurement of Play fields and Specifications of Sports Equipment.
4. Fundamental Skills of the Game/Sport
5. Related Sports Terminologies
6. Important Tournaments and Venues
7. Sports Awards.

Part C

1. Healthful Living

1.1 Concept of Environment
1.2 Scope of Environment-Living Environment, Work Place Environment for Leisure Activities.
1.3 Essential Elements of Healthful Environment—Safe Water, Low Levels of noise, Clean Air, Sanitary Surrounding, Low Levels of Radio active Radiations and Absence of Hazards Responsible for Accidents in (i) home and neighbourhood in rural and urban areas (ii) school and work place (iii) during leisure time activities recreation and sports.

1.4 Role of Individual in Improvement of Environment for Health Promotion and Prevention of Accidents related to Transportation Swimming and Water sports.
1.5 Disaster preparedness and health care during disasters.

2. Family Health Education

2.1 Meaning of Functions of Family and its Importance as a Social Institution
2.2 Needs and Problems of Adolescents and their Management.
2.3 Human Reproduction-Menstruation, Conceptional and Prenatal care
2.4 Problems Associated with Pre-marital Sex and Teenage Pregnancies
2.5 Preparation of Marriage
2.6 Role of Parents in Child Care.

3. Prevention and First-Aid for Sports Injuries

3.1 Soft Tissue Injuries-Sprain and Strain
3.2 Bone Injuries
3.3 Joint Injuries

4

School Health Services and Healthful School Environment

4.1 IMPORTANCE OF SCHOOL HEALTH SERVICES

The quality and quantity of health services in the school have a great bearing on the development of emotional, mental and physical health of the students and also of the entire school personnel. The school health services influence the parents as well as the community. We cannot afford to allow the students to remain underdeveloped. All efforts must be made to ensure that the students do not become a prey to any disease. The protective measures regarding health should be taken on a large scale and of a good quality to maintain and improve the health of the students. The school must establish good quality health services to ensure a sound healthful environment.

4.2 AGENCIES OF SCHOOL HEALTH SERVICES

Agencies of School Health Services

(1) School Medical Department under the charge of School Doctor (Exists only in well established schools)

(2) School Health Doctor (only in well established schools)

(3) School dispensary under the charge of school Doctor (Normally part-time Doctor)

(4) Red Cross Society of the School

(5) Physical Education/Sports Department under the charge of the Physical Education Teacher

4.3 PROGRAMME COMPONENTS OF SCHOOL HEALTH SERVICES

The School health services include:

1. Medical inspection of the students.
2. Maintenance of records of medical inspection and health of the students.

3. Sending reports of the medical inspection of the students to their parents.
4. Follow up programme on the medical inspection of the students *i.e.* remedial steps.
5. Protective measures to prevent communicable diseases by timely immunization.
6. First Aid and Emergency care.
7. Health examination of school staff.
8. Provision of health guidance services.
9. Provision of mid-day meals or nutritional services.
10. Provision of healthful school conditions.
11. Referral of serious cases for clinical treatment.
12. Correcting medical defects among students.
13. Indentification and education of the handicapped students.

School health services differ from school to school depending upon the resources of the school.

4.4 MEDICAL INSPECTION OF THE STUDENTS

Objectives of Medical Inspection of the Students: Following are the main objectives of medical inspection of the students:

1. Evaluation of the health status of the students.
2. Treatment of disease if any, when possible in the school.
3. Isolating the students suffering from any communicable disease.
4. Advising the parents of the appropriate action to be taken by them.
5. Identification of any special handicap.

General Defects observed in Medical Inspection

Systematic medical examination is one of the most important means of taking care of the physical well-being of the students. Although this system has been in existence for many years, it has failed to achieve the desired results.

The Secondary Education Commission (1952-53) has observed the following defects in the prevailing system:

(i) It is done in a very superficial manner.
(ii) The remedial measures suggested are often not carried out.
(iii) Follow up work is practically absent.
(iv) Effective cooperation has not been established between the parents and the school authorities.

The defects pointed out by the Commission still exist though more than half a century has elapsed.

Suggestions to Make Medical Examination Effective

Medical inspection to be effective should be done in the following manner:

1. It should be thorough and comprehensive and should not be treated as a mere routine. It should not merely concern itself with the height, weight and chest measurements but should also concern itself with ears, teeth, eyes, nose, heart and lungs etc. In fact no part of the body should be left unexamined as

far as possible. The first inspection should be at the time of admission of the child in a school. If it is found out that the child is suffering from some chronic disease, he may be refused admission. Child should be examined every year. The last inspection will be just prior to leaving the school which reveals the strength and weakness of the child and helps him to choose some vocation suited to his physical development also.

2. Students with serious defects should be examined more frequently.

3. Remedial measures should be taken to remove defects.

4. Three copies of the report should be prepared. One should be sent to the parents, another should be kept by the teacher-in-charge and the third one should be kept by the medical officer.

Follow-up Work

A few words may be said regarding 'follow up' work. It has been rightly stated that medical inspection is of little or no use unless proper 'follow-up' work is undertaken. In many cases, it does not call for any extra burden. A slight care of the child brings about good results. The parents and the teachers should cooperate. Immediate action should be taken after the medical inspection is over. When the parents are unable to take remedial steps due to poverty, school should take upon itself the responsibility of looking after the health of the child. The State may arrange mobile hospital ambulances for the purpose. "In any case such remedial measures as the school medical officer may suggest should be adopted, and the school authorities should see that they are carried out," thus remarks the Secondary Education Commission.

Daily/Weekly Health Inspection by the Teachers

Apart from medical inspection by the physician, daily inspection of the general cleanliness of the child should be made by the teacher. This costs nothing and can be done in a few minutes.

Utilising the Health Services of Hospitals by School Students

The Secondary Education Commission suggested that the schools should make efforts to utilise the child health services provided in the nearby hospitals. In cases where defects of somewhat serious nature in medical examination by the school doctor have been noted and medical treatment is required, children may be taken by the teacher, or the school medical officer or the physical education teacher of the school to the hospital concerned on one or two afternoons in the week.

4.5 SCHOOL HEALTH SERVICE AND THE RURAL COMMUNITY

There are several fields in which the school can serve the community and the community can also serve the school. It is important to remember that in regard to the health and care of the children, the activities of the school should be extended to their homes, neighbourhood and to the village as a whole. The reason for this is obvious. The health of school children is determined not only during the hours spent at school but even more so during the time spent at home and in the neighbourhood and at work. If the school neglects the home and community factors, those out of school influences may prevent or offset many of the beneficial effects of the school's endeavour to improve the health of the students. It is not suggested that schools can directly control the conditions outside but they 'can' influence them by educating both the students and their parents, by cooperating with the physicians and health authorities of the village or group of villages. The school can also influence by educating the public to a better appreciation of the health problems of the students and the efforts of the school. The school dispensary can also be made available to the village community.

The Secondary Education Commission is of the view that if the school could actually do something to improve the conditions of the sanitation in the neighbourhood or locality, it would be the best health education service.

4.6 SCHOOL CLINIC OR DISPENSARY

Every school should establish a school clinic to look after the health of the pupils and for the treatment of minor diseases. Several schools in a town may combine and set up a dispensary under the charge of a qualified medical officer.

Medical examination should be conducted free of charge. In case any teacher finds a students suffering from some disease, he should report it to the doctor and ensure that the treatment at the clinic/dispensary is carried out.

4.7 JUNIOR RED CROSS SOCIETY

The Junior Red Cross Society is the school children's branch of the Red Cross Organisation. The Red Cross Organisation is a world-wide organisation. It is voluntary, non-governmental, non-political, non-sectarian and international in character.

Aims of the Junior Red Cross Society

(a) Promotion of health, personal hygiene, school hygiene and community hygiene.
(b) Service to others especially in relation to health.
(c) Promotion of fellowship among, and friendly helpfulness towards other young people of all countries.

Activities of Junior Red Cross Society: For the propagation of health rules, a Junior Red Cross Society takes the aid of posters and charts. Health plays are also staged.

The members of the Junior Red Cross Society can render a very useful assistance to the medical officer at the time of medical inspection of the students. Usually a Junior Red Cross Society runs a small dispensary and a library containing books dealing with health, the rules of health, diseases, their causes and remedies.

The students are encouraged to exchange letters, photos, seeds, plants and handwork with students of other countries in order to promote international friendliness. It also arranges lectures on various diseases and their cures. Its members are expected to set good examples before others by visiting the sick students of the school. The members of a Junior Red Cross Society render first-aid when the students receive minor injuries.

4.8 FIRST AID (*See Chapter 7*).

4.9 HEALTHFUL SCHOOL ENVIRONMENT OR HEALTHFUL SCHOOL LIVING

All Round Attractive, Calm, Captivating, Enchanting, Serene, Spiritual and Vibrant Environment of the School

It is an established fact that school environment has a direct bearing on ethical, mental, physical, social and spiritual development and well-being of students. Next to home, students spend most of their time in school and therefore the school environment and its programme have a great impact on them. Proper conditions for healthy physical life in the school are: proper location and building of the school, sanitation, water supply, recreation programmes, games and sports, emotional set-up and happy group relations, along with effective teaching-learning process.

1. *Physical Environment of the School:* This includes:
   - (i) *The site of the school*: The school should be located in an attractive, clean, congenial, healthy and pleasant environment. As far as possible, its natural surrounding should have a touch of beauty. The site should be free from dampness, dust, noise, smoke and other unhygienic conditions.
   - (ii) *The school building*: The building in its totality-classrooms, laboratory, library and playgrounds etc. should be beautiful, clean, neat and spacious to a reasonable extent. Its maintenance should be properly attended to. There should be suitable arrangement for its annual repairs and white washing.
   - (iii) *Light and air*: Adequate arrangements for light and ventilation should exist. There should be no glare from light. During summer there should be no scope for the sunlight to enter the rooms. The purpose should be to have maximum sunlight in winter and minimum in summer. There should be provision for both artificial and natural light and ventilation.
   - (iv) *Furniture*: The seats should be comfortable for the students. It should be possible to keep the entire furniture neat and clean. There should be arrangement for its annual repairs and polishing. Blackboard should be of appropriate size and colour and placed in such a location that the students do not have to tax their eyes to see the writings on it.

(v) *Canteen*: Regular supervision of the school canteen is very important from the point of view of hygiene, cleanliness, and nutrition.

(vi) *Drinking water*: Suitable provision of clean and fresh water has to be ensured.

(vii) *Toilet*: The hygienic environment of the school toilets is an index of the state of its concern for health of the child. Toilet facilities should not only be adequate but also its cleanliness and disinfection should be ensured.

(viii) *Dustbins*: Dustbins should be provided at suitable spots so that it may be convenient to the students to throw pieces of waste paper etc. in them.

(ix) *Hygiene and sanitation*: There should be no places or spots in the school where water may stagnate and provide a breeding place for mosquitoes and other germs. Disinfectants should be regularly used at all the places where necessary.

(x) *Hygiene and sanitation*: There should be no places or spots in the school where water may stagnate and provide a breeding place for mosquitoes and other germs. Disinfectants should be regularly used at all the places where necessary.

(xi) *Condition of the laboratories, farm and workshops*: All these places of work should be kept neat and clean. Appropriate safety measures should be adopted.

2. *Instruction and Supervision of Personal Hygiene of the Students*: This includes: (i) Cleanliness of body, (ii) Cleanliness of clothes, (iii) Check on unhygienic habits like blowing of noise everywhere, spitting, passing of urine at any place and the like bad habits.

3. *Emotional Environment:* The emotional development of the students is greatly influenced by the emotional balance of the teachers. Sense of humour of the teacher is very helpful in creating and maintaining a healthy classroom environment. He should pay due regard to the personality of the child. He should be fair and just. His own healthy habits generate similar habits among students.

4. *Healthy Postures of the Students:* Suitable postures of reading, writing, sitting, standing, walking, running and lying in the bed should be stressed upon as they form an essential part of any physical and health education programme. A wrong posture is very harmful and it may lead to deformities and stunted growth.

5. *Games, Sports and Exercises:* Physical education including games, sports and exercises go a long way in enabling the students to enjoy reasonable good health.

6. *Mid-day Meals:* Proper arrangement of nutritive mid-day meals should exist in the school. The school should supplement and enrich the lunch packets of the students. A comfortable seating or standing arrangement as the case may be should also be provided for the students to take the lunch.

7. *School Time-Table:* The school programme and time-table should be so organized that it may not cause fatigue to the teachers and students. The school-hour should be adjusted to the age-level of the students and seasonal changes. The entire teaching and non-teaching programme should be made interesting and inspiring.

8. *Medical Inspection:* Medical inspection and its follow-up should be done carefully and regularly.

9. *Social Environment:* Good teacher-pupil relationships keep children mentally healthy. Relationships among other groups have also a great bearing on students.

10. *School Health Services:* School health service programme plays a very important role in achieving the aim of promotion of physical, emotional, mental and social health of the students.

4.10 ENVIRONMENTAL CLEANLINESS AND PREVENTING ILLNESS/ DISEASES

'Prevention is better than cure' is a true saying. There are a large number of environment factors which influence our health.

However, it costs nothing to take care of the cleanliness of our environment. A few importnt suggestions are given below to prevent illness by attending to cleanliness.

1. Illness can be prevented by washing hands with soap and water after contact with faeces (solid waste matter passed out of the body) and before handling food

Washing hands with soap and water removes germs from the hands. This helps to stop germs from getting into food or into the mouth. Soap and water should be easily available for all members of the family to wash their hands.

It is especially important to wash hands after defecating, before handling food, and after cleaning the bottom of a baby or child who has just defecated.

Children often put their hands into their mouths. So it is important for the child to wash hands often, especially before giving food.

A child should wash his face at least once every day. This helps to keep flies away from the face and prevent eye infections. Soap is helpful for washing, but not absolutely essential.

2. Illness can be prevented by using latrines

The single most important action which families and schools can take to prevent the spread of germs is to dispose of faeces safely. Many illnesses, especially diarrhoea, come from the germs found in human faeces. Pupils can swallow these germs if the germs get into water, into food, into the hands, or into utensils and surfaces used for preparing food.

To prevent this:

(i) Use latrines.

(ii) If it is not possible to use a latrine, adults and children should defecate well away from houses, paths, water supplies, and anywhere that children play. After defecating, the faeces should be buried. Contrary to common belief, the faeces of babies and young children are even more dangerous than those of adults. So even small children should be asked to use the latrine. If children defecate without using a latrine, then their faeces should be cleared up immediately and either put down the latrine or buried.

(iii) Latrines should be cleaned regularly and kept covered.

(iv) Keep the faeces of animals away from homes and water sources.

3. Illness can be prevented by using clean water

Families and schools who have a plentiful supply of safe piped water, and know how to use it, have fewer illnesses.

Schools and families without a safe piped water supply can reduce illness if they protect their water supply from germs by:

(a) Keeping wells covered. Keeping faeces and waste water (especially from latrines) well away from any water used for cooking, drinking, bathing or washing.

(b) Keeping buckets, ropes and jars used to collect and store water as clean as possible (for example, by hanging up buckets rather than putting them on the ground).

(c) Keeping animals away from drinking water.

(d) Families and schools can keep water clean in the home and in the schools by:

 (i) Storing drinking water in a clean, covered container.

 (ii) Taking water out of the container with a clean cup.

 (iii) Not allowing anyone to put hands into the container or to drink directly from it.

 (iv) Keeping animals out of the house.

4. Illness can be prevented by boiling drinking water if it is not from a safe piped supply

Even if water is clear, it may not be free from germs. The safe drinking water is from a piped supply. Water from other sources is more likely to contain germs.

Boiled water kills germs. So, if possible, water drawn from sources such as ponds, streams, springs, wells, tanks or public standpipes should be boiled and cooled before drinking. It is especially important to boil and cool the water which is given to babies and young children, because they have less resistance to germs than adults.

If boiling is not possible, store drinking water in a closed or covered container of clean plastic or glass, and leave it standing in sunlight for two days before using it.

5. Illness can be prevented by keeping food clean

Germs on food can enter the body and cause illness. But food can be kept safe by:

(i) Making sure that food is thoroughly cooked, especially meat and poultry.
(ii) Eating food soon after it has been cooked, so that it does not have time to go bad.
(iii) If food has to be kept for more than five hours, it should either be kept heated or kept cooled.
(iv) If already-cooked food is saved, it should be thoroughly reheated before being used again.
(v) Raw meat, especially poultry, usually contains germs. So it should not be allowed to come into contact with cooked meat. Utensils and food preparing surfaces should be cleaned after preparing raw meat.
(vi) Keeping food-preparing surfaces clean.
(vii) Keeping food clean and covered and away from flies, rats, mice and other animals.

6. Illness can be prevented by burning or burying household refuse

Germs can be spread by flies, which breed in refuse such as food scraps and peelings from fruit and vegetables. Every school having mid-day meal arrangement should have special pit or other mechanism where refuse is buried or burned everyday.

4.11 FUNCTIONS, ROLES AND RESPONSIBILITIES OF THE TEACHERS

Many-sided Efforts for the Health and Physical Development of Pupils

In a school, a child comes into contact with his friends, teachers and the other school staff. All these contacts, besides the physical environment of the school have far reaching effects on the emotional, mental, physical, spiritual and social health of a child. As a matter of fact all these facets of the life of the child are very closely interlinked, and are greatly influenced by the teachers. The teachers, their role in the health and physical development of the child is as important as, their role in his academic or intellectual development. It is a wrong notion that the physical education teacher alone is responsible in this regard.

Measures to be adopted by the Teachers for the Promotion of Health and Physical Fitness of Students

The following measures should be adopted by the teachers for the promotion of health and physical fitness of the students:

1. *Personal Cleanliness:* The daily morning inspection of the cleanliness of the students by the teacher is very helpful in enforcing personal cleanliness. A rapid survey of the class should be made. Competition may be introduced

among the students. Cleanliness chart may be prepared and marks are allotted to them.

2. *Development of Habits regarding Air:* Stress should be laid on the need of fresh air at all times and especially while sleeping. The students should be asked not to cover their mouth at night. They should be taught to breathe through their noses.

3. *Training in First-Aid Habits:* The students should be instructed to give immediate attention to cuts and bruises.

4. *Vaccination and Inoculation:* At time of epidemics precautionary measures should be suggested to them and they should be vaccinated and inoculated.

5. *Development of Habits of Hygienic Feeding:* The students should be taught to take right type of food in a suitable quantity. They should be warned of the dangers of over-eating. They should be asked not to take sour food. They should be made to understand the importance of drinking plenty of water.

6. *Selection of Suitable Physical Exercises:* A variety of physical activity programmes should exist in a school so that the students may choose activity of their liking.

7. *Formation of Good Classroom Habits:* A wise teacher would always pay due attention to the postures of the students. The students may be instructed to keep pens and pencils out of the mouth and to use handkerchiefs while coughing. Such other matters should be attended to.

8. *Development of better Human Relations in Matters Concerning Health:* Every child should be asked to make it a point to do his best for the betterment of the health of his friends, relatives, neighbours and the whole community.

9. *Medical Inspection and Follow-up Work:* Medical examination should be thorough and the follow-up work taken up seriously.

10. *Training in First Aid:* Teachers themselves should get training in first aid, give first aid training to students and render emergency service.

11. *Vaccination and Inoculation:* Teachers should ensure that each child is regularly vaccinated and inoculated through the arrangements made by the school.

12. *Physical Exercises:* Whenever feasible, all teachers should supervise physical education programmes.

13. *Special Methods of Teaching Health:* The teachers should be on the look out of using a variety of methods of teaching health.

14. *School Dispensary:* Teachers, in turn, can look after the school dispensary.

15. *Assistance to Medical Officer or School Doctor:* At the time of medical inspection of students and its follow up, teachers can render very useful help.

5

Safety Education

5.1 MEANING AND IMPORTANCE OF SAFETY

'Safety implies the condition of being secure from undergoing or causing hurt, injury or loss. It implies free from accidents.

Accidents involve persons of all age groups and these may occur at any place in the home, on the road, on the job, in the school or during recreation. However most of the accidents can be prevented. Accidents are a great economic burden on the individual, his family and also on the society. Safety precautions, therefore, should be the part of our daily life. The school is an important place for providing learning and instruction in this regard.

Developing positive attitude towards safety and learning to operate new technological devices is sure to go a long way in making our life free from most of the common accidents.

Guidelines for Safety Habits: The following may be considered as acceptable guidelines to make safety a habit:

1. Looking for possible hazards in whatever we may be doing
2. Taking precautionary measures for making adjustment in our behaviour.
3. Observing proper safety measures needed for a specific situation.

5.2 ACCIDENTS AND NEED FOR SAFETY AT DIFFERENT AGE GROUPS

In general it may be stated that boys are involved in two to three times as many accidents as girls. Every age has its particular hazards. It is important to be acquainted with main dangers that beset children at each age level and we should do all in our power to eliminate them.

Under one year: Choking and suffocation are the chief hazards. Falls cause most of the injuries and even account for several deaths.

One to four years: The child is struck in the lane, street or road. Most accidents involve motor vehicles. The menace of fire is the next cause. Drownings in fish ponds or tanks near the home is the third cause. Poisoning is the fourth cause.

Five to nine years: Motor vehicles are responsible for most fatal accidents. Drownings come next. Cuts are the most frequent injuries.

Ten to fourteen: Motor vehicles continue to be the instruments of death. Drownings run second. Fire accidents come third.

5.3 MEASURES FOR MINIMISING ACCIDENTS AT HOME AND SCHOOLS

1. Adequate lighting in stairs.
2. Stairways clear of toys, bottles and brooms etc.
3. Handrails on sides.
4. No electrical equipment near bathroom.
5. Disconnecting appliances when not in use.
6. Replacing worn out cords.
7. No slippery throw of rugs.
8. Wiping up immediately Liquids spilled on floor.
9. Highly polished floors to be avoided.
10. Gas burners turned off tightly.
11. Handles of cooking utensils on stove turned inward.
12. Sharp knives, razor blades, scissors and matches out of reach of children.
13. Medicines safely stored.
14. Children should not be allowed to go to the street or road without any escort.

5.4 COMMON ACCIDENTS AT HOME

A large majority of accidents occur in homes. Common accidents in homes are on account of falls, fires, choking, suffocation, poisoning and cuts. Carelessness is a major cause on the part of elders and lack of knowledge and experience on the part of children.

Safety from Falls. To prevent falls inside the home, things should be kept at proper places after their use. Floors should be kept dry and cleaned. Discarded furniture and other trash should be properly stored and disposed off. A sturdy step-stool should be used for reaching high points. Staircases should be kept ventilated and suitable handrails provided on both sides. Toys and brooms etc. should never be left on the steps. Gates should be provided at the bottom and top of the stairways. Window should be provided with iron bars or grills to protect chidlren from falling. A non-skid rubber mat or even a towel or gunny bag may be kept on the floor of the bathroom to prevent skidding. Children should not be allowed to fly kites on top roofs if there are no high walls surrounding the roof. A torch may be kept at a convenient place in case it is needed to get up at night on account of any reason.

Safety from Fire: Fires and burns involve life and property. By following common safety mesures in our homes we can prevent loss from fire. Match boxes, burning stoves, open flames and electrical appliances when connected with electricity should be kept out of reach of children and should never be left unattended to. A flame should never be left before going to bed. Curtains should not be allowed to blow over open flame. Kerosene lamp, candles, and wick lamps can cause havoc when turned down by wind. Inflammable articles like kerosene, petrol, varnishes and turpentine oil, etc., should be kept stored properly in air tight containers.

Kitchen should be well ventilated. While cooking, synthetic garments or bangles of inflammable material like lac should not be worn. In case gas is used for cooking, match stick may be ignited first before opening the gas and not otherwise. Leaking gas should not be checked with a lighted match stick. Looking into an oven may be avoided when lighting it.

Kitchen appliances like pressure cookers should be used according to directions indicated by the manufacturer. Handles of pots and pans should be turned backward to prevent brushing against or getting bumped or getting caught on clothing. A cover should be used on the pots and pans while pouring out hot liquids.

Many fires take place on account of faulty electrical gadgets and their improper and careless handling. Electrical wiring and fuses should be maintained in proper order. Worn out insulations and faulty gadgets should always be disconnected. Appliances like electric iron should not be left unattended even for a short while when it is on. When working with electricity we should not stand on a metal or wet concrete or wet ground. It is wise to stand on a rubber or dry wooden platform when using electric equipment.

Safety from Poisoning: Most of the victims of poison accidents are children between two and five years of age. All the containers of poisonous substances should be kept out of the reach of the children. The bottles of medicines should be kept very carefully. Children should be instructed not to eat the heads of matches and bright coloured papers because poisonous substances are used to make dyes.

Safety from Choking and Suffocation: Sometimes young children swallow small objects like coins. To avoid this, such things should be kept out of reach of the children. Many a time children cover their heads with empty plastic bags and suffocate to death. Choking and suffocation is also caused by too much of smoke. A kerosene or coal stove to warm the room during winter and especially when doors and windows are closed can be dangerous.

5.5 COMMON ACCIDENTS IN SCHOOL

Generally same types of accidents take place in the school as in the home. However in the school there are special situations which need special care. Such special situations in the school are on account of the school workshops, school canteen, chemical laboratory, school gymnasium and playground, school transport etc. uncommon to home.

Safety in the Laboratory: All experiments should be performed under the guidance of the teacher. As a matter of fact laboratory should not be opened for use if there is no teacher available. Students should not be allowed to mix up two chemicals when the result of such a combination is not known. Glass should be handled with care so as to avoid cuts.

Safety in Workshop: Sufficient space should be provided for movements. Tools should be maintained in proper condition and at their proper places. Students should be given suitable instructions in the use of tools.

Safety During Recess and at the Close of the School: It is generally observed that when the bell rings to announce recess or end of school, students are so much excited that sometimes there is a 'mini' stampede to rush out of the classes and several students are hurt. Teachers should be very vigilant on such occasions.

Students' Fights: When the discipline in the school is loose, children get several chances to fight among themselves. It is, therefore, very essential that a close watch is kept on the students.

A First-Aid Box must be kept in every institution.

5.6 SAFETY AT PLAYGROUND

School ground should not be slippery. It should be free from thorns and pebbles. All games and sports should be played under the guidance of teachers. All apparatus and equipments should be kept in proper condition.

5.7 SCHOOL TRANSPORT SAFETY

In recent years, especially in cities, quite a large number of students use school transport. Trained drivers and cleaners/helpers should be engaged. Speed should also be kept within the prescribed limit. Overloading should not be done. Necessary precautions should be taken at the time of boarding and dropping children at the spots free from heavy traffic.

5.8 SAFE DRINKING WATER

Importance: Safe and adequate water supply is very essential for health both of the individual and the community. Drinking unclean water spreads several diseases of the gut and the digestive tract. Drinking unclean water may lead to jaundice. Water intended for human-consumption should be safe and wholesome, and it is defined as water that is (a) free from diseases carrying germs; (b) free from harmful chemical substances; (c) pleasant to taste, and (d) usable for domestic purposes.

Sources of Safe Drinking Water: The water used for drinking and in the preparation of eating and drinking products should come from a tested safe source of water and in case of doubt it should be treated by the individual to make it safe before using it. On a large scale water is usually purified and treated in water supply systems under the control of local bodies or any other approved authority. This water is supplied to the households through water taps.

6

Postures

6.1 MEANING AND IMPORTANCE OF PROPER POSTURES

Posture means an individual/child balancing his/her body specifically. Proper posture is that in which the child does not feel any effort in balancing his body weight or both the feet with equilibrium. In the proper posture, the trunk of the body that is spine is parallel to the head and neck like a perpendicular line. All parts of the body work harmoniously. The normal child does not feel any kind of fatigue or strain, when he/she is in the proper postural position. Proper postures result in good appearance, efficiency in movement, 'physical fitness' and 'alertness'. We can hardly ignore the seriousness of poor postures. They adversely affect health, physical efficiency, mental attitude and appearance of an individual. Most of our diseases are the outcome of poor postures. A teacher can do much in the classroom work and physical instruction period to prevent bad postural habits in the students. As a result of poor postures says, Dr. Mosher, "constipation, diarrhoea, flatulence, disturbance of the circulation, nervous irritability and, most marked of all fatigue out of proportion to the effort expended, lessen the efficiency of the individual and often make life a burden."

6.2 CHARACTERISTICS OF GOOD POSTURES

1. A good posture implies that body is held without any sort of effort, with its weight, equally distributed over both the legs and feet so as to produce least fatigue.
2. A good posture keeps equilibrium among all parts of the body.
3. A posture is dynamic and it varies with every activity.
4. It is not necessary that we may always stand in a certain position or sit firmly in a chair in order to have a good posture.
5. The secret of good posture is a frequent change of positions.
6. Remaining in one posture for a long time is fatigue-causing.
7. Posture is more than a more physical condition.
8. A posture reflects the emotions and moods of an individual.
9. A posture indicates the attitudes of both body and mind.
10. A good posture makes it possible for the alignments and muscles to maintain position of the body which are conducive to efficient movement.
11. Good postures keep us in natural state or in working conditions.

12. Good posture is largely an individual matter of common sense.
13. Certain postures may be inherited.
14. Postures can be modified through training.

6.3 MAJOR ADVERSE EFFECTS OF POOR POSTURES

Some of the main adverse effects of poor postures are given below:

(i) They interfere in the normal working of respiration, circulation and digestion.
(ii) They badly affect the eye-sight.
(iii) They spoil handwriting because the students will not be able to hold the pen properly.
(iv) They lead to round shoulders and drooping body.
(v) They decrease physical efficiency and develop laziness.
(vi) They develop crooked bodies which are not normal in shape, and look very unpleasant.
(vii) They result in undesirable traits, e.g. timidness, lack of courage, etc.

6.4 CAUSES OF POOR POSTURES

1. Congenital postural deformities i.e. by birth
2. Postural defects on account of diseases.
3. Postural defects through accident or injury.
4. More mental work.
5. Wrong postural habits due to lack of information regarding correct positions.
6. Defective desks and seats compelling the students to stretch or cramp their bodies.
7. Wrong writing positions.
8. Wrong reading positions.
9. Defective eye-sight.
10. Defective hearing.
11. Illegible writing of the teacher on the black-board.
12. Wrong postures of the teachers leading to depressing effects on the students.
13. Illness of the students.
14. Wrong type of dress of the students.
15. Fatigue.
16. Physical weakness.
17. Lack of proper diet.
18. Lack of proper light.
19. Lack of adequate air.
20. Unhygienic school conditions.
21. Wrong type of punishment.
22. Unscientific time table.
23. Unsupervised exercises.
24. Insufficient sleep.
25. Fashion regarding wearing of clothes.

Classification of Postures of Students

(1)	(2)	(3)	(4)	(5)
Sitting Postures	Standing Postures	Reading Postures	Writing Postures	Walking Postures

6.5 IDENTIFICATION OF COMMON POSTURAL DEFECTS AMONG CHILDREN AND THEIR CLASSIFICATION

It is very important to identify common postural defects of students. There are certain common postural defects which can be easily identified by just having a glance on the reading, writing, listening, sitting and standing movements of the students.

These are some defects which come to light through medical examination.

6.6 GENERAL REMEDIAL MEASURES FOR PROPER POSTURES

(i) The students should be asked to take regular exercise to strengthen muscles.
(ii) Suitable furniture should be provided.
(iii) Good postural habits should be developed.
(iv) Stools should be provided for smaller children so that they may learn to sit without reclining against the chair.
(v) Suitable corrective postural exercises should be recommended to the students.
(vi) Students having defective eye-sight and hearing should be seated on the front benches.
(vii) Rooms should be suitably ventilated.
(viii) Bold type books should be selected.
(ix) Help of school medical officer should be sought.
(x) Time table should be so arranged that students do not feel the impact of fatigue.
(xi) Causes of students' tension should be removed.
(xii) Sufficient sitting space should be provided to the students.
(xiii) Nutritious and balanced mid-day meals should be provided to students.
(xiv) Proper arrangement for sufficient light should be made in the classroom.
(xv) Teachers should check wrong postures of the students.
(xvi) Small children should not be engaged too much in drill.

6.7 PROPER POSTURES IN VARIOUS SITUATIONS

Sitting Postures: In sitting postures, different organs of the body and the body as a whole are balanced; the legs are crossed, the hips are comfortably and properly placed at the seat; the head, the shoulders and hips are in a straight vertical line and the vertebral column is perfectly vertical. The thigh should remain at the right angles and upper parts of the body.

Standing Posture: (1) In correct standing posture, the body weight should equally fall on both the legs. (2) The entire body should be erect and vertical, (3) The heels should rest evenly on the flat floor, (4) The two arms should rest on the thighs in a straight line, (5) The head and the body should not bend forward, body should not bend on one of its sides and body as a whole should be balanced.

Reading Posture: (1) While reading the students should sit straight, (2) The book should not be placed very close to the eyes. It should be placed at least 12 inches away. (3) The hand handling the book should form an angle of 45 degrees with the eyes. (4) The desk should be placed on 'plus distance' from the chair, (5) Proper print should be given to students so that they do not have to exert to read the pointed material.

Writing Posture: While writing, the position of the desk or table should be quite close to the body and bent in an upright position and not bent over the note-book. The legs should be on the ground. The note-book should be at a distance of 12 inches from the eyes. The paper should be placed parallel to the edge of the desk and the pen should be held in between the thumb and fingers. Thighs should be horizontal and lower part of the leg should be in perpendicular position and the feet should rest on the floor. The writing should be straight and not oblique.

Walking Posture: While walking, the body as a whole should be erect and upright. The eyes should look straight at an angle of 90 degrees. The arms should swing alternately along with steps preferably upto an angle of 90 degrees with the body. The heels should reach the ground first and then the middle portion and the toes. One should take steps of normal dimension.

6.8 SPECIFIC POSTURAL DEFECTS AND PHYSICAL EXERCISES FOR IMPROVING POSTURES

It is hardly necessary to stress the early detection of postural defects and to take remedial measures. A.S. Daniels and E.A. Davies have made very useful suggestions in this regard.

1. Improving the Head and Neck Postures

(i) The student should sit with head and neck erect. He should then turn head and neck to right and left, turn by turn, check chin to clavicle.

(ii) The student should stand with back to wall, touching with buttocks, shoulders and back of head. Then he should raise chest, flatten lower back, pull in the abdomen and press the back of the head against the wall. He should hold this position for a few seconds and repeat.

(iii) Lying on back, the students should stretch arms sideways and palms down. Then he should raise chest, arching upper back. He should support weight on back of head, arms and hips. This position should be held for a few seconds and repeated.

(iv) The student should adopt the standing position with a sand bag/ pitcher balanced on top of head. Then he should walk.

2. Improving Round Upper Back and Kyphosis

(i) The student should lie down on back with knees drawn up and feet flat on the floor and hands at sides. Then he should move arms side horizontal and even with shoulders, palms up. The he should move arms along floor to position overhead, palms still up, remain for a few seconds and repeat.

(ii) The student should pronate hands on hips and then raise head and trunk (with chin in) several inches from door, bring down and repeat.

(iii) The student's sitting position should be such as neck firm and finger's laced behind head. Then he should stretch trunk, neck, head and elbows upwards, keeping back straight and trunk erect.

(iv) The student should sit with a wand held in horizontal position over head, hands well spread. Then he should lower and raise wand behind head and shoulders, with head and trunk quite erect.

3. Improving Lordosis (Hollow Back)

(i) The student should stride standing position, flex trunk, grasp lift ankle with both hands and pull trunk downwards for the counts and repeat to opposite side.

(ii) The student should be in a sitting position, with knees extended and feet spread. Then he should reach forward, grasp ankles, pull trunk forward relaxed bounce for three counts. This exercise can also be done with feet together, instead of spreading.

(iii) The student should sit in a position with knees extended, feet together and hands at sides. Then he should bend forward, touching fingers to toes, hold three counts, relax and repeat.

4. Improving Kypholordosis (Abnormal backward curvature of spine)

(i) The student should pronate hands under abdomen, keep hips and shoulders down, press hands up on abdomen and raise lower back.

(ii) The student should lie down on back, knees drawn up, arms overhead with elbows bent. He should then separate knees, touching soles of feet together. While exhaling, he should draw knees towards chest, keeping hips on floor.

(iii) The student should pronate hands clasped behind lower back, press elbow together, drawing shoulder/blades together, pushing hands towards the feet.

5. Strengthening the Abdominal Wall

(i) The student should lie down on back, knees bent and feet flat on floor. Then he should contract the abdominal muscles and relax.

(ii) The student should lie down on back with hands placed behind head. Then he should flex knees and side heels along floor till they touch buttocks. Back should be kept flat.

(iii) The student should lie down, legs extended, feet together and hands at side. Then he should raise legs so that the heels are just above the floor. Feet should be spread well apart, feet brought together, lowered to floor. The student should thus relax and repeat.

6. Improving Scoliosis

(i) The student should pronate, right arm upward, left arm at side. Then he should move right arm in an arch towards the left over head, press down with left hand and slide up over left hip .

(ii) The student should pronate right arm extended forward, left arm at side, feet firmly held to floor. Then he should extend the trunk, the right arm pushed forward and the left arm pushed backward, hold three counts, relax and repeat.

(iii) The student should stand in a position with feet few inches apart, raise left heel and left hip. Then he should extend right arm in an arc overhead to the left and press left hand against ribs on left.

7. Improving the Feet

(i) Student's standing position should be with knees fixed, feet together and flat on the floor. Then he should place hands on floor behind the back, raise inner border of feet, keeping toes and heels on floor.

(ii) The student's standing position should be with toes turned in. Then he should rise on balls of feet, shifting weight to outside of each feet, holding position and then returning heels to floor.

(iii) *Walking*: The student should walk about distances with heels raised and weight on outer border of the balls of feet.

(iv) *Sitting*: The student should sit with legs extended. Then he should cross the left leg over the right one with toes fixed. There should be foot circling, in and up, out and down. Movements should be alternated for each foot.

7

First Aid—Meaning, Scope and Principles of First Aid in Various Situations

7.1 MEANING AND ORIGIN OF FIRST-AID

Meaning: First-Aid is the immediate and temporary care given to the victim of an accident or sudden illness. Its purpose is to preserve life, assist recovery and prevent aggravation of the condition, until the services of a doctor can be obtained, or during transport to hospital or the casualty's home.

The First-Aider's responsibilities end as soon as medical aid is available; but he should stand by after making his report to the Doctor in case he can be of further assistance.

First-Aid is definitely limited to the assistance rendered at the time of emergency with such material as may be available. It is not intended that the First-Aider should take the place of the Doctor and it must be clearly understood that the re-dressing of injuries and other such after treatment are outside the scope of First-Aid.

Originator of the First Aid: The originator of First-Aid was Esmarch (1823-1908). He was born in Schleswing Holstein; became a distinguished surgeon and was appointed Surgeon General in the German Army on the outbreak of the Franco-Prussian War. Later he was appointed Consulting Surgeon to the large military hospital near Berlin and was recognised as one of the greatest authorities on hospital management and military surgery. However, no part of his work was more widely valued than his two manuals, entitled "*First Aid on the Battlefield*" and "*First Aid to the Injured*". The triangular bandage was invented in 1831 by Dr. Mayor of Lausanne, Switzerland, but was later popularised by Esmarch.

Origin of the Term: The term 'First-Aid' was adopted officially in England for the first time in 1879 by the St. John Ambulance Association. The expression "First-Aider" was not coined till 1894 and was intended to designate "any person who has received a certificate from an authorised association that he (or she) is qualified to render first hand aid."

7.2 THE SCOPE OF FIRST AID

The Scope of First Aid

- (1) Diagnosis of the Case
- (2) Treatment of the Case
- (3) Disposal of the Case

The Diagnosis: In the first instance, the first aider must know how the accident or sudden injury has occurred. This information can be obtained from the victim if he is in a position to do so or from a witness or witnesses. This is known as the 'history of the case'.

The next step in diagnosis is to observe the 'symptoms' like faintness, pain, shivering or thirst.

Treatment: With a view to prevent the condition from becoming worse, special attention should be paid to cases of severe bleeding, failure of breathing, unconsciousness and shock etc.

Disposal: After rendering first aid, the doctor should be called in to examine the casualty or victim. However if this is not possible, the patient should be immediately removed to his home, dispensary or hospital depending upon the situation. The members of the family of the victim or his relatives should also be informed at once. In any case, immediate treatment is a must.

7.3 QUALITIES OF THE FIRST AIDER

The first-raider must try to imbibe the following qualities to discharge his functions effectively and efficiently.

1. *Promptness and Quickness:* The first aider should render help to the victim without any loss of time.
2. *Calmness and Composeness:* The first aider should take speedy action without any tension.
3. *Intelligence and Wisdom*: He should intelligently and wisely decide upon the action to be taken to render help to the victim.
4. *Resourcefulness*: For providing immediate relief to the victim of the accident, the first aider should utilise all the available resources that he can think of.
5. *Sympathy*: The first aider should display an attitude of helpfulness and consideration to the victim so that the victim feels comfortable.
6. *Sweetness.* The first aider should say sweet words to the victim.
7. *Skilfulness and Tactfulness*: The first aider should be skilful to provide first aid and should be tactful to control the crowd which usually gathers around the victim and causes undue delay in providing immediate help.
8. *Dextrality*: The first aider should handle the patient as well as the appliance without causing any pain to the victim.

7.4 BASIC PRINCIPLES OF RENDERING FIRST AID OR MANAGING THE ACCIDENT

1. Principle of removing the cause of injury.
2. Principle of stopping bleeding immediately.
3. Principle of ensuring the free supply of air to the patient.
4. Principle of keeping the patient warm.
5. Principle of removal of clothes including shoes of the patient without causing him unnecessary pain.
6. Principle of covering the wound with clean dressing.
7. Principle of supporting and placing the injured limb in a natural position as far as possible, with bandages, splints and slings.
8. Principle of keeping the patient in a restful position.
9. Principle of making efforts to take out the poison.
10. Principle of saving broken parts of limbs till proper medical aid is available.
11. Principle of giving warm milk or tea to the patient.
12. Principle of possessing adequate knowledge of anatomy and physiology.
13. Principle of not taking the place of the doctor.
14. Principle of making immediate arrangements to remove the patient to a hospital.

7.5 FIRST AID BOX: CONTENTS

First Aid Box: Contents

(1) Apparatus or Equipment	(2) Medicines
1. Adhesive dressings	1. A.P.C.
2. Bandages (Different types)	2. Belladona plaster
3. Camel hair brush	3. Bicarbonate of soda
4. Cotton wool	4. Burnoil
5. Dressing forceps	5. Caromine drops or tablets
6. Glass graduated	6. Common salt
7. Kidney basin	7. Dettol
8. Measuring tape	8. Dusting powder
9. Needle	9. Glycerine
10. Note book and pencil	10. Gum paint
11. Pads of various sizes	11. Iodex
12. Safety pins	12. Johnson violet
13. Scissors	13. Locula
14. Splints	14. Mercury chrome lotion (or red lotiom)
15. Spoon	15. Olive oil
16. Thermometer	16. Potassium permanganate
17. Tourniquet	17. Smelling salt
18. Tweezers	18. Tincture of iodine
	19. Throat paint
	20. Vicks Vaporub or Balm

7.6 FIRST AID FOR DIFFERENT TYPES OF ACCIDENTS/NEEDS/ EMERGENCIES

I. Drowning

Following steps are considered important in case of drowning treatment.

1. If the victim is still in water, all efforts should be made to take him/ her out of water with a rope or stick. In case a boat is available, it may be used to the best advantage.
2. When out of water, the victim's mouth or throat should be cleaned of mud or any other thing which might have gone in with water.
3. The patient after the above treatment should be put on his stomach, with the back up and face on one side.
4. After step 3, the back should be pressed to bring out water from the lungs.
5. Artificial breathing may be given to the patient, if he/she is not breathing. This may be done by laying the patient on his/her back after taking out the water and bringing chin forward and up.
6. The nose of the patient should be held firmly while breathing gently into his mouth, about 15 times a minute. This helps in inflating the lungs and helping in restoring the circulation.
7. If the heart has stopped breathing, mouth to mouth breathing may be continued and some other person be asked to give cardiac massage, by pressing firmly with the heel of the hand over the middle of the breast bone. This may be done about 50 times a minute. After each pressure hand must be lifted off.
8. The patient's wet clothes should be removed and dry clothes put while artificial respiration is being given.
9. The patient must be kept warm.
10. It must be ensured that respiration does not stop.
11. As early as possible, the patient should be removed to the hospital in an ambulance.

II. Poisoning

Symptoms

1. Eyes become red.
2. The body becomes inactive and unconsciousness develops.
3. Speech sensation is lost.
4. Foam may come out of the mouth.
5. The lips and the tongue get choked and assume scarlet colour.

Common Poisons and their Treatment

1. *Acids (Strong)*
   (i) Do not make the patient vomit.
   (ii) Give plenty of water to dilute the acid.

(iii) Add if possible, 2 tablets of chalk, milk of magnesia, plaster or white wash to a pint of water.

2. *Lead*

(i) Make the casualty vomit.

(ii) Give a desert spoon of Epson salt in a cup of waer.

3. *Mercury*

Take white of an egg in water, followed by milk. Then make the causality vomit.

4. *Opium*

(i) Give a few crystals of permanganate of potash dissolved in a tumbler of water.

(ii) Give hot coffee.

(iii) Make the causality awake.

III. Burns and Scalds

Meaning of 'Burn': When the body is burnt with some thing hot or a flame, it is called 'burn'.

Meaning of Scalds: 'Scald' implies burning with steam, hot liquid matter like ghee, milk, oil and water etc. Generally speaking no difference is made between the terms 'burn' and 'scald'.

Types of Burns

(1)	(2)	(3)
Minor burns First degree burns)	Burns that cause blisters (Second degree burns)	Deep burns (Third degree burns)

1. *Minor burns that do not form blisters (1st degree)*: To help ease the pain and lessen damage caused by a minor burn, put the burned part in cold water at once. No other treatment is needed. Give aspirin for pain.

2. *Burns that cause blisters (2nd Degree)*:

(i) Do not break blisters.

(ii) If the blisters are broken, wash gently with soap and boiled water that has been cooled. Sterilize a little vaseline by heating it until it boils and spread it on a piece of sterile gauze. Then put the gauze on the burn.

(iii) If there is no vaseline, put some gentian violet, leave the burn uncovered.

(iv) It is very important to keep the burn as clean as possible. Protect it from dirt, dust, and flies.

(v) If signs of infection appear—pus, bad smell, fever, or swollen lymph nodes—apply compresses of potassium permanganate solution 3 times a day. If potassium permanganate is not available, you can use warm salt water (1 teaspoon salt to 1 litre water). Boil both the water and cloth before use. With great care, remove the dead skin and flesh. You can spread on a little antibiotic ointment such as neosporin. In severe cases, consider taking an antibiotic such as penicillin or Ampicillin by mouth.

3. *Deep burns (3rd degree)*: These destroy the skin and expose raw or charred flesh and are always serious. They cover large areas of the body. Take the pupil to a health centre at once. In the meantime wrap the burned part with a very clean cloth or towel.

If it is not possible to get medical help, treat the burn as described above. If you do not have vaseline, put some gentian violet and leave the burns in the open air, covering it only with a loose cotton cloth or sheet to protect it from dust and flies. Keep the cloth very clean and change it each time it gets dirty with liquid or blood from the burn. Give penicillin.

Never put grease, fat, hides, coffee of feces on burns.

IV. Shocks

Shock is that feeble condition of nervous system which is the result of sudden accident or dreadful disease. Electric shocks are very common and their reason is well-known.

Symptoms of Shock

(a) Weakness after fainting especially on standing up
(b) Vomiting feeling
(c) Cold damp skin
(d) Too much sweating even in cold weather
(e) Severe thirst
(f) Restlessness, mental confusion or loss of consciousness
(g) Weak rapid pulse (more than 100 per minute)

Treatment of Shock

(i) Have the pupil lie down with his feet higher than his head. If the shock is due to a head injury do not raise his feet. Make him sit propped up (half sitting position against a pillow).
(ii) If the pupil feels cold, cover him with a blanket.
(iii) If the pupil is conscious, give him warm water or other lukewarm drinks. If shock is due to injury (accidents, stab wounds) then do not give him anything to drink. He may need surgery. Get medical help fast.
(iv) If the pupil is in pain, give him aspirin or another pain medicine.
(v) Keep calm and reassure the pupil.

V. Fainting or Loss of Consciousness

Symptoms: When a person faints, his blood pressure falls. He becomes pale and his pulse becomes weak and rapid.

Common causes of loss of consciousness are:

(a) A hit on the head (getting knocked out)

(b) Shock
(c) Poisoning
(d) Diabetes
(e) Fainting (from fright, weakness, etc.)
(f) Heat stroke
(g) Stroke
(h) Heart attack
(i) Epilepsy

Treatment: If pupil is unconscious and you do not know why, immediately check each of the following:

1. Is he breathing well? If not, tilt his head way back and pull the jaw and tongue forward. If something is stuck in his throat, pull it out. If he is not breathing, use mouth-to-mouth breathing at once.
2. Is he losing a lot of blood? If so, control the bleeding.
3. Is he in shock (moist, pale skin; weak, rapid pulse)? If so, lay him with his head lower than his feet and loosen his clothing.
4. Could it be heat stroke (no sweat, high fever, hot, red skin)? If so, shade him from the sun, keep his head higher than his feet, and soak him with cold water (ice water if possible).
5. It is best not to move him until he becomes conscious. If you have to move him, do so with great care, because if his neck or back is broken, any change of position may cause greater injury.
6. Look for wounds or broken bones, but move the person as little as possible. Do not bend his back or neck.
7. Never give anything by mouth to a person who is unconscious.

VI. Snake Bite

Hundreds of deaths occur in our country on account of snake bite. Although majority of snakes are not poisonous, yet their bite leads to death, mostly due to shock.

Snake Bite Treatment

1. If bitten on a limb, arrest the circulation of blood immediately in the arteries and veins by means of a constriction placed round the upper arm, between the wound and the heart but not round the forearm or leg.
2. The constriction may consist of rubber tubing or elastic braces or of non-elastic strips of clothing, e.g., pugree, puttee, a tie or handkerchief, tied loosely round the limb tightened with a stick.
3. Wash the wound with a solution of potassium permanganate in order to remove any venom.
4. Make an incision ¾ inch deep into the bitten area with a sharp knife or razor blade.
5. Rub crystals of potassium permanganate into the incision as a neutralising agent.
6. Keep the patient warm.

7. Keep the patient at rest.
8. Give hot drinks such as tea, coffee, or milk if the patient is able to swallow.
9. Reassure the patient with encouraging words.
10. Apply artificial respiration if breathing is falling.

Treatment of Rabies and Dog Bites

1. Immediately send for the doctor.
2. Wash the whole abraded surface with soap and water whether licked, scratched or lacerated.
3. Paint carefully the abraded surfaces if pure carbolic acid is available.
4. Crystals or a saturated solution of permanganate potash may be applied.
5. If the dog is known, insist on the owner to chain it for the doctor's inspection and to prevent any further mischief.

VII. Headache

It may be on account of poor sleep, too much exertion, fatigue, eye disease, defective vision etc.

1. Rest should be taken and one should lie down on a dark quiet place.
2. Light food should be taken.
3. Asprine tablets may be taken.

VIII. Vomiting

It is often due to a problem in the stomach or guts.

Treatment

1. Nothing should be eaten when vomiting is severe.
2. Some tea may be sipped with sugar but without milk. Ginger or lime juice may be added.
3. Frequent sips of cola, tea may be taken.

IX. Heat Cramps

In hot weather people who work hard and sweat a lot sometimes get painful cramps in their legs, arms, or stomach. These occur because the body lacks salts.

Treatment: Put a teaspoon of salt in a litre of boiled water and drink it. You can add a little sugar and lime juice to the drink.

X. Heat Exhaustion

Signs: A person who works and sweats a lot in hot weather may become very pale and weak and perhaps feel faint. The skin is cool and moist. The pulse is rapid and weak. The most striking thing is that on a very hot day the skin is cold and moist.

Treatment: Have the person lie down in a cool place, raise his feet, and rub his legs. Give salt water to drink: 1 teaspoon of salt in a litre of water. (Give nothing by mouth while the person is unconscious.)

XI. Heat Stroke

Heat stroke is not common, but is very dangerous. It occurs especially in older people and alcoholics during hot weather.

Signs: The skin is red, very hot, and dry. Not even the armpits are moist. The person has a very high fever, sometimes more than 42°C. Often he is unconscious.

Treatment

1. The body temperature must be lowered immediately.
2. Put the person in the shade.
3. Take off his clothes and pour cold water over him.
4. Fan him.
5. Give ice cold water enema.
6. Take the temperature every 10 minutes.
7. When the temperature comes down to 38°C, stop pouring cold water on him.
8. Seek medical help.

XII. Cuts, Scraps, and Small Wounds

1. Cleanliness is of prime importance in preventing infection and helping wounds to heal.
2. To treat a wound, first, wash your hands very well with soap and water. Then wash the wound well with soap and boiled water.
3. When cleaning the wound, be careful to clean out all the dirt. Lift up and clean under the flaps of skin. You can use a clean tweezer or other instruments to remove bits of dirt, but always boil them first to be sure they are sterile.
4. If a pupil gets a cut, scrap or wound, give him an injection of tetanus toxiod immediately. If he has not been immunized against tetanus, give him one injection each month for the next two months.

XIII. When Something Gets Stuck in the Throat

When food or something else sticks in a person's throat and he cannot breathe, quickly do this:

1. Stand behind him and wrap your arms around his waist.
2. Put your fist against his belly above the naval and below the ribs.
3. Press into his belly with a sudden strong upward jerk. This forces the air from his lungs and should free his throat. Repeat this several times, if necessary.
4. If the pupil is a bit bigger than you, or is already unconscious, quickly do this:
   (a) Lay him on his back.
   (b) Sit over him like this, with the heel of your lower hand on his

belly between his naval and ribs.

(c) make a quick, strong upward push. Repeat several times if necessary.

(d) If he still cannot breath, try mouth-to-mouth breathing.

XIV. Nose-bleeding

1. Patient should sit quietly.
2. Pinch the nose firmly for 10 minutes or until the bleeding has stopped and if this does not control the bleeding, pack the nostril with a wad of cotton, leaving part of it outside the nose. If possible, first wet the cotton with hydrogen peroxide, Vaseline, cardon cactus juice or lidocaine with epinephrine. Then pinch the nose firmly again. Do not let go for 10 minutes or more.
3. Leave the cotton in place for a few hours after the bleeding stops; then take it out very carefully.
4. Do not dig into the nose or try to remove clotted blood. Bleeding will start again.
5. If a pupil's nose bleeds often, smear a little vaseline inside the nostril twice a day.

8

Common Sports Injuries and Road Safety Rules

8.1 INTRODUCTION

Injuries occur in sports as they do occur in everyday life. They are common in almost every sport. It is also true that quite a large number of injuries can be avoided in sports. Injuries in sports primarily occur on account of lack of knowledge on the part of sports persons. As observed by leonardo De Vinci, "If you are enamoured of practice without scientific knowledge, you are just like a pilot who goes into a ship without rudder and a compass and does not know his destination."

8.2 TYPES OF SPORTS INJURIES

Types of Sports Injuries

- (1) Soft Tissue Injuries
- (2) Bone Injuries
- (3) Joint Injuries

Soft Tissue Injuries: Their Classification

- (1) Abrasion
- (2) Bruises
- (3) Contusion
- (4) Sprain
- (5) Strain

8.3 SOFT TISSUE INJURIES

Abrasion is a superficial (not deep) injury of skin or mucous membranes due to rubbing or scraping. It is normally a minor injury but can be serious if some foreign matter gets stuck in it. It may be caused by a fall on a hard or rough surface. It may also occur on account of friction with certain equipment.

Such injuries occur in sports like cricket, football, hockey wrestling, track, and field etc.

(a) Abrasion

(i) Scraping of skin with some burning pain.
(ii) Some bleeding or oozing at the abrasion spot.

Prevention

(i) Wearing protective gear.
(ii) Avoiding poorly maintained fields.

Treatment

(i) Washing area of abrasion with soap and warm water.
(ii) Cleaning and applying antibiotic ointment.
(iii) Covering the wound lightly during day time and uncovering it at night.
(iv) Taking medical assistance if infection is suspected.

(b) Bruises

1. The injured spot appears to be blue.
2. Blood spreads under the skin because blood vessels are also broken.
3. Bruise is not clearly visible because in this injury, inner tissues are damaged.

Bruises are common in boxing, football and hockey.

Prevention of Bruises

1. The player should have the ability to anticipate the danger of occuring the bruise.
2. The player should use proper protective equipment.
3. The player should remain careful.

Treatment of Bruises

1. Application of ice or cold compressing should be given immediately to the injured player for 10 to 20 minutes.
2. After two days, massage should be done lightly on the spot of bruises for reducing swelling and stiffness.

(c) Contusion

Meaning of Contusion: Contusion implies a direct hit or blow anywhere on the body, causing bleeding from ruptured small capillaries below the skin without any breaking of skin.

Such injuries take place in sports like baseball, boxing, cricket, hockey and gymnastics etc.

Symptoms

(i) Discolouration under the skin which starts from redness to turning black or blue gradually.
(ii) Swelling and pain on the contused part.
(iii) Stiffness over the area.

Prevention

Use protective gear like batting gloves, elbow guards, helmets and skin guard etc. as per requirements.

Treatment

(i) Apply a cold compression or ice or lint soaked in equal quantity of spirit and water at the time of injury.
(ii) Continue ice massage three to four times a day.
(iii) After three days, apply heat instead of ice massage and massage gently to reduce swelling.

(d) Sprain

Meaning of Sprain: Sprain is an injury of the ligaments. It occurs due to over stretching of ligaments. During exercise, ligaments sometimes become tense and get injured near the joint with a bone or from a weak spot in the ligaments themselves.

Sprain may occur in tennis, field, track and weight lifting. It may take place at joints or any part like ankle joint, elbow or knee joint.

Types of Sprain

(1) Mild sprain
(2) Moderate sprain
(3) Severe sprain

Mild Sprain: In mild sprain, there is slight tearing of some of the ligament fibres and there is no loss of function of joint.

Moderate Sprain: In moderate sprain there is some rupture of ligaments and is accompanied with some loss of function.

Severe Sprain: In severe sprain there is total rupture of ligaments and they also get separated from bone and there is total loss of movement.

Symptoms

(i) Acute pain in the spot injured.
(ii) Swelling on the spot.
(iii) Softness at the spot and pain on touching.

Prevention

(i) Long term specific training or conditioning.
(ii) Warming up before participation.
(iii) Wearing knee caps, elbow caps or bandages etc.

Treatment

(i) Do not move the injured part.
(ii) In case of mild sprain, apply ice compression 3 to 4 times in a day

for three days and cover the affected part by elastic crepe bandage after treatment.

(iii) After three days apply heat.
(iv) Consult the doctor.

(e) Strain

Meaning of strain: Strain is a muscle injury. It is the result of stress or force applied on tissues. Application of force results in some deformity in tissues. This deformation is termed as strain. Strain may also be termed as an injury to muscles or tendons connected to the bones. Application of a violent or extra force results in such injuries.

Such injuries take place in track and field, gymnastics, weight lifting, skiing and tennis etc.

Strains occur at joints and any part like elbow, knee or ankle joint etc. may be affected.

Types of Strain

- (1) Mild strain
- (2) Moderate strain
- (3) Severe strain

(i) *Mild strain*: In mild strain, there is a slight muscle pull without any tearing of muscle or tendon.
(ii) *Moderate strain*: In moderate strain, there is slight tearing of muscle or tendon and there is some loss of strength.
(iii) *Severe strain*: In severe strain, the muscles or tendons rupture. In such a case, loss of strength is considerable.

Symptoms

(i) Pain in moving the body part such as arm or leg.
(ii) Swelling in the area
(iii) Feeling as something broken inside.
(iv) Loss of strength in movement.

Prevention

(i) Proper conditioning
(ii) Warming up before participation.
(iii) Using appropriate protective gear.

Types of Strain

- (1) Sternocostal joint strain
- (2) Bicep muscle strain
- (3) Tricep muscle strain
- (4) Facia lata strain
- (5) Medical ligament strain
- (6) Calf muscle strain

Treatment

(i) Place the injured in a comfortable position.
(ii) Stop any movement of the injured part.
(iii) For mild strain, use ice massage 3 to 4 times daily.
(iv) After two days, stop ice massage and apply heat instead.
(v) Wrap the affected part by crepe bandage.
(vi) Give some pain killer, if pain persists.

8.4 BONE INJURIES

Bone injuries are usually caused by a direct blow to the bone either in a fall or a kick. Important types of bone injuries are as under:

1. Simple fracture.
2. Compound fracture.
3. Complicated fracture.
4. Comminuted fracture.
5. Impacted fracture.
6. Green stick fracture.

Types of Fractures on the Parts of the Body

(1) Ankle fracture
(2) Collarbone fracture
(3) Foot fracture
(4) Knee fracture
(5) Radius bone fracture
(6) Scaphoid fracture

Simple fracture: When the bone is fractured without any wound, it is called simple fracture.

Compound fracture: Compound fracture is that fracture in which the bone is broken along with the damage to the muscles and skin.

Complicated fracture. In complicated fracture, the broken bone damages an internal organ. Such fractures usually occur in high jump and pole vault.

Comminuted fracture: When a bone gets broken into more than two pieces, it is called comminuted fracture. This type of fracture occurs in events like cycling and motorcycle racing.

Impacted fracture: When the end of a broken bone enters into another bone, it is called impacted fracture.

Green Stick fracture: In a green stick fracture, bones are bent immediately whenever there is any pressure on them. Such types of fractures are common among children because their bones are delicate and soft.

Symptoms of Fracture

1. Usually unbearable pain occurs at the place of fracture.
2. It becomes impossible to move the broken part of the limb.
3. Inflammation or swelling occurs immediately at the site and the near by part.

4. The fractured limb does not remain in its normal shape. Deformity of the bone can be observed very easily.
5. The sensation of the crepitus can be felt easily by keeping the finger on the broken bone.

Prevention of Fracture

1. To some extent, fracture can be prevented by using protective equipment needed in a sport, for instance, head gear and teethguard.
2. Fracture can be prevented to some extent by having sports equipment of good quality.
3. A scientific knowledge of the game and its application is also helpful in preventing fracture.

Treatment of Fracture

1. If there is a fracture in the limb of a sports person, it should be located by touching the site very gently and slowly.
2. When the fracture is located, attempt should not be made to move it to any side.
3. If there is any bleeding, it should be stopped immediately.
4. Efforts should be made to keep the fractured part stable by using splints and bandages.
5. In case of compound fracture, neither the wound should be washed, nor any antiseptic used.
6. In case of a fracture in the vertibrae, the injured player should be lifted and moved in such a way as to avoid bending, twisting or displacement of the damaged vertibrae.
7. Immobilising bandage should be applied when there is rib's fracture. Thereafter the victim should be shifted to hospital.
8. For the ankle bone fracture, a splint should be applied.
9. For the fracture of metatarsal, the foot and ankle joint should be immobilised. When it is not feasible, then the foot can be immobilised by binding it with a triangular bandage.
10. For the fracture of the thigh bone (femur), the injured person should be given anaesthetics and his leg immobilised. Immobilisation lessens the additional damage to the victim.
11. Pain killer should be given to the victim.
12. Injured person should be kept warm for lessening felt shock.

8.5 JOINT INJURIES

Classification of Joint Injuries

(1) Finger dislocation
(2) Hip joint dislocation
(3) Knee cap dislocation
(4) Lower jaw dislocation
(5) Radio humeral joint injury
(6) Shoulder joint dislocation
(7) Shoulder separation

1. *Finger Dislocation*: Finger dislocation is usually caused by a blow to the front of the finger, e.g. catching a baseball or cricket ball. The finger immediately looks deformed because the bones at one of the joints are dislocated. Initially there is a great pain in the joint.

2. *Hip Joint Dislocation*: Dislocation of the hip joint is caused by strong force. In this dislocation, the limb seems to be shortened. There is pain at the site of dislocation.

Treatment: The complete lower limbs should be immobilised. The victim should be taken promptly on a stretcher to hospital.

3. *Knee Dislocation*: The knee is very vulnerable to damage during a twisting injury. In this type of dislocation, recovery is not very quick. Several types of fracture can occur within the knee joint. It is mostly caused by direct blow to knee, although it can occur with ligament injuries or dislocated knee cap. There is swelling in the joint just after the injury. Immediate medical treatment is needed rather than waiting until stiffness has set in.

4. *Lower Jaw Dislocation*: Low jaw dislocation generally occurs when the chin is struck or the mouth has been opened too wide.

Treatment

Symptoms: (i) Pain is felt at the site of the joint, (ii) There is inability to close the mouth, and (iii) There is forward displacement of the chin.

Preventive Measures: (i) Protective equipments should be used, and (ii) Mouth should not be opened too wide.

The victim should be seated on a low place and the first aider should stand behind him holding his head and the lower jaw bone firmly inserting his thumbs into the victim's mouth. The first aider should then depress the lower jaw bone of the victim by slow and strong pressure.

5. *Radio Humeral Joint Injury*: Radio humeral joint injury is caused on account of damage either to the ligaments around outside of the joint or the shiny surface of the joint itself. Pain is felt over the outer side of the joint over the bony knob. It is usually caused by twisting the arm downwards such as during a forearm tennis or badminton shot.

6. *Shoulder Joint Dislocation*: In the field of games and sports, dislocation of the shoulder joint frequently occurs.

Symptoms of Shoulder Joint Dislocation: (i) Dislocation is observed from the forced position of the arm and change in the position of the joint, (ii) The injured person keeps his arm bent at the elbow and a little to one side of the trunk, (iii) There is sharp pain when the joint is moved, (iv) The shape of the shoulder gets distorted because the head of the humerous is displaced forward and down in relation to the socket of the joint.

Treatment

(i) The injured player should be supported by triangular bandage.

(ii) No attempt should be made to reduce the dislocation.

(iii) The victim should be promptly taken to hospital.

7. *Shoulder Separation*: Shoulder separation or acrimio-clavicular joint separation is caused by direct blow to shoulder such as falling on shoulder in sports and games like boxing, judo and *kabbadi etc.* There is lot of pain and swelling at the end of the collar bone. End of collarbone may be swollen and end of bone may be seen out of position. The injured person should be taken immediately to the hospital.

8.6 BANDAGES

1. Bandages are used to help keep wounds clean. For this reason, bandages or pieces of cloth used to cover wounds must always be clean. Cloth used for bandages should be washed and then dried with an iron or in the sun, in a clean, dust-free place.
2. If possible, cover the wound with a sterile gauze pad before bandaging. These pads are often sold in sealed envelopes in pharmacies. Or prepare your own sterile gauze of cloth. Wrap it in thick paper, seal it with tape, and bake it for 20 minutes in an oven. Putting a pan of water in the oven under the cloth will keep it from charring.
3. If a bandage gets wet or dirt gets under it, take the bandage off, wash the cut again, and put on a clean bandage.
4. Be careful that a bandage that goes around a limb is not so tight it cuts off the flow of blood.
5. Many small scrapes and cuts do not need bandages. They heal best if washed with soap and water and left open to the air. The most important thing is to keep them clean.

8.7 ROAD SAFETY RULES

Factors on which Road Safety Depends

Road safety primarily depends upon the following factors:

1. Observance of traffic rules.
2. Driving habits of the people.
3. Volume of traffic on the road.
4. Type of traffic on the road.
5. Situation/location of the road.
6. Condition of the road.

Role of the School in Training Safety Rules

The school can play an important role in training the students in the observance of road safety rules. Following methods can be used in this regard:

1. Instruction in road safety rules.
2. Taking the students at a suitable place to observe the traffic police in controlling the traffic at strategic crossing.
3. Giving actual training to elder students to control traffic by assisting the traffic police.

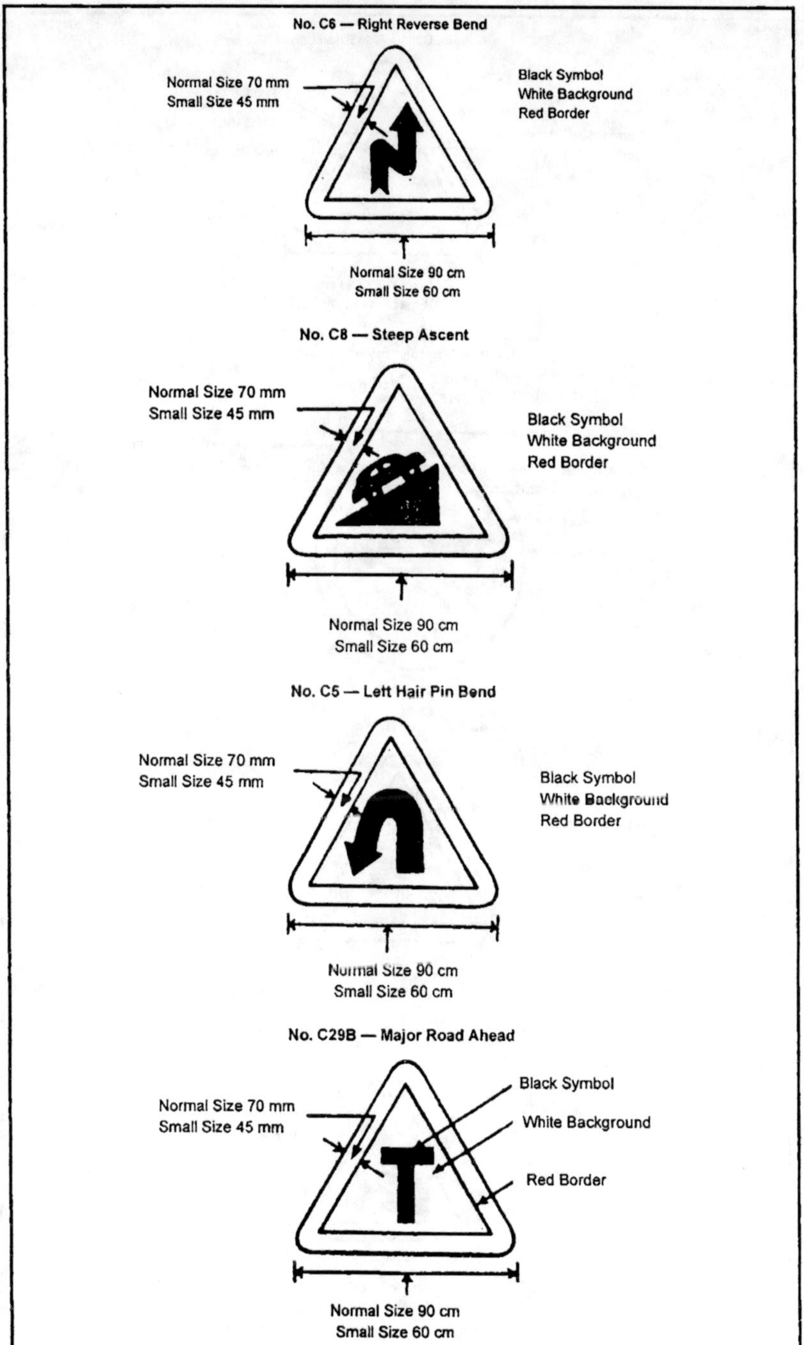

Fig. 8.1: Road Safety Signs

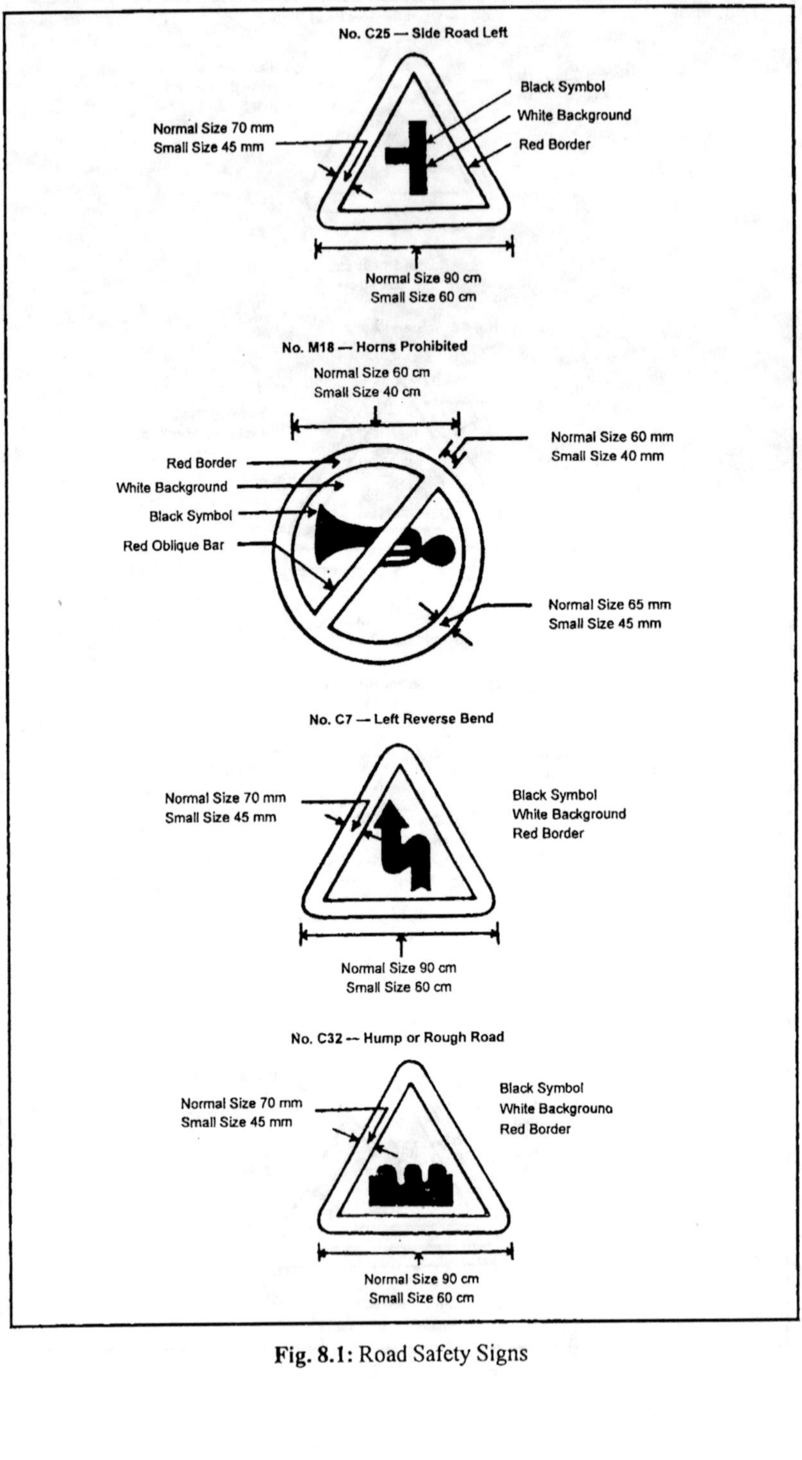

Fig. 8.1: Road Safety Signs

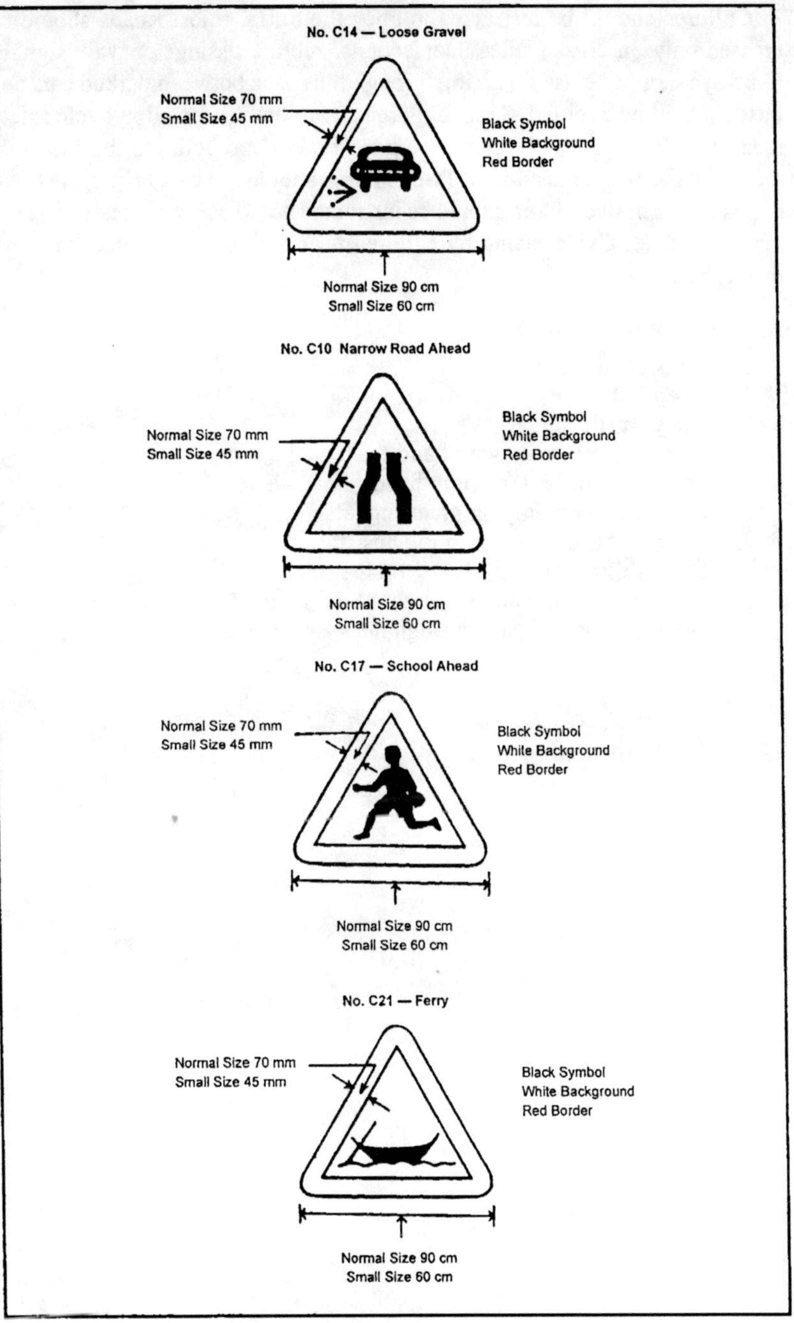

Fig. 8.1: Road Safety Signs

Children should be instructed to obey the traffic rules. Roads should be crossed only on cross walks, intersections, zebra crossings or walk signals. Subways should be used. Passing through the space between parked cars and buses should be avoided. Small children should be instructed in cycle safety measures also. The cycle must have good brakes and bell. During the night there must be proper headlight. Two children should not ride on a cycle as far as possible. Small children should be instructed not to use cycle on the road as far as possible. Cycle racing by children near the congested places is very dangerous.

Road Safety Rules and Signs

1. Walk on the footpath.
2. Keep left
3. Obey traffic signals
4. Signal clearly with your hand for taking a turn.
5. Overtake only by the right handside.
6. Cross the road only on green signals.
7. Always stand in queue at the bus stop.
8. Do not throw fruit peels etc. on the road.
9. Don't play, jump and loiter about on the road.
10. Do not walk and pass through heavy vehicles.

9

Concept of Physical Education

9.1 IMPORTANCE OF PHYSICAL EDUCATION

Importance of physical education in the all round development of an individual is recognised by all thinkers. Here we quote the views of some prominent thinkers including educators and philosophers.

Rousseau states, "It is the sound constitution of the body, that makes the operation of the mind easy and certain."

Spencer is of the view, "To be a good animal is the first requisite to success in life and to be a nation of good animals is the first condition to national prosperity."

Montaigue writes, "Physical education does neither train up the soul, nor body but the whole man."

"The physical welfare of the youth of the country should be one of the main concerns of the State and any departure from the normal standards of physical well-being at this period of life may have serious consequences," observed the Secondary Education Commission.

Hall has very emphatically observed, "A ton of knowledge bought at the expense of an ounce of health which is the most ancient and precious form of wealth costs more than its value."

Similar views have been expressed by Carlyle when he writes, "We manufacture clever devils by the thousand because health is not the object of party politics."

The great saint Swami Vivekananda has also stressed the importance of well-built bodies when he remarks, "What India needs today is not the *Bhagwad Gita* but the football field." Our Indian schools must give due importance to this aspect of education. There is a great need of a general philosophy of physical education in India, though it appears to be very strange in a country famous for ancient Yogic system. There is no denying the fact that of late we have been ignoring this side. This has led W.M. Ryburn to remark, "We need in Indian education a general physical education—a conception of education in which physical education takes its rightful place and in which its vital importance is recognised."

Regarding the significance of physical education, H.C. Buck has observed that a properly directed physical education should result in health, happiness, efficiency and character.

Froebel says, "If we wish to develop the whole being, we must exercise the whole human being."

In brief, physical education is important on account of the following benefits.

First: It helps in building individual and national character and strength.

Second: It helps to develop desirable qualities and values like agility, elegance, endurance, initiative, resourcefulness and smartness.

Third: It makes a significant contribution to the social adjustment of an individual.

Fourth: It helps in the spiritual development of an individual.

Meaning of Physical Education

The views of great thinkers given below throw adequate light on the meaning of physical education.

1. *R. Cassidy*, "Physical education is the sum of changes in the individual caused by experience which can bring in motor activity."

2. *C.L. Brownwell,* "Physical education is concerned with strength and endurance (the principal objectives of physical training). But physical education regards these qualities as a means to an end—the means of obtaining greater satisfaction in a specific activity, and the end which represents the all-round educational development associated with participation in the activity. In short, physical education means the physical activities that have characterised the immemorial history of mankind."

3. *Delbert Obertenffer,* "Physical education is the sum of those experiences which come to the individual through movement."

4. *Jesse Feiring Williams,* "Physical education is the sum of man's physical activities selected as to kind and conducted as to outcomes."

5. *Jay B. Nash*, "Physical education is that field of education which deals with big muscle activities and their related responses."

6. *Charles A. Bucher*, "Physical education is an integral part of the total education process and has as its aim the development of physically, mentally, emotionally and socially fit citizens through the medium of physical activities which have been selected with a view to realizing these outcomes."

7. *C.C. Cowell*, "Physical education is the social process of change in the behaviour of the human organism, originating primarily from the stimulus of social big-muscle-play and related activities."

8. *Clark, W. Hetherington*, "Physical education is that phase of education which is concerned, first, with the organization and leadership of children in big muscle activities, to gain the development and adjustment inherent in the activities according to social standards, and second with the leadership of the activities so that the educational process may go on without growth handicaps."

9. *Nixon and Cozens*, "Physical education should be defined as that phase

of the whole process of education which is concerned with vigorous muscular activities and related responses and with the modifications in the individual resultant from these responses."

10. *Edward F. Voltmer*, Arthur A. Esslingor, "Physical education is that part of education which proceeds by means of, or predominantly through physical activity, it is not some separate, partially related field. Physical education is but one aspect of the larger problem of education in general, and any system which divorces or tends to divorce, the physical from the moral and intellectual aspects of life, is thoroughly unsound."

11. *Websters Dictionary*, "Physical education is a part of education which gives instruction in the development and care of the body ranging from simple calasthemic exercises to a course of study providing training in hygiene, gymnastics, and the performance and management of athletic games."

12. *A.R. Wayman*, "Physical education is that aspect of education which is concerned with the development and education of the entire personality of a man by physical activities."

13. *Hasley and Porter*, "Physical education is that part of the educational programme in which the child is not merely encouraged to move but is taught to move effectively. Through physical education we make sure that a child's movements are the most suitable ones for stages of developments."

9.2 CONCEPT OF PHYSICAL EDUCATION

The *Secondary Education Commission* (1952-53) made it clear "that unless physical education is accepted as an integral part of education, and the educational authorities recognize its need in all schools, the youth of the country, which forms its most valuable assets, will never be able to pull their full weight in national welfare". The old concept of physical education as 'mere drill or a series of regulated exercises' has been rejected. "It includes all forms of physical activities and games which promote the development of the body and mind." The Commission recommended that physical education should be comprehensive enough to include all aspects of health education; full records of physical activities should be maintained; teachers of physical education should be given the same status as other teachers of similar qualifications; and other teachers of the school along with the physical instructor should actively participate in the physical activities of students.

The *Education Commission* (1964-66) points out: 'There has been a tendency in recent government schemes of physical education to emphasize only the physical fitness value of physical education and ignore its educational value'. The concept of physical education has been made broader, as it should contribute 'not only to physical fitness but also to physical efficiency, mental alertness and the development of certain qualities—perseverance, team spirit, leadership, obedience to rules, moderation in victory and balance in defeat." The Commission was aware of the hard realities which one encounters while preparing programmes of physical education in schools and colleges, and, therefore, it suggested that the programmes 'should take into account not only what is useful but also what is possible in view of limitations of facilities, time and number of teachers.' It also emphasized the need for re-examining and re-designing the programmes of physical education in the light of certain basic principles of child growth and development.

The revised National Policy on Education (1992) emphatically stated, "Sports and physical education are an integral part of the learning process."

Helen Manley, former Director of Health and Physical Education, Missouri (U.S.A.), stated, "Physical education is bigger than free play, exercises or races. It recognises that a child is an integre (a whole) and as such cannot be torn into parts, with mind, body and soul, and educated separately. The unique contribution of physical education is in educating boys and girl through physical activities. The body is the vehicle, the larger motor areas the tools. The activities must promote organic vigour, neuro – muscular skills and social experiences, promotive of democratic living."

Present Concept of Physical Education and Its Contents

As already observed, physical education is a very wide concept. It is not correct to equate physical education with games and sports, gymnastics, mass drill, 'yoga', physical exercise, physical training and physical culture. None of these terms convey the correct concept and scope of physical education. Physical education encompasses all these programmes.

The term physical education includes activities like exercises—fitness as well as curative, games, informal play, movement education, informal play, rhythmetic activities, sports and 'yoga'; health oriented activities which help for the emotional, mental, physical, social and spiritual development of the individual. Physical education is much more than building a healthy and strong body.

From the views expressed above it will be obvious that physical education is not only concerned with helping the child to grow and develop physically but also learning to fit in with his social environment and adjusting to life around, acquiring the capacity to be mentally alert to all environmental responses, expressing emotions without prejudice to others and otherwise reaching his maturity progressively.

9.3 BRIEF HISTORY OF PHYSICAL EDUCATION

Physical Education in the Ancient Period

Physical education, in one or the other form, formed an integral part of general education in the *'Gurukulas'* in ancient India.

The ancient Greeks had developed a well-organised physical education programme by 800 BC. Special training institutions called gymnasiums were set up where boys and girls were given physical and military training. Physical programmes also included jumping, running and wrestling etc. Discuss throws and javelin throws were also practised in these gymnasiums.

The town of Olympia in Greece is the ancient site of Olympic games. The earliest records of Olympic Games date back to 77 B.C. when CORIBUS, a citizen of Elis, became the champion of foot race of 192.25 metres.

Modern Olympic Games began in the 19th century. The credit for reviving the ancient Olympic Games goes to Pierre de Coubertin (1863-1937) of France. He believed that intelligence cannot exist without training the body.

The main objectives of the revival of Olympic Games were:

1. To create interest of public, educators and governments of different countries in establishing national programmes of physical training and competitions for promoting health and morals.
2. To exhibit the principles of fair play and sportsmanship which could be adopted in other spheres also.
3. To organise games with the noble idea of taking part in the games, without the temptation of financial or material gains.
4. To link sports with the social movement of spreading friendship and fraternity among the youth of the world.
5. To create international friendship and goodwill, that can lead to a happier and peaceful world.

Physical Education Programmes in Schools in the Modern Times

During the 1800s, physical education programmes were introduced in schools in several countries like Germany, the United Kingdom, Sweden, etc. These programmes included athletics, gymnastics and some sports.

During early 1900s, separate physical education programmes were introduced for females. During this period, several national and international sports associations came into being.

At present, physical education is considered as an integral part of education.

All possible efforts are made to provide maximum opportunities to each student to take part in a variety of physical education programmes.

New Physical Education is aimed at sharing with other disciplines its contribution to the cognitive, connative and affective development of the students.

Following are the major programmes included in physical education.

1. Calisthenics
2. Athletics
3. Games
4. Aquatics
5. Rhythmic Activities
6. Gymnastics
7. Yogic Exercises
8. Judo

9.4 AIMS AND OBJECTIVES OF PHYSICAL EDUCATION

The determination of objectives in every activity/programme/endeavour is very essential. So is the case with the educational programme. Objectives in education including physical education in general are based on the national aspirations, ideals and values. They are the guiding force behind every activity. An objective as observed by Dewey, is a foreseen end that gives direction to an activity or motivates behaviour. There is an intimate relationship between an activity and its aim. An objective or an aim is a conscious purpose which is apt to set before us while launching an activity. We set our hearts on achieving some specific result and this desired end is the aim or objective. It is, therefore, very essential to understand the general objectives of physical education.

In the following paragraphs, general objectives of physical education are given in brief.

1. *Development of Physical well-being*: This implies providing physical education to students for normal physical growth and development, in developing endurance and strength to do normal tasks of life as well as to meet the demands of the stress of life, without feeling undue strain and in maintaining and developing proper and sound functioning of organs and organic systems.

2. *Development of motor qualities*: Physical education aims at developing motor qualities such as endurance, strength, speed, coordinative abilities, flexibility and power, etc.

These qualities are essential for participating effectively in sports and games as well as for leading a healthy and productive life in society.

3. *Development of neuro-muscular coordination*: Neuro-muscular coordination is essential in order to accomplish a work gracefully. Such activities are developed only through physical exercises and that too at the younger age to a considerable extent.

4. *Maintenance of health and fitness:* Physical activities aim at helping in a large measure to slow down the degenerative process.

5. *Development of functional knowledge*: Physical education aims at providing opportunities to acquire knowledge of first-aid and proper health procedure related to physical exercises.

6. *Cultural pursuits:* As observed by Cozens and Stempt, "Sports and physical activities belong to the 'arts' of humanity. Such activities have formed a basic part of all cultures, including all racial groups and historical ages, because they are as fundamental a form of human experience as music, poetry and painting. Every age has its artists, its adherents and its enemies. While wars, systems of government, plagues and famines, have come and gone in the long record of mankind, these fundamental things have always been present, in greater or lesser degree."

7. *Sublimation of emotions*: Gregarious instinct in the adolescent is very predominant. This expresses the desire of the growing boys to form groups. If

no opportunity is provided to the students, they may form gangs. Physical activities enable them to work in appropriate groups.

8. *Social and Civic Training Aim*: By participating in a variety of physical activities, students learn valuable lessons of cooperative and team work.

9. *Aim of Development of Worthy recreational interests*: Recreational interests developed through physical activities prove to be very beneficial in the leisure hours of adult life and make life fuller and richer.

10. *Aim of Development of Sentiment of Loyalty*: Physical education aims at developing the sense of loyalty among the students. Tournaments foster this sentiment.

11. *Vocational Aim of Physical Education*: Physical education aims at developing skills which prepare students for a vocation.

12. *Spiritual Development Aim of Physical Education*: Physical education being an integral part of the total educational processes, should help in the spiritual development of the student.

13. *Participation in Construction Social Programme*: '*The Programme of Action: NPE (1992)*' has observed that studies have shown a positive correlation between participation of students in constructive social programmes and in sports and games.

Summing up: We may sum up the objectives of physical education with a statement from Sultan Mohiyuddin, "The object of physical education and training is to help in the protection and maintenance of health in body and mind. The condition of modern civilization, involving crowded localities, sedentary occupations, increase of study and mental work, restricted opportunities for natural physical growth—all these require that children, and young people should receive physical education. They must be encouraged to devote special attention for maintaining the health of the mind and the body."

9.5 AIMS AND OBJECTIVES OF PHYSICAL EDUCATION AT DIFFERENT STAGES

I. Objective of Physical Educational Primary Stage (Class I to V)

1. To develop in the students proper regular habits and attitudes to meet the natural needs of the body.
2. To train how to keep their hands, feet, eyes, nose, ears and hair clean.
3. To develop awareness and sensitivity towards the immediate environment and understand the inter-dependence between humans and the environment.
4. To develop respect for physical work, dignity of labour and hard work.
5. To develop values such as cooperation, team work and tolerance.
6. To develop physical, mental and emotional well-being through 'yoga' and games.

7. To develop qualities of enterprise, initiative, followership as well as leadership.
8. To develop an attitude of living in clean environment.
9. To be able to naturally accept failure and success.
10. To exhibit characteristics of calm and quietness at times of turmoil.
11. To maintain regularity and punctuality in all kinds of activities.

II. Objectives of Physical Education at the Upper Stage (Class VI to VIII)

1. To enable the students understand the meaning and importance of physical education.
2. To enable the students acquire healthy practices relating to exercise, rest, recreation, relaxation, sheep, posture, safety.
3. To develop skills in providing first-aid in athletic and other common childhood injuries that occur in the home, school and outside the home and school.
4. To develop organic fitness.
5. To cultivate habits of engaging in appropriate exercises so that immediate and future health needs are met.
6. To develop neuro-muscular skills and promote the ability to perform the work with ease and grace.
7. To develop attitudes of cooperation, good sportsmanship and fair play.
8. To develop a spirit of self-sacrifice and tolerance.

III. Objectives of Physical Education at the Secondary Stage (Class IX and X)

1. To bring the overall awareness of values and inculcate among students the desired habits and attitudes towards physical fitness and to raise their physical fitness status.
2. To develop a scientific point of view regarding physical education.
3. To identify personal, family and community physical fitness problems and acquire scientific knowledge and information to control these problems to stay physically fit.
4. To take action, individually and collectively to protect and promote (i) their own physical fitness, and (ii) physical fitness of their family members, (iii) physical fitness of those around them in the community, seeking help when required from available community resources.
5. To develop awareness regarding transfer of fundamental processes to physical activities of one's choice.
6. To develop interest in exercise, sports and games for self-satisfaction and making it a part of life.
7. To enable the student to enhance qualities of courage, discipline, efficiency and self-confidence.
8. To enable the students to develop and display a sense of responsibility and self-sacrifice.

9. To develop an awareness of good postures and to strive for them.
10. To enable the students to develop an active and sturdy life.
11. To enable the students to practise socially behavioural patterns in an impressive manner.

Objectives of Physical Education for Elementary Teachers Training

1. To enable the students to appreciate the need of physical education in the total curriculum.
2. To enable the students identify common postural defects among the students and suggest remedial treatment.
3. To enable the students to provide First-Aid for minor accidents and injuries.
4. To enable the students to plan, organise and conduct activities and practices directly related to children's games and sports.
5. To enable the students to organise various indigenous and modern games, combatives, drill marching and calisthenics display.

Objectives of Physical Education for B.Ed. as laid down by University Grants Commission (UGC)—2002

To develop in student teacher:

1. The theoretical assumption behind the practice of modern physical education.
2. The abilities required for organising various physical activities.
3. The abilities required for organising physical education meets and events.
4. The abilities required for evaluating attainments in physical education.

10

Methods of Teaching Physical Education

10.1 MEANING

The word method is often used very loosely. Without going into a detailed discussion on the definition of method of teaching, we may quote Herbert and Frank Rose, "While it is true that good method is not merely a collection of mechanical devices and that every teacher must devise his own method, it is important to remember that good method can result only from the constant observation of certain principles." According to these authors the principles of a good method are:

One—Orderly procedure in teaching

Two—An arrangement of subject – matter which will avoid waste of time and energy.

Three—Maximum involvement of the students.

Four—Active interest of the students.

Five—Mutual healthy interaction between the teacher and the learner.

10.2 OBJECTIVES

1. Methods of teaching aim at adapting to 3 A's—age, ability and aptitude of the student.
2. They should aim at developing love for work.
3. They should aim at inculcating the desire to do work with the maximum efficiency which one is capable of. The motto before the teachers and students should be, "Everything that is worth doing at all is worth doing well."
4. They should aim at teaching 'how to learn through one's efforts.'
5. They should develop the capacity to think logically and scientifically.
6. They should make the students active participants in the lesson.
7. They should aim at expanding the interests of the students.
8. They should aim at correlating different aspects and subjects.
9. They should aim at transforming schools into activity schools.
10. They should aim at making the contents as vivid as possible.

10.3 REVOLUTION IN METHODS OF TEACHING

The impact of recent developments in communication and information technology (CIT) has been revolutionary on methods of teaching. Earlier developments in educational psychology brought about the slogan 'The century of the child'. The essence now is on enabling the child 'to learn how to learn.'

Progressive methods of teaching aim at providing suitable opportunities for 'learning by doing', 'learning by observation', 'learning through experimentation' and 'learning through cooperation'.

As observed by Ruskin, "Teach the pupil not only to answer questions but also to question answers".

Montaigue has pointed the essence of good methods of teaching as, "A tutor should not be continually thundering instruction into the ears of his pupils, as if he were pouring it through a funnel but induce him to think to distinguish and to find out things for himself, sometimes opening the way, at other times leaving it for him to open."

10.4 CLASSIFICATION OF METHODS OF TEACHING

There is no clear-cut distinction between devices, techniques and methods of teaching as they overlap. However, following are some of the important methods which have found general acceptance as methods of teaching:

1. Assignment Method, 2. Dalton Plan, 3. Demonstration Method, 4. Discussion Method, 5. Experiment or Laboratory Method, 6. Lecture Method, 7. Montessori Method, 8. Observation Method, 9. Play-way Method, 10. Problem Method, 11. Project Method, 12. Question Method, 13. Review Method, 14. Socialised Classroom Method, 15. Source Method, 16. Story Telling Method, 17. Supervised Study Method, 18. Team Teaching Method, 19. Textbook Method, 20. Unit Method.

A Word of Caution

Regarding the use of methods of teaching in the classroom or outside, it must be emphasised that there is no single method which could serve all purposes. Methods have to be used in combination. Likewise, a teacher should not remain wedded to a particular method. He may device his own method keeping in view the environment of teaching-learning. Lastly it must always be remembered that a method of teaching is a 'servant' and not 'master'.

10.5 SUPPLEMENTARY METHODS

Apart from methods mentioned above, following methods may be used in imparting physical education.

1. Physical education postures etc.
2. Physical education weeks.
3. Maintaining physical book relating to each child.
4. Physical environment of the school, the classroom, the play-field etc.
5. Physical education film and filmstrip.
6. Education trip for physical education purposes.
7. Physical education clubs.

8. Physical education through radio.
9. Physical education through T.V.
10. Physical education through models.
11. Physical education through cartoons.
12. Physical education through dramatics.
13. Physical education through story telling.
14. Physical education through group discussion.

10.6 WHOLE OR PART METHOD OF TEACHING-LEARNING

There are two methods of memorizing any content of learning which are known as the Whole method and the Part method. We may give an example of rules of safety at home, in the school and in the playground.

According to the Whole method the child may learn all the rules of the lesson again and again from the beginning to the end and thus memorize it.

According to the Part method, the lesson may be divided into smaller units and the child may try to memorize each part intelligently until the skill related to that learning has been fully acquired.

The Whole Method: Advantages

1. The parts are combined into one and give a meaning to the child.
2. If the child has learnt some content material by heart, this method works.

Limitations: This method does not operate if the subject matter for memorization is too long and difficult.

The Part Method: Advantages

1. It works well when the subject matter of learning is short.
2. It gives better results if the learner is young and the subject matter is difficult.

Limitations: 1. The structure of the entire poem is not clear to the child till the end of the learning, 2. The child finds it difficult to link the parts of the lesson into the whole one, and 3. It is psychologically unsound.

Latest Researches

1. Aveling came to the conclusion that nearly one-fifth of the time of learning can be economized with the wise use of the Whole method.
2. Pyne and Syner came to the conclusion that the Whole method is more effective in the case of a poem having about 24 lines.

The Part Progressive Method or Mediating Method

A modification of the Whole method is suggested which is known as Part Progressive or Mediating Method. The outlines are as follows:

1. The difficult words or phrases may be mastered or understood before hand and then the whole method may be employed.

2. The learner should make a cautious approach while making use of the whole method.
3. The lesson may be sub-divided into three units. The child may combine 1 and 2 and later on combine 2 and 3 and finally 1, 2 and 3.

10.7 DEMONSTRATION

Meaning of Demonstration. Demonstration is the process of talking and explaining of an idea or skill or an object by the teacher to the students by means of showing them how to do it themselves.

It involves verbal or facial expressions and doing some concrete activity. Examples of demonstration: (i) How to do an exercise, (ii) How to do an 'Asan', (iii) How to deliver a speech, (iv) How to write legibly, (v) How to prepare a map, (vi) How to prepare food (vii) How to perform an experiment, (viii) How to write a letter.

Various Elements of Demonstration

1. *Objective.* The primary objective is to promote understanding and skills among students. It also enables the teacher to maintain interest of the students.

2. *Demonstration* Strategies: (i) Doing some physical exercise, (ii) Illustrating something by comparing and giving examples, (iii) Asking questions, (iv) Presenting the working model of something, (v) Conducting some experiment.

3. *Role of the Teacher.* Teacher's role is very important. He should demonstrate effectively and efficiently by collecting and setting the relevant materials of demonstration. Demonstration should be illustrated by verbal explanation.

Verbal illustrations should be educative, interesting, and relevant to the topic. Proper sitting arrangements should be made so as to ensure that all students can see the demonstration.

4. *Role of the students.* (i) The students should observe very keenly all the processes involved in demonstration (ii) They may put relevant questions.

5. *Evaluation.* (i) The teacher may ask a few questions on the topic, (ii) He may ask a few students to demonstrate a few acts involved in the physical exercise or the experiment.

Guidelines in Effective Demonstration

1. Plan all the activities relating to demonstration in great detail.
2. Ensure that all the equipment, illustrations and other relevant materials are procured in time and kept ready before the demonstration begins.
3. Make proper seating arrangement of the class.
4. Make proper arrangement for placing demonstration table with the equipment.

5. State clear objectives of the demonstration.
6. Pace the demonstration *i.e.* neither too fast nor too slow.
7. Breakdown the process of demonstration slowly so that all the students may grasp the details.
8. Wherever possible, involved students in demonstration.
9. Ascertain after every step whether the students have grasped the meaning, contents and explanation. Repeat if they have not followed it.
10. Give suitable verbal explanations for heightening the interest of the students.
11. Encourage students to analyse, record and tabulate the results of their observation.
12. Make assignments based on the demonstration.

Merits of Demonstration: Demonstration enables the students to acquire knowledge, skill and attitude in the first hand form. It establishes a close relationship between theory and practice. It helps in fixing facts and principles. It fosters creativity. It brings an element of reality. It is based on the principle of 'Learning by doing'.

11

Lesson Planning

11.1 MEANING

One of the most important elements in good teaching is good lesson planning. Lesson planning is essentially an 'experience in anticipatory teaching'. It is teacher's experience in advance, mental and emotional. The eager faces, the questions that will arise, the difficulties the pupils will encounter, the way these difficulties are to be met—all these the teacher will experience in imagination and thereafter fully tinge these with realism.

A lesson plan is based on (i) The operational philosophy of the teacher (ii) Teacher's understanding of his pupils (iii) Teacher's knowledge of the material to be taught (iv) Teacher's knowledge of the methods of teaching.

A lesson plan may be envisaged as:

(a) a blue print
(b) a guide map for action
(c) a comprehensive chart of classroom teaching-learning activities
(d) an elastic but systematic approach for the teaching of concepts, skills and attitudes etc.
(e) An emotional and mental visualisation of the teacher regarding classroom experiences as he hopes to occur.

11.2 SIGNIFICANCE

Regarding the importance of proper lesson planning, Bagley states, "however, able and experienced the teacher, he could do never without his preliminary preparation." J.K. Davis is very right when he observes, "lesson must be prepared for there is nothing so fatal to a teacher's progress as unpreparedness." R.L. Stevenson gives a very useful advice to teachers on lesson planning, "Always plan out your lesson before-hand but do not be slave to it."

The lesson plan affects the teacher's skill, intelligence, ability and his personality. Following are the chief functions of planning:

1. It delimits the field of work of the teacher as well as of the students and provides a definite objective for each day's work.
2. As the goal is determined, the teacher gets impetus to realise his goal.

3. It tends to prevent wandering from the subject and going off the way. It serves as a check on the possible wastage of time and energy of the teachers and students. It makes teaching systematic, orderly and economical.
4. Planning helps the teacher to organise and systematise the learning process. The activities in the lesson are well-knit, interconnected and associated. The continuity of the educative process is ensured.
5. Planning helps to avoid needless repetition.
6. Planning helps the teacher to overcome the feeling of nervousness of insecurity. It gives him confidence to face the class.
7. Lesson planning gives opportunities to the teacher to think out new ways and means of making the lesson interesting and to introduce thought-provoking questions.
8. Lesson planning ensures a definite assignment for class and availability of adequate materials for the lesson.
9. Lesson planning enables the teacher to link the new knowledge with the previous knowledge acquired by students.
10. Lesson planning ensures a proper connection of the new lesson with the previous lesson.
11. Lesson planning enables the teacher to prepare a suitable scheme of selection and organisation of subject-matter, materials and activities.
12. Lesson planning enables the teacher to prepare pivotal questions and illustrations.
13. Lesson planning makes it possible to provide for individual differences in pupils.
14. Lesson planning enables the teacher to provide for suitable summaries.
15. Lesson planning provides for an adequate checking of the outcomes of instruction.
16. Lesson planning helps the teacher as well as the taught in fixing new learning by making adequate provision for drill work, practice and revision.

11.3 PREPARATION OF LESSON PLAN

Questions to be Considered in Planning

1. What are the needs, difficulties, problems and interests of the students?
2. In what way can the requirements of the subject-matter be made suitable to the capacity and growth of the students?
3. What preparations have the students made for attacking the subject?
4. What are their experiences of the past which can be of assistance in the present situation?
5. How can the subject-matter be presented economically and effectively?
6. What type of material aids should be prepared and used in the lesson?
7. What incidents should be related?

8. What comparisons can be drawn and what similarities can be shown?
9. What type of application work should be used to fix, to clear up and to make real the grasp of the students of the general principles of the lesson?
10. What methods should be used to make the students active participants in the lesson?

Essentials of a Good Lesson Plan

Generally speaking the following are the characteristics of a good lesson plan:

1. *It should be written:* A lesson plan should preferably be written and should not remain at the oral or mental stage. Panton writes, "The teacher is strongly advised, at least in the early stages, to make a written note of his preparation. Memory sometimes proves a treacherous servant, especially when his attention is divided." It is advisable, however, not to teach from notes. Excessive reliance upon these may undermine the teacher's confidence so that he can never do without them. If, however, the teacher has occasion while teaching to refer to his notes, it is better for him to do so openly than to take a suspicious look at them. He loses nothing in the eye of the children by the former method whereas by the second he is likely to be misjudged by his pupils. Writing helps in clarifying thoughts and concentration.

2. *It should have clear aims:* The lesson plan should clearly state the objectifies, general and specific, to be achieved.

3. *It should be linked with the previous knowledge:* The plan should not let the lesson remain an isolated one. It should have its basis on the background of the class. It should grow out of what the pupils have already learnt.

4. *It should show techniques of teaching:* It should state clearly the various steps that the teacher is going to take, and also various questions that he will ask.

5. *It should show the illustrative aids:* The illustrative aids to be used should be shown in the lesson plan.

6. *It should contain suitable organised subject matter:* The materials of instruction or subject matter should be carefully selected or organised.

7. *It should be divided into units:* The plan should be divided into units; but care should be taken to see that the lesson remains an integrated whole and every unit develops from the previous and submerges into the next one.

8. *It should provide for activity:* The children must be given enough scope to be active. It should not make them mere passive listeners.

9. *It should provide for individual differences:* The plan should be prepared in such a way as it does full justice to all the students of varied abilities.

10. *It should show certain routine things:* The plan should indicate the duration of the period, the period itself, average age of the students, subjects and the class.

11. *It should be flexible:* The plan is a means and not an end. It is wrong to

follow it slavishly. It is an instrument and should be used as such. The teacher should be prepared to change his teaching method from those as referred to in the plan, if need be.

12. *It should include the summary*: The lesson plan should include the summary of the whole lesson which is to be developed on the blackboard with the help of students.

13. *It should refer to reference material:* The plan becomes more useful if it refers to other reading material. This will moativte the bright students to do extra reading. Care should be taken to suggest only that material which is available in the school library.

11.4 PRESENTATION OF A LESSON PLAN

Skill Lesson

Objective of a skill lesson: A skill lesson aims at forming and developing some kind of manual or other skill. Examples of skills are: physical exercises, 'Yoga Asanas', gymnastics, games skills, dancing, modelling, running etc.

As observed by L.P. Jacks, "The human body is naturally skill – hungry and until that hunger is satisfied, it will be ill-at-ease, craving for something it has not got and seeking its satisfaction in external excitements which exhaust its vitality and diminish its capacity for joy. Short of skill, the perfect health, even of body, is impossible."

Steps in Skill Lesson

1. *Preparation*: The mind of the children should be prepared to learn the new skill. The preparation or introduction may take different forms:
   - (i) The students may be taken to gymnasiums or swimming pools etc.
   - (ii) A model of some good work may be shown to the students.
   - (iii) In the project method there are various skills the knowledge of which is required for the performance of various plans.
   - (iv) It is just sufficient to show the room, the tools etc. to create a proper attitude for the work in the students.

2. *Statement of the aim*: The students must know clearly what they are going to learn; otherwise they will be groping in the dark and their co-operation will be half-hearted.

3. *Presentation and statement of rules*: The teacher presents the new form of skill. The teacher should give a few instructions to the students so that they may properly watch and observe the demonstration given by him. Sometimes the students may handle the model for close observation. This stage consists largely of observation, listening and seeing on the part of the students. The teacher is doing things and explaining things. The teacher may give the statements of the rules to be observed in practising the skill. But they should be very brief and should not be such, as Raymont puts, "There is a sense in which rules are the death of true art."

4. *Practice*: The students will imitate what the teacher has demonstrated before them. This is the most important step and will also take a longer period. The teacher will not remain passive at this stage. He will supervise and guide the practice of each individual student.

5. *Correction*: It is a sort of representation. The teacher will point out the defects and show the correct ways of performing the activity. He may restate the rules.

6. *Consolidation and refinement*: Then again will come practice and the students may practise the skill and acquire improvement. The two steps 'correction' and 'practice' may be repeated a number of times.

The following considerations should be kept in view in this type of lesson—

(a) The sudents must feel the urge for learning the skill. They must be properly motivated.
(b) The skill set for the children should not be too difficult.
(c) The time required to perform the activity should not be too long.
(d) The skill should provide a sort of channel for self expression, if possible.

Creative Aspect in Skill Lessons: Hughes and Hughes write, "Any form of practical work in which skill has been acquired becomes a vehicle for the expression of beauty. It provides scope for the highest type of self expression." Imitation helps to develop and improve a power which already exists but it cannot create it. The teacher should encourage students to create things for themselves and should not set unnecessary rules and techniques. Real and creative art is free and spontaneous and breaks through shackles of rules, formulae and conventions.

12

Food and Nutrition

12.1 MEANING AND FUNCTIONS OF FOOD

Food may be described as the nutritive material solid or liquid, taken into the human body. Nutritive material relates to nutrition. Nutrition may be defined as "food at work in the body." Nutrition is also defined as a process by which an organism takes the food and utilises its nutrients for growth, development and maintenance of the body.

Nutrients are the constituents in food that must be supplied to the body in suitable amounts. These are proteins, carbohydrates, fats, minerals, vitamins and water.

Good Nutrition: This term is applied to the quality of nutrition. Good nutrition is important for happy and healthy life. Good nutrition means nutrition which contains essential nutrients in correct amounts.

In order to be healthy and stay energetic, we need to take proper food. Eating too little or too much makes one sick due to deficiency or excess of food. Our food should be such that it takes care of our daily energy needs.

12.2 COMPONENTS OF FOOD

We eat food in the form of cereals, pulses, vegetables, fruits, milk and milk products etc. These foods contain certain organic substances and minerals known as nutrients.

Nutrients are the components of food that must be supplied to the body in suitable amounts. The main nutrients of food are:

1. Carbohydrates
2. Proteins
3. Fats
4. Vitamins
5. Minerals
6. Roughage (dietary fibre)
7. Water

Roughage and water do not only provide energy but are also essential for the body.

12.3 BASIC FOOD GROUPS

Nutrients are present in all foods in varying proportions.

Depending on the relative concentration of nutrients in foods, they have been classified into three broad groups (Fig. 12.1). These are:

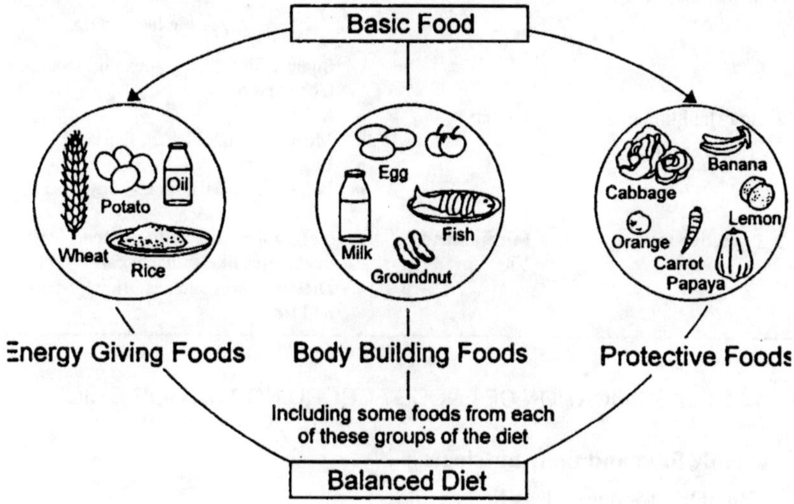

Fig. 12.1: Basic Food Groups.

(i) Energy giving foods, (ii) Body building foods, (iii) Protective foods.

(i) *Energy giving foods:* They include carbohydrates and fats. They provide energy to the body. Body needs energy for all functions like digestion, respiration and circulation etc. In fact body needs energy even at rest or while sleeping.

(ii) *Body building foods:* These include proteins which are required for tissue building, growth and repair of the body. Wear and tear occurs in the body all the time. Proteins help in building new cells and in the repair of the damaged parts.

(iii) *Protective foods:* Vitamins and minerals form the protective foods. They play a vital role in regulating various body processes like growth, eyesight, formation of teeth and bones, good digestion etc. They do not provide energy but are essential for good health and normal growth. A balanced diet must contain all vitamins and minerals in required amounts. Even if any one of them is absent or present in less quantity than required, they cause "deficiency diseases".

12.4 FOOD GROUPS ACCORDING TO THEIR FUNCTIONS AND SOURCES

Food groups according to their function	*Major nutrient*	*Food containing the nutrient*
1. Energy giving foods	Carbohydrates and	• Starch – Cereals like rice and wheat – Vegetable like potato
	Fat	• Sugar-Fruits like grapes and banana Ghee and oil
2. Body building goods	Protein	• Milk • Meat-mutton, chicken, fish • Egg white • Pulses like dals, gram, soya bean, peas
3. Protective foods	Minerals and Vitamins	• Vegetables-especially green leafy vegetables like spinach, cabbage etc. • Dietary Fibres such as brinjal, beans and fruits.

12.5 CLASSIFICATION OF FOODS ACCORDING TO THEIR ORIGIN

Vegetable food and their nutrients

Vegetable food are classified as under:

1. Cereals
2. Pulses
3. Roots and Tubers
4. Green Vegetables
5. Fruits
6. Nuts
7. Fungi

Cereals: Cereals are in the form of grains like maize.

Pulses: Pulses include beans, lentils and peas. They are a rich source of protein. When fresh they contain a lot of vitamins A, B, and C. They have minerals and sugar but little starch.

Roots and Tubers: Roots and tubers include arrowroot, beetrot, carrot, radish, sweet potato and turnip. They contain a high percentage of starch and proteins but no fats.

Green Vegetables: Green vegetables comprise buds, leaves, leaf-stalk or the whole plant. They are rich in vitamins A, B, C, E and K. They contain a high percentage of water and some protein, starch and fat.

Fruits: Fruits are rich in acids, salts, sugar and vitamins.

Nuts: Nuts possess a high percentage of proteins and fats but less carbohydrates.

Fungi: Fungi are the mushrooms which contain over 90 per cent of water and little protein. They have no food value.

Animal Foods

Animal foods includes: (i) Meat, (ii) Fish, (iii) Egg and (iv) Milk

Meat: Meat usually means mutton or pork. It is rich in protein and iron. It contains some vitamins of B group.

Fish: Fish consists mainly of fat, protein and water. The amount of fat varies greatly in different kinds of fish.

Eggs: Eggs possess a high nutritive value. They are rich in iron and phosphorus. They contain Vitamin A and D.

Milk: Milk is obtained from buffalo, cow, goat and reindeer. It contains all the nutrients. It is generally given to babies and children as complete food. It is rich in minerals, proteins and vitamins A and B. Its products like cream, butter, curd, cheese and ghee are rich sources of energy.

12.6 NUTRIENT COMPONENTS OF FOOD AND THEIR IMPORTANCE

1. Carbohydrates

Carbohydrates are the heat and energy providing foods that mainly exist as glucose (commonly called as simple sugar), sucrose (common sugar or cane-sugar) and starch in our diet. Both glucose and sucrose are known as sugars although glucose is a simple sugar and sucrose a compound sugar. Starch is a complex carbohydrate with a high molecular weight.

Main Characteristics of Carbohydrates

- Carbohydrates are made up of carbon, hydrogen and oxygen. The composition of hydrogen and oxygen is same as is present in water (H_2O). So the general formula of carbohydrates is $CnH_{2n}O_n$ or $C_nH_2O)_n$-1.
- Carbohydrates are also known as hydrates of carbon.
- Carbohydrates are the principal source of energy in our body. They are the first one to be oxidized during respiration.
- The complex carbohydrates like starch that we consume are broken down to simple sugars and absorbed.
- Most of the carbohydrate absorbed by the blood stream is present in the form of glucose in blood. Glucose is converted to glycogen and stored in the muscles.
- During respiration, glucose is oxidised to release energy.

On complete oxidation, 1 gm of glucose yields 4.2 kcl of energy.

Sources of Carbohydrates

- *Starch* is the most important carbohydrate in our diet. Cereals like rice, wheat, corn, millet are a rich source of starch. Starch is also present in potato, sweet potato, tapioca, beans, peas and pulses.
- *Sucrose* is present in sugarcane, cane-sugar (common sugar that we consume everyday), sugar beet etc.

- *Glucose* is found in sweet fruits and vegetables like banana, grapes, berries, oranges, sweet corn. Honey also contains large amount of glucose.
- *Lactose*. Milk contains lactose, also known as milk sugar.

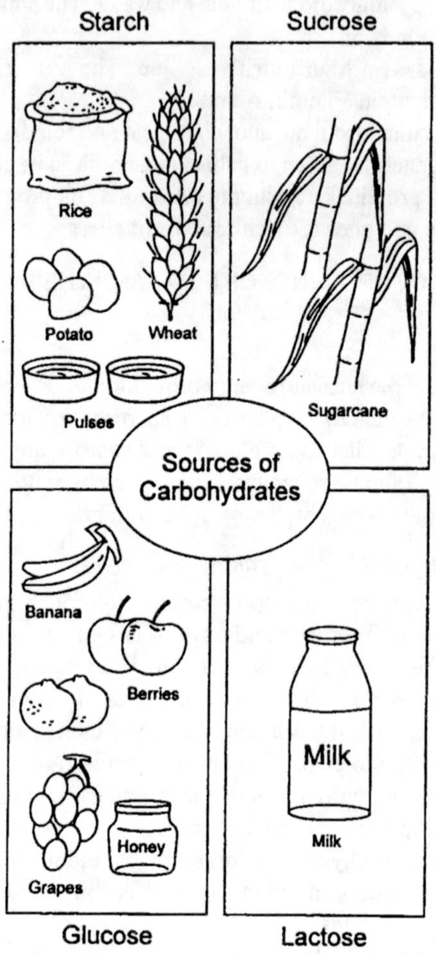

Fig. 12.2: Sources of Carbohydrates

2. Proteins

Proteins are the growth promoting foods. They are made up of smaller units called amino acids. The term protein was given by J. Berzelias (1938). Most proteins present in the body of living organisms are made up of 20 amino acids. Out of 20 amino acids, 12 can be made by the body but 8 need to be provided through the food. Since these 8 amino acids cannot be synthesised and must be present in food, they are called *essential amino acids*. Others that can be synthesised from carbohydrates metabolites or other components are called *non-essential amino acids*.

Functions of Proteins: Proteins are not only required for making building blocks like cell membranes but also in many other molecules like haem or haemoglobin. Though proteins are always required and considered essential for body growth and functioning, their need increases tremendously during pregnancy and lactation. The infants and children need a high protein diet due to their growing body needs. Their deficiency causes retardation of physical and mental growth.

The deficiency of proteins leads to diseases like *Kwashiorkar* and *Marasmus* in children.

Sources of Proteins

Proteins are found in abundance in cheese, beans, peanut, gram, peas, pulses, egg white and chicken. All proteins do not contain the same amino acids. Proteins have been divided into two main groups-first class or complete proteins and second class or incomplete proteins.

(a) *First class or complete proteins:* These are the proteins that contain high proportion of essential amino acids. Generally animal proteins like milk, meat and fish are complete proteins. Among plant proteins, soya protein is as good as animal protein.

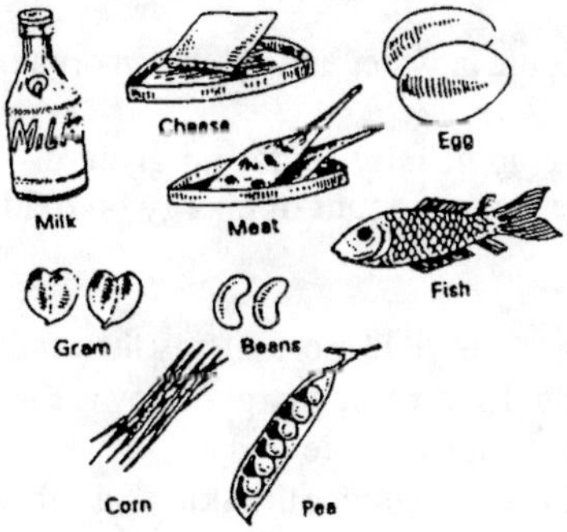

Fig. 12.3: Sources of Proteins

(b) *Second class or incomplete proteins:* These are the proteins that lack certain essential amino acids. Generally plant proteins are considered inferior as they are not well balanced in their amino acid content. For instance cereal proteins (like corn) are poor in amino acid lysine, while pulse proteins (like beans) are poor in methionine, although they are rich in lysine. Such proteins individually are therefore incomplete proteins.

Vegetarians need to select the diet with care to have a mix of vegetables to get all essential acids Fig. 12.4.

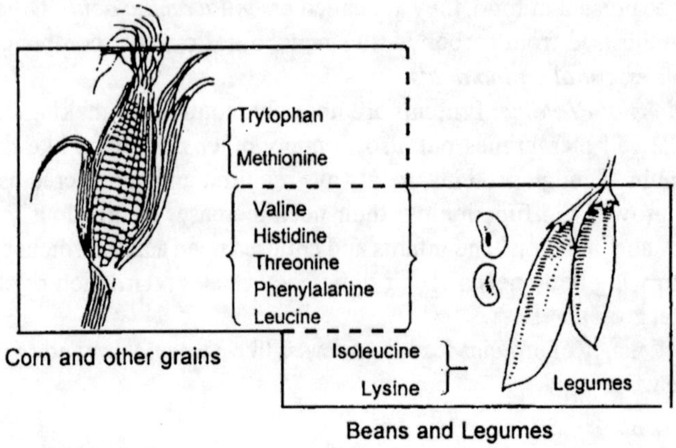

Fig. 12.4: Combination of Foods to get Essential Amino Acids

3. Fats

Like carbohydrates and proteins, fats are a necessary ingredient in our diet. Fats are members of a heterogenous groups of chemicals called lipids. The term lipids includes fats, oils, fat like substances, steroids, waxes etc.

- Fats are energy rich compounds, made up of carbon, hydrogen and oxygen.
- The number of oxygen atoms in fats is very small compared to carbon atoms.
- Fats are insoluble in water and soluble in organic solvents like acetone, ether etc.
- Fats are made up of fatty acids and glycerol.
- Fats release a large amount of energy on oxidation.

Functions of Fats

1. *Source of energy*: Fats yield more energy than carbohydrates and proteins. They are a concentrated source of energy. They are less readily available in a cell and are difficult to digest in the body.

2. *Insulation*: Fat is stored under the skin as a subculaneous layer and acts as an insulating layer (*i.e.* does not allow body heat to escape).

3. *Protection*: Fat forms a protective shock absorbing cushion around a number of organs like eye-ball, kidney and ovaries.

4. *Structure of cell membrane*: Fats form a part of the phospholipid molecules of the cell membranes.

Sources of Fats: Fats are found in various foodstuffs like groundnut, butter, mustard seeds, vanaspati ghee, desi ghee, egg, milk and various types of oils used for cooking. Depending on the source, fats can be divided into two groups. These are:

(i) Animal fat, and
(ii) Vegetable fat.

FAT

Animal fat (derived from animal or animal products

Examples: Milk, cheese, butter, eggs, meat and fish oil.

Vegetable fat (derived from plants)

Examples: Nuts like walnut, almonds, groundnut and coconut. Seeds like mustard seeds and sesame (til) seeds. Vegetable oil extracted from nuts or seeds like mustard oil, palm oil, coconut oil etc.

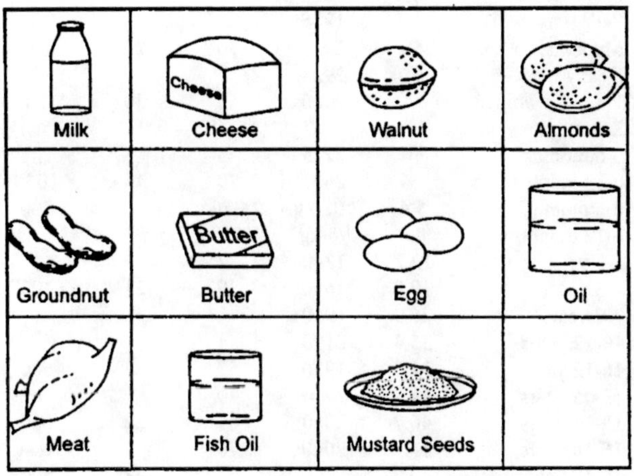

Fig. 12.5: Sources of Fats

Fats are generally solid at low temperatures like less than 20°C (you must have seen butter and ghee solidifying in winters). If they are liquid at this temperature, they are called oils. This property of fats and oils is due to the type of fatty acids they contain. Fats are rich in saturated fatty acids while oils contain unsaturated fatty acids. Coconut oil and palm oil are the only saturated vegetable oils.

Fats as storage molecules: Fats and oils are high concentrated energy foods. They yield more than twice about 2.25 times more energy than carbohydrates.

- one gm of carbohydrate (glucose) yields 4 kcal.
- one gm of fat yields 9.3 kcal.

Fat is a compact and a more suitable form to store food. Amount of food stored depends on the energy requirement of the body and intake of food. If more food energy is taken, this extra energy is largely converted into fats for storage. Nowadays the so called snack food or junk food is high calorie carbohydrate food, the surplus of which is converted into fats, that leads to obesity.

The nutritional value of fats depends on the kind of fatty acids present, whether saturated or unsaturated. Saturated fats like butter, ghee etc., increase the blood cholesterol level. Cholesterol is said to create abnormal thickening on the walls of arteries causing *arteriosclerosis*. It may cause high blood pressure and lead to heart disorders.

Table 12.1: Recommended Dietary Nutrients for Indians as per Indian Council of Medical Research (ICMR)

Group	*Particulars*	*Body Wt kg*	*Net energy kcal/d*	*Protein g/d*	*Fat g/d*	*Calcium mg/d*	*Iron mg/d*
Man	Sedentary work	60	2425				
	Moderate work	60	2875	60	20	400	28
	Heavy work	60	3800				
Women	Sedentary work		1875				
	Moderate work	50	2225	50	20	400	30
	Heavy work		2925				
	Pregnant women		2500	65	30	1000	38
	Lactation						
	0-6 months	50	2275	75			
	0-12 months		2600	70	45	1000	30
Infants	0-6 months	5.4	108/kg	2.05/kg		500	
	6-12 months	8.6	98/kg	1.65/kg			
Children	1-3 years	12.2	1240	22			12
	4-6 years	19.0	1690	30	25	400	18
	7-9 years	26.9	1950	41			26
Boys	10-12 years	35.4	2190	54			34
Girls	10-12 years	31.5	1970	57	22	600	19
Boys	13-15 years	47.8	2450	70			41
Girls	13-15 years	46.7	2060	65	22	600	28
Boys	16-18 years	57.1	2640	78			50
Girls	16-18 years	49.9	2060	63	22	500	30

g/d = grams per day

4. Vitamins

Vitamins are life-giving substances. They are of vital importance to the proper growth of the body. They facilitate the digestive system and tune the nervous system. They resist body diseases. It is very essential to include them in food in order to maintain life. Lack of sufficient vitamins in the diet results in deficiency disease.

The term vitamins was given by Casimir Funk (C. Funk) a Polish bio-chemist in 1911.

Vitamins are organic substances required in small trace amounts in the diet.

Vitamin B-complex

These are a group of vitamins that have related functions and are often found together in the same food. They are grouped together as Vitamin B-complex. These are water solubles.

Table 12.2: Functions and Deficiency Diseases of Various Vitamins

S. No.	*Name of vitamin*	*Functions*	*Deficiency*	*Sources*
1.	Vitamin A (Retinol)	• Maintenance of normal healthy eyesight. • Maintains normal secretary epithelium of eye. • Synthesis of visual pigment like Rhodopsin	Xerophthalmia Night blindness	• Cod liver oil, shark, liver oil, liver, milk, butter, dairy products; • Yellow vegetables and fruits like carrot, ripe mango, papaya. • Green leafy vegetables like spinach
2.	Vitamin B (Thiamine)	• Acts as a coenzyme • Esseantial for carbohydrate metabolism • Required for aerobic respiration • Required for well-being of nerves.	Beri Beri	• Milk, whole cereals, yeast, nuts, sprouted beans, green vegetables. • Sea food, liver (In cereals, present mainly in the bran i.e. outer cover of grains) • •
3.	Vitamin B_2 (Riboflavin)	• Maintains healthy skin and oral mucosa of mouth • Essential for carbohydrate, protein and fat metabolism to release energy.	• Sores at the corner of mouth • Inflammation of tongue	• Milk, yogurt (curd, peas, beans, yeast, green leafy vegetables, egg, liver, meat •
4.	Vitamin B_5 (Niacin)	• Associated with several metabolic reactions • Along with Thiamine and Riboflavin participates in metabolism of food to release energy	Pellagra	• Potato, tomato, green vegetables, whole grain, groundnut; • Meat, fish, fowl (chicken) Vit. B_5 can be synthesised in the body from amino acid tryptophan;

(Contd.)

(Contd.)

S. No.	*Name of vitamin*	*Functions*	*Deficiency*	*Sources*
5.	Folic acid	• Helps in multiplication and maturation of R.B.C. (Red Blood Cell) • Necessary for metabolism of proteins.	Megaloblastic anaemia (Large immature, nucleated R.B.C. in blood)	Green leaf vegetables, sprouted pulses; liver, yeast fish
6.	Vitamin B_{12}	• Like folic acid involved in maturation of R.B.C.	Permicious anaemia	Milk, Meat, kidney, liver, eggs, fish
7.	Vitamin C	• Important for formation of collagen, a cementing material that holds cells together • Necessary for calcification of bones and teeth	Scurvy	Citrus fruits especially amla, lime, lemon, orange; Other fruits like gooseberry; guava, (heating or drying of fresh fruits and vegetables destroys most or all of vitamin C)
8.	Vitamin D	• Increases calcium and phosphorus absorption from intestine • Important for bone and teeth formation.	Rickets in children Osteomalacia in adults	Milk, cod liver oil, shark liver oil, fish, egg. "Vit. D is also made by the action of sunlight in the skin".
9.	Vitamin E	• An antioxidant, maintains normal cell membrane structure. • Essential for rapid division of cells. When the fertilized ovum begins to multiply itself to produce a new individual this vitamin is very necessary.	Increased haemolysis of R.B.C. in man	Green leaf vegetables, milk, brown flour, germinated wheat and seeds, vegetable oil, tomato
10.	Vitamin K	• Known as 'coagulation vitamin'. Needed for normal coagulation of blood.	Profuse bleeding due to delayed blood clotting	Leafy vegetables like cabbage, spinach, coriander, radish. Also synthesized in the body.

Vitamin B-complex includes vitamins B_1, B_2, B_3, folic acid, B_{12} and some more B-group vitamins. Some of these are important in human nutrition.

Most B-group vitamins are present in the skin or husk (bran) of the grains. To get vitamin B-complex, whole grain is preferred to refined flour.

The deficiencies of some of these vitamins frequently overlap, hence in clinical practice it is customary to treat cases presenting one or more of these deficiencies with a mixture of B-complex vitamins, rather than individual vitamins.

5. Minerals

Minerals are known as protective foods. They are inorganic molecules that are important for the formation of complex organic molecules in the body. Like vitamins, minerals are very vital to the body. Mineral like sodium chloride (table salt-NaCl) is consumed directly and in large amount everyday. Minerals must be present in the diet in the required amount.

Characteristics of Minerals

- Minerals constitute about 4% of the total body weight.
- Minerals are water soluble and the excess is excreted through urine. Hence they have to be supplied in the daily diet.
- The body contains about 21 minerals, all of which must be derived from the food.
- Like vitamins, minerals do not supply any energy to the body but are essential for various metabolic activities and for growth and development of the body.
- The minerals required in small amount or traces are called micro-nutrients while the ones required in large amounts like sodium, potassium and calcium etc. are called macro-nutrients.

  "*Fats and sugars have no minerals. Highly refined cereals and flour are also poor sources*".

Functions and sources of some important minerals are given in Table 12.3.

Importance of Minerals

1. They help to maintain balance of acids and alkalies in the body.
2. They make possible normal rhythm in the heart beat.
3. They help to maintain a normal response of nerves to stimuli.
4. They constitute bones which act like pillars of the body, e.c. calcium and phosphorus.
5. They help in the production of digestive juices.
6. They constitute body cells of which muscles, blood corpuscles, livers, etc. are composed, *i.e.*, minerals like calcium, phosphorus and iron.
7. They help in providing stability to the body, e.g., chlorine, phosphorus, potassium and sodium.
8. Some minerals like copper and iron have their own functions for the formation of blood, iodine and thyroxine.

Table 12.3: Functions, Sources and Daily Requirement of Various Minerals

S. o.	*Mineral*	*Daily requirement*	*Food source*	*Functions*	*Deficiency diseases*
1.	Calcium	1-2 g	Milk, cheese, eggs, green vegetables, whole-grain, cereal, ragi, tapioca, some fish, "Vitamin D is necessary for proper absorption of calcium".	(i) Along with vitamin D it is essential for building of bones and teeth. (ii) Helps in clotting of blood. (iii) For heart muscles to contract, the tissue fluid around them should have enough calcium (iv) Regulates conduction of nerve impulse and muscle contraction. (v) Essential for action of many enzymes.	—Poor skeletal growth, may lead to rickets—When calcium levels fall below normal, muscles get irritated and it results in convulsion in the body.
2.	Iodine	20 mg	Salt water, fish, sea food, green leafy vegetables, iodized common salt.	(i) Essential for the formation of thyroxine harmone secreted by thyroid gland. (ii) Controls oxidation of carbohydrates and energy metabolism – the basic metabolic rate (BMR).	Deficiency of iodine causes Goitre.
3.	Iron	35 mg for girls 25 mg for boys	Liver, kidney, egg yolk, whole meal bred, bajra, ragi, apple, banana and other green vegetables and jaggery	(i) Essential for formation of haemoglobin in R.B.C. (ii) responsible for tissue respiration. (iii) Iron is present in muscles in myoglobin which store O_2 in the muscles. (iv) Haeme enzymes like catalase, peroxides, cytochrome have iron in them. They bring about oxidation of proteins, fats and carbohydrates within the cell.	Deficiency of iron causes anaemia.
4.	Phosphorus	1-2 g	Milk, cheese, green leaf vegetables, bajra, ragi, oatmeal, nuts, liver and kidney	(i) In association with calcium, gives strength and rigidity to teeth. (ii) Helps to maintain constant composition of body fluid. (iii) Regulation of heart beat	Rarely deficient in human beings.

(Contd.)

(Contd.)

S. No.	*Mineral*	*Daily requirement*	*Food source*	*Functions*	*Deficiency diseases*
				(iv) Constituent of nucleic acids. Coenzymes, ATP, and cell membranes.	
5.	Potassium	1g	Banana, dates, potato, spinach, orange, beans, molasses and widely distributed in all goods	Most commonly occurring action in intracellular fluid (indise the cytoplasm of cell) (i) Mainly associated with membrane functions like maintenance of electrical potential across the membrane Na+/K+ pump. (ii) Necessary for enzymatic reactions within the cell. (iii) Required for contraction of muscles. (iv) Associated with trasmission of nerve impulse	Potassium is rarely deficient in diet.
6.	Sodium (taken as sodium chloride NaCl)	2.5 g	Common salt (NaCl) Fish, meat, eggs, milk	(i) Maintains normal osmotic pressure. (ii) Protects against excessive loss of water. (iii) Associated with transmission of nerve impulse. (iv) Important for contraction of muscles. (v) Maintains electrical potential across the membranes (sodium potassium pump)	Muscular cramps

6. Roughage

Roughage includes the "dietary fibres" present in the food that are not digested by the enzymes.

These are non-nutritive substances but an important part of a balanced diet. They are required for proper digestion of food.

Roughage is present in the form of cellulose in fruits and vegetables and in the connective tissue in meat and fish. Human beings do not have an enzyme to digest cellulose and hence it remains undigested and forms roughage of the food.

Sources of Roughage: The skin of vegetables and fruits that we eat contains a high fibre content. Salads, leafy vegetables like cabbage and fruits like apples, peaches and pears and whole-grain cereals, corncob (bhutta), porridge (Dalia) provide good amount of roughage. The basic component in all these is cellulose that cannot be digested and hence acts as roughage.

Roughage is an important part of food and is good for digestion because-

(i) The indigestible part of food-the cellulose in roughage can hold a lot of water and thus helps in retaining water in the body.

(ii) The fibres in roughage add bulk to the food. They increase the motility of the small intestine and promote elimination of faeces and bowel movement, thus preventing constipation.

7. Water

Water is an important constituent of our diet. It makes about 75% of an infant's body and 60% of an adult body. From this amount of water, a loss of 15-20% may prove to be fatal. Water forms the major structural constituent of our body. All tissues of our body including bones and teeth contain water. In our body water is present in two forms.

- In intracellular fluids *i.e.* the fluids present within the cells.
- In extracellular fluids *i.e.* the fluids present outside the cells, like plasma, lymph, secretions of glands etc.

Functions of Water

1. Water helps in the elimination of poisonous elements and waste products from the body.
2. Water helps in the digestion of food. All digestive juices are in the watery form.
3. Water helps in the circulation of blood.
4. Water forms the basis of the body fluids like plasma of the blood, the lymph, digestive juices and other secretions.
5. Water helps in maintaining the body temperature by distributing the heat in the body. Sweating and evaporation help in lowering of the body temperature.
6. Water acts as a medium for a number of bio-chemical reactions in the body. It acts as a reagent for the action of hydrolytic enzymes.
7. The waste products of the body are excreted in the form of urine and perspiration and water is a medium for both of these.
8. Water acts as an excellent solvent in which a number of food nutrients dissolve. Body contains number of water soluble vitamins and minerals.
9. Water acts as a carrier for the products of digestion helping in transporting them to various cells of the body.
10. Water is an important part of mucus and saliva. Mucus lubricates the digestive and respiratory tracts and saliva makes it possible for us to swallow food.

13

Balanced Diet and Malnutrition

13.1 MEANING OF BALANCED DIET

A complete diet or balanced diet may be defined as the one which contains all the nutrients in the correct amount. A balanced diet can also be defined as the one which contains different types of food in such quantities and proportions that the need for calories, minerals, vitamins and other nutrients is adequately met and a small provision is made for extra nutrients to withstand short duration of leanness. Following are the main characteristics of a balanced diet.

- It includes carbohydrates, proteins, fats, minerals, salt, vitamins, water and roughage in the right amount.
- Carbohydrates in the diet provide energy.
- Proteins are the building foods that provide material for growth and development and for the repair of damaged tissues.
- Fats are the high concentrated energy food and act as storage molecules.
- Vitamins and minerals play an important role in a number of body functions. Some minerals like calcium and phosphorus form bones and teeth.
- Water forms 65% of all the cells and is necessary for all vital functions like digestion, excretion and respiration etc.
- Roughage in the form of dietary fibre is important for proper digestion and helps in bowel movement.

The nutrients in a balanced diet differ according to age, health and occupation. Also there are additional requirements for special situations, for example:

1. A person doing hard physical work needs more energy and this extra energy can be provided by taking in more carbohydrates and fats in the diet. Hence food of this person requires greater carbohydrate content in the diet.
2. Pregnant women need additional supply of milk, proteins, calcium, iron and vitamins to take care of the developing embryo.
3. Nursing mothers also need additional supply of calcium, proteins, rich milk and vitamins to breast-feed the body. Mother's milk is a rich source of vital nutrients and antibodies for the baby.

4. Growing children up to the age of 12 need extra protein for their growth. They need extra calcium and iron for growing bones and red blood cells.

13.2 RECOMMENDED BALANCED DIET BY ICMR

Table 13.1 gives the recommended daily diet of balanced food in grams for adult men and women by Indian Council of Medical Research (ICMR).

Table 13.1: Balanced Diets as Recommended by ICMR in terms of Food Items (*grams*)

Sl. No.	*Food item*	*Adult Men*			*Adult Women*		
		Sedentary	*Moderate Work*	*Heavy Work*	*Sedentary*	*Moderate Work*	*Heavy Work*
1.	Cereals	460	520	670	410	440	575
2.	Pulses	40	50	60	40	45	50
3.	Leafy vegetables	40	40	40	100	100	50
4.	Other vegetables	60	70	80	40	40	100
5.	Roots and tubers	50	60	80	50	50	60
6.	Milk	150	200	250	100	200	150
7.	Oil and fat	40	45	65	20	25	40
8.	Sugar or jaggery	30	35	55	20	20	40

Note: Non-vegetarians may substitute some of the above items with eggs, meat or fish.

For example, pulses or dals can be partly replaced. About 25g of pulses can be substituted by one egg or by 30g meat or fish and 5g or extra fat or oil.

Table 13.2: Balanced Diet for a Normal and Healthy Person

	Food Item	*Vegetarian Diet*	*Non-Vegetarian Diet*
1.	Bread	14 oz.	14 oz.
2.	Milk	14 oz.	10 oz.
3.	Vegetables without leaves	06 oz.	06 oz.
4.	Vegetables with leaves	04 oz.	04 oz.
5.	Meat and fish	-	03 oz.
6.	Eggs	-	01 oz.
7.	Cereal	03 oz.	02 oz.
8.	Sugar	02 oz.	02 oz.
9.	Fruit	02 oz.	02 oz.
10.	Liquids	02 oz.	02 oz.
	Total	47 oz.	46 oz.

Changes should be made in the above list according to the profession, body build, sex, age, climate etc.

Table 13.3: Balanced Diet for Adolescent Boys and Girls (In *gms*)

		Boys : 13-18 years		*Girls: 13-18 years*	
S.No.	*Item*	*Veg.*	*Non-Veg.*	*Veg.*	*Non-Veg.*
1.	Cereals	450	450	350	350
2.	Pulses	70	50	70	50
3.	Green Leaf vegetables	100	100	150	150
4.	Other vegetables	75	75	75	75
5.	Roots and Tubers	100	100	75	75
6.	Fruits	30	30	30	30
7.	Fats and Oils	45	50	35	40
8.	Meat and Fish	-	30	-	30
9.	Eggs	-	30	-	30
10.	Sugar and Jaggery	40	40	30	30
11.	Groundnuts	50	50		

Note: Additional 30 gms of fats and oils can be included in place of groundnuts.

Table 13.4: Balanced Diet for Children upto 12 years of Age (*grams*)

S. No.	*Food Items*	*1-3 yrs.*	*4-6 yrs.*	*7-9 yrs.*	*10-12 yrs.*
1.	Cereals	175	270	420	380
2.	Pulses	35	35	45	45
3.	Leafy vegetables	40	50	50	50
4.	Other vegetables	20	30	50	50
5.	Roots and Tubers	10	20	30	30
6.	Milk	300	250	250	250
7.	Oil and Fat	15	25	40	35
8.	Sugar or Jaggery	30	40	45	45
9.	Fruit	50	50	50	50

Note: as in Table 13.3.

13.3 BALANCED DIET: CALORIE REQUIREMENTS

Heat is the chief end product of foods we eat. The unit of heat used in nutrition is a large Calorie consisting of 1000 calories and defined as the amount of heat required for increasing the temperature of a kilogram of water from 15°C to 16°C. It is called a kilocalorie or a calorie. A calorie is the amount of heat required to increase similarly the temperature of one gram of water. When the Calories in the diet are less than the calories needed, body tissue is broken. This results in undernourishment or malnutrition. The Indian Council of Medical Research has suggested the calories needed for different groups as under:

Table 13.5: Calorie Requirements

Age Group	*Type of Work*	*Net Calories*
Children		
(a) 1-3 years		1,200
(b) 4-6 years		1,500
(c) 7-9 years		1,800
(d) 10-12 years		2,100
Adolescent		
Boys 13-15 years		2,500
16-18 years		2,850
Girls 13-15 years		2,100
16-18 years		2,200
Adults		
Male	– Sedentary Work	2,400
	– Moderate Work	2,800
	– Heavy Work	3,900
Female	– Sedentary Work	2,000
	– Moderate Work	2,200
	– Heavy Work	2,900
	– Pregnancy	2,700
	– Lactation	2,750

13.4 THINGS TO BE AVOIDED IN DIET

1. *Too much greasy food, hot spices and coffee.* These things can cause stomach ulcers and other problems of the digestive tract.
2. *Too much sugar and sweets.* These spoil the appetite, rot the teeth, can cause heart problems and may be part of the cause of intestinal cancer.
3. *Too much use of salt.* Consumption of excess salt is not good for everyone.
   People with high blood pressure, certain heart problems or swollen feet should use little or no salt.
4. *Alcohol.* Alcohol causes or makes worse diseases of the liver, stomach and nerves. It also causes emotional and social problems.
5. *Smoking.* It can cause chronic (long-term) coughing or lung cancer and other problems. Smoking is especially bad for people with lung diseases like tuberculosis, asthma and bronchitis. It is very harmful for pregnant woman.
6. *Stomach ulcers and diabetes.* These ailments require special diet.

13.5 PRINCIPLES OF DIET PLANNING

Diet planning implies the use of right foods, at the right time, in the right manner and in right quantity. It is true that in the family, there are individual differences regarding food habits. Yet there are broad principles which must be observed in planning. These are:

1. Principle of nourishment.
2. Principle of selection of food item from broad categories.
3. Principle of age, *i.e.*, diet for an infant will be different from that of a child.
4. Principle of sex which implies that there may be slight variations for a few food items according to sex requirements.
5. Principle of occupation meaning thereby that number of calories depends on the type of work involved, *i.e.*, light work, heavy work and intellectual work.
6. Principle of flexibility which means that diet is determined by climatic and seasonal factors.
7. Principle of economy meaning thereby that inexpensive food-items can also give the same amount of calories as given by expensive food items. Efforts should be made to tap alternative sources of food items. Better foods can be had at low costs.
8. Principle of regularity in taking diet.

13.6 PROBLEMS CAUSED BY NOT EATING A BALANCED DIET OR EATING WELL

1. Diarrhoea.
2. Ringing or buzzing in the ears.
3. Headache.
4. Bleeding or redness of the gums.
5. Nose bleeding.
6. Stomach discomfort.
7. Dryness and cracking of the skin.
8. Fits or convulsions in small children.
9. Palpitation (heavy pulsing of the heart).
10. Anxiety (nerve worry) and various mental or nerve problems.
11. Liver disease.
12. Frequent infections.

13.7 NUTRITIONAL VALUE OF LOCALLY AVAILABLE DIET: GETTING BETTER FOOD AT LOW COST

It is observed that a large number of people cannot afford costly food which is nutritious. However there are several items of nutritious food which the poor people get at low cost and gain strength. Here are some of the ways for getting more proteins, vitamins and minerals at low cost.

1. *Breast Milk:* This is the cheapest, healthiest and the most complete food for the baby. Breast feeding is not only best for the baby, it also saves money. The mother can eat plenty of plant protein and turn it into the perfect baby food-breast milk.

2. *Ragi and Bajra:* They are very rich in minerals, especially calcium and

iron. They are cheaper than rice or wheat and are also more nutritious. These can be substituted for rice and wheat for a good diet.

3. *Rice, Wheat and Other Grains:* They are more nutritious if they are not polished.

4. *Dried Maize (Corn):* It, when soaked in slaked lime before cooking, allows more of the vitamins and protein to be used by the body.

5. *A Mixed Cereals Diet*: A mixed cereal diet is better than just one cereal. A mixture of different cereals will supply the body with all the proteins it needs.

6. *Beans etc.:* Beans are a good cheap sources of protein, especially soyabeans and winged beans. They are higher in vitamins when allowed to sprout before cooking them well, peeling of their skins and mashing them. Besides providing proteins at low cost, growing these crops makes the soil richer and other crops grow better afterwards.

7. *Dark Green Leaves Vegetables:* These contain a modest amount of protein, some iron and a lot of vitamin A. The leaves of beans, peas, pumpkins and sweet potatoes are especially nutritious. They can be dried, powdered and mixed with babies gruel (Kanji) to add to the protein and vitamin content.

8. *Green Leaves of Root Vegetables:* Tapioca leaves contain seven times as much proteins and more vitamins than the root. When eaten together with the root, they have more value at no additional cost.

9. *Cooking, Vegetables, Rice and other Foods in some quantity of Water:* Vegetables should be cut just before cooking. They should not be overcooked. This way fewer vitamins and minerals are lost. Soup may be made of the leftover water and may be drunk. A little 'tamarind' may be added to the cooking vegetables. This way fewer vitamins are lost. Fresh vegetables have more nutrients than the old and stale ones.

10. *Wild Fruit and Berries:* They provide vitamin C as well as natural sugar.

11. *Jaggery:* It contains a lot of iron as it is made in iron pots. It may be used in place of commonly used white sugar.

12. *Eggs and Chicken*: At many places eggs are available at cheap rates. They can be mixed with food given to babies who cannot get breast milk. They can also be given along with breast milk as the baby grows older.

If the family raises its own chickens, it can serve as a fairly cheap form of animal protein.

13. *Fish:* Fish is often cheaper than other meat but is just as nutritious. In certain parts of India, dried fish is very cheap. This is a good food.

13.8 COSTLY FOOD ITEMS AND THEIR SUBSTITUTES

Table 13.6 reflects costly food items and their substitutes.

Table 13.6: Costly Food Items and Their Probable Substitutes

Food Group	*Costly Food Items*	*Substituted Cheap Sources*	*Predominant Nutrients*
1. Cereals	Rice and Wheat	Maize, jawar and bajra	Carbohydrates and proteins
2. Pulses and beans	Rajmah, urad, green peas	Moong, moth, masoor, arhar, soyabean and other bean products, sprouted pulses	Protein, Carbohydrates, Vitamin B
3. Green leafy vegetables	Cabbage	Amaranth (chola), bathus, Kalfa, palak, methi, radish, and carrot leaves, mustard leaves, etc.	Vitamins and minerals
4. Roots and tubers	Sweet potatoes	Potato, drum stick leaves, turnip, radish	Carbohydrates mineals and vitamins
5. Other vegetables	Fresh beans, lady's finger, cauliflower	Turnip, tinda, gourds, brinjal	Minerals, vitamins, carbohydrates and proteins
6. Fruits	Apple, pear, orange, mossumi, pineapple, mangoes	Amla, banana, guava, pappaya, lemon	Carbohydrates, vitamins and minerals
7. Nuts and oil seeds	Almonds, cashewnuts, chilgoza, khurmani	Walnut, til, groundnuts	Fats, vitamins, proteins
8. Fish food	Meat, fish, mutton, eggs	Fish (cheaper in costal areas), soyabean	Proteins, fat, vitamins and minerals
9. Milk and milk products	Milk, cheese, curd	Soyabean milk and its products, groundnut and its products.	Carbohydrates, proteins, fats, vitamins, minerals
10. Jaggery sugar and honey	Sugar, honey	Jaggery	Carbohydrates, minerals
11. Fats and edible oils	Butter, ghee, hydrogenerated oil (vanaspati), cooking oils (til and coconut)	Mustard, groundnut oil	Fats and vitamins

13.9 FOOD EXCHANGE SYSTEM

While planning a balanced diet, the food groups are classified into food exchange system. In a food exchange system, the foods of specific serving size *i.e.* quantity, are decided and then standardized in terms of the energy (kcal) the food contains and its composition in terms of carbohydrates, proteins and fats.

Examples:

(i) Half cup of green leafy vegetables contains 30-40 kcal of energy; 6 g of carbohydrates, no protein and no fat.

(ii) 25 g of cereal contains 85 kcal of energy; 19-21 g of carbohydrates, 2-3 g of protein and no fat.

Refer Table 13.7 for energy values and the content of nutrients in some foods in the food exchange system.

Table 13.7: The Food Exchange System

S. No.	*Exchange list*	*Serving size or raw weight in (g)*	*Carbohydrate (g)*	*Protein (g)*	*Fat*	*Energy (k.cal)*
1.	Vegetable Green Leaf	½ Cup	6	Nil	*	30-40
	Other	½ Cup	6-10	Nil	Nil	50-60
2.	Fruit	Varies	10	Nil	Nil	40
3.	Cereal	25	19-21	2-3	*	85
4.	Legumes and Pulses	25	15	6	*	85
5.	Milk and	½ cup	6	3.5	4.0	65
	Meat	75	Nil	7.5	6.0	85
6.	Fat and	10	Nil	Nil	10.0	90
	Sugar	10	10	Nil	Nil	40

Table 13.8: Suggested Substitution for Non-Vegetarian

Food item which can be deleted from non vegetarian diets	*Substitution that can be suggested for deleted item or items*
50% of pulses (20-30g)	1. One egg or 30g of meat or fish. 2. Additional 5g of fat or oil.
100% pulses (40-60g)	1. Two eggs or 50g of meat or fish. One egg or 30g meat.2. 10g of fat or oil.

Table 13.9: Malnutrition in India: Availability of Food Per Person in Selected Countries

Country	*Food available for human consumption (kcal/day per person)*	*No. of people undernourished (millions)*	*Undernourished (% total population)*
Malaysia	2,920	0.5	<2.5
Romania	3,340	0.2	<2.5
Saudi Arabia	2,840	0.6	3
Russia	2,940	6.2	4
Nigeria	2,770	9.1	8
China	2,970	135.3	11
India	**2,490**	**213.7**	**21**
Nicaragua	2,250	1.5	29
Tajikistan	1,720	4.3	71
Congo, Dem. rep.	1,570	38.3	75

Source: FAO

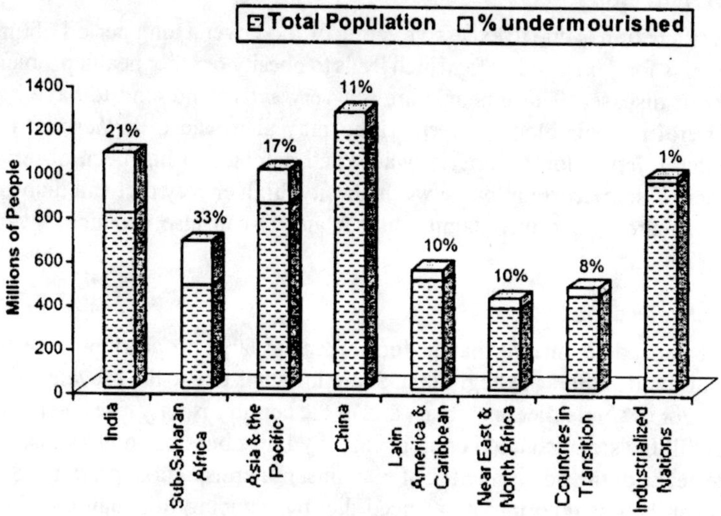

Fig. 13.1: Percentage of Undernourished People in India vis-à-vis Selected Countries

13.10 MALNUTRITION, UNDERNUTRITION, OVERNUTRITION UNBALANCED DIET AND SPECIFIC DEFICIENCY IN DIET

Malnutrition is not same as undernutrition. Malnutrition occurs when the diet is not balanced and does not contain the right amount of nutrients. It can be due to:

(i) faulty or inadequate diet that does not supply normal quantities of all nutrients, or

(ii) physical inability of persons to absorb or metabolise nutrients because of some disease. Malnutrition can be of four types:

1. Undernutrition 2. Overnutrition
3. Imbalanced diet 4. Specific deficiency

1. Undernutrition

When insufficient food is taken over a long period of time, it is called undernutrition. It results in reduced body weight and multiple nutritive disorders. The individual becomes weak and sickly. In extreme cases when no food is taken for days, it may lead to starvation. There are many parts of the world especially developing countries where there is not sufficient food to eat and people are undernourished, hence they suffer from deficiency diseases. Protein-energy malnutrition (PEM) affects large number of third world countries. *Kwashiorkar* and *Marasmus* are two very serious PEM diseases. Undernutrition leads to retardation in growth and physical and mental disabilities in children.

2. Overnutrition

Overnutrition is due to excessive eating of food over a long period of time. The excess food is stored as fat which leads to obesity or other health problems like heart diseases. These people are not very active and tend to have high cholesterol in their blood. Overnutrition may also lead to *artheroma* (*i.e.* cholesterol deposition on arterial walls) and diabetes. It has been observed that there is some correlation between obesity, high energy diet and diabetes. Excess intake of certain vitamins like A and D can also produce adverse symptoms.

3. Unbalanced Diet

Unbalanced diet means that the food taken has large proportions of certain nutrients while others are negligible. Sometimes it is due to the prevalent food habits. For example diet in certain parts of the country is only rice and potato. It may fill the stomach and is rich in carbohydrates but does not take care of all the needs of the body in terms of vitamins, minerals, fats or proteins. Such a diet can be changed into a balanced diet by reducing the quantity of one food and substituting it by certain other foods with specific necessary nutrients.

4. Specific Deficiency

Specific deficiency is a type of malnutrition that results from a diet that contains negligible or none at all of a specific nutrient and leads to specific deficiency symptoms.

13.11 MALNUTRITION

Meaning of Malnutrition. Malnutrition means insufficient and unwholesome feeding. When a person does not eat the right foods or does not eat enough, he is said to be undernourished. In our country, a large number of people are unable to get proper diet. They are ill-fed, ill-clothed and ill-housed. They are unable to give proper diet to their children with the result that they are malnourished. This affects their physical and mental health.

Causes of Malnutrition and Undernourishment

1. Improper diet.
2. Insufficient amount of food.
3. Poor preparation of food.
4. Irregular meal times.
5. Random lunching and snacks.
6. Worry or psychological disturbance-parental coercion.
7. Digestive problem or disease.
8. Excessive activity interfering with meals.
9. Inadequate rest.
10. Mealtime tensions in the home.
11. Wrong examples set by others.

Symptoms of Malnutrition

Causes of malnutrition may be detected by both physical and mental conditions.

(a) *Physical Conditions*

(i) Bad postures
(ii) Laziness.
(iii) Easily fatigued.
(iv) Susceptibility to diseases.
(v) Pale and charmless face.
(vi) Drowsiness.
(vii) Under-weight

(b) *Mental Conditions*

(i) Gloomy nature
(ii) Unenthusiasm.
(iii) Forgetful memory.
(iv) Lack of concentration.
(v) Slow comprehension.
(vi) Irritability.

Deficiencies and Problems of Malnutrition Among Children

1. Failure of the child to grow or gain weight.
2. Slowness in talking, thinking, or walking.
3. Thin arms and legs.
4. Swollen bellies.
5. Sadness.
6. Lack of energy.
7. Swelling of face, feet and hands.
8. Often marks or sores on the skin.
9. Thinning or loss of hair or loss of its colour or shine.
10. Dryness of eyes and sometimes blindness.
11. Loss of appetite.
12. Desire to eat dirt.
13. Night blindness.

Diseases Especially Infections Caused by Malnutrition or Poor Nutrition

Poor nutrition weakens the ability of the body to resist the following diseases:

1. Poorly nourished children are much more prone to severe diarrhoea and also to die from it than children who are well nourished.
2. Measles are especially dangerous in children who are malnourished.
3. Tuberculosis is more common and gets worse more rapidly in those who are undernourished.
4. Minor problems like the common cold are often worse and last longer in children who are poorly nourished.

Characteristics of Wet Malnutrition and Dry Malnutrition

Wet Malnutrition or Kwashiorkor	*Dry Malnutrition or Marasmus*
1. Swollen 'moon' face	1. Face like an old man
2. Miserable	2. Always hungry
3. Growth stops	3. Pot belly
4. Sores and peeling skin	4. Very underweight
5. Swollen hands and feet	5. Very thin
6. Colour loss in hair and skin	
7. Thin upper arms	
8. Wasted muscles but may have some fat	

Often a child may indicate the signs of wet malnutrition as well as dry malnutrition.

Prevention of Malnutrition Among Children

In solving the problems of undernourishment and malnutrition, it is necessary to climinate the causes leading to it. Malnutrition can be prevented and treated by giving children enough body-building and protective foods like milk, beans, lentils, fruits, vegetables, eggs, meat and fish.

Following are some of the measures for checking malnutrition:

1. Maintaining a balanced diet, concentrating on high-calorie food.
2. Using inexpensive but nutritional food items and getting good foods at low cost.
3. Regular mealtimes.
4. Well prepared and attractively served foods.
5. Adding light snacks between meals and at bed time.
6. Making mealtime environment calm, cheerful and encouraging.
7. Supplementing school meals.

13.12 SCHOOL MID-DAY MEALS

Why School Meals: It is now generally recognized that in the wake of 'under-nutrition and malnutrition of a large number of Indian children, the school must take up the responsibility to make up this deficiency. This will not only assist in improving the health and physical development of the child but also assist him in making quick and sounder progress in his studies because a child who is better-fed and healthier makes rapid progress. It also provides motivation to parents to send their children to school. It is, therefore, essential that we must develop a programme of school meals as an integral part of its programme of universal, free and compulsory primary education.

Various Schemes of School Meals

Free Milk: With the help of United Nations International Children's Emergency Fund (UNICEF) which provided milk powder free of charge, milk was distributed to about 7 lakhs of primary school children for several years.

Contents of Mid-day Meals: The School Health Committee (1960) recommended that it should be based on cheap, nutritious and locally available foods. A menu may comprise a minimum of cereals and millets-2.5 oz; pulses-1 oz; non-leafy vegetable-1 oz; Oil-1 oz. and condiments and salt.

Subsidy by the Government: The Committee recommended that the Government should support the school meal programme besides the contribution of the community at the rate of 50 per cent of the total cost.

Special Nutrition Programmes (SNP): This programme was launched in 1970-71 to provide supplementary nutrition to children below six years of age and expectant/nursing mothers living in rural slum, tribal areas and backward rural areas. Under the programme, supplementary feeding is given for 300 days in a year to provide about 300 calories and 10 grams of protein per child per day and about 500 calories and 20 grams of protein to a mother.

Wheat Based Supplementary Nutrition Programme: The programme has two components-Centrally funded component and state funded component. Under the Centrally funded component, Central assistance for the programme consists of supply of free wheat and supportive costs for other ingredients such as sugar, pulses, oil, etc, to make different kind of recipes and also to meet expenditure on cooking and transport, etc.

Balwadi Nutrition Programme (BNP): This programme has been implemented since 1970-71 through The Central Social Welfare Board and four national level voluntary organisations including the Indian Council of Child Welfare.

World Food Programme (WFP): Under this project, World Food Programme provides food commodities to beneficiaries.

CARE (Cooperative for American Relief Everywhere) Assisted Nutrition Programme: Under the Indo-CARE Agreement 1950, supplementary nutrition is provided to pre-school children below 6 years.

Tamil Nadu Integrated Nutrition Project (TNNP): It has been undertaken as a State Sector Project in Tamil Nadu with World Bank Assistance.

NSPE: The Government of India, initiated the scheme 'Nutritional Support to Primary Education' (NSPE), popularly known as the Mid-day Meals Scheme on August 15, 1995 on a nation-wide scale. The programme intends to give a boost to the universalization of primary education by increasing enrolment, retention and attendance and also to improve the nutritional status of students in the primary classes (I to V).

The Central support under this scheme is:

(i) Provision of foodgrains free of cost.

(ii) Reimbursement of transport cost to district authorities for moving foodgrains from godowns of Food Corporation of India to Schools.

The Scheme aims at covering 10 crore children. In 2002, the scheme was in operation in Chattisgarh, Delhi, Karnataka, Kerala, Madhya Pradesh, Orissa and Tamil Nadu. The remaining States were distributing foodgrains/wheat/rice.

Supreme Court Directions on Compulsory Midday Meals:

In 2003, the Supreme Court gave directions to all States and Union Territories to supply mid-day meals in all primary schools (Classes I to V).

14

Diet Deficiency Diseases

14.1 MEANING OF DIET DEFICIENCY DISEASES

Diet deficiency diseases or disorders are those diseases or disorders which are caused on account of malnutrition. Adequate nutrition is essential for maintaining healthy state of human body. Balanced requirement of proteins, carbohydrates, fats, vitamins and minerals is needed for proper growth and maintenance. A prolonged diet deficiency of any of these nutrients results in deficiency diseases.

14.2 TYPES OF DEFICIENCY DISEASES

Types of Deficiency Diseases

(1) Protein Deficiency Diseases
(2) Mineral Deficiency Diseases
(3) Vitamin Deficiency Diseases

14.3 PROTEIN-ENERGY MALNUTRITION (PEM) OR DEFICIENCY ON ACCOUNT OF LACK OF PROTEIN

Protein-energy malnutrition (PEM) is common among children in underdeveloped and developing countries. It causes several disorders in children. It affects children in the age group of 1-5 years. The children remain underweight and are susceptible to infections. In many countries, nearly half the children do not survive to the age of five years due to PEM.

Marasmus and *Kwashiorkor* are two common disease due to PEM.

1. Marasmus

Marasmus is a nutritional disease that occurs due to protein-energy malnutrition (PEM). There is undernourishment of both proteins and carbohydrates or total food calories. It is common in children below one year of age on account of inadequate diet and less spacing of children and replacement of mother's milk with calorie deficient food. One of the reasons why babies are weaned too soon from breast milk to subsist on a deficient diet, is frequent pregnancy. Premature deprivation of mother's milk because of early arrival of the next child is an important cause.

Symptoms (Fig. 14.1)

1. The child gives a shrivelled appearance as the body becomes very thin. The stored fat and tissue protein are utilised for the energy production as the diet is insufficient to proteinaceous food.
2. The ribs are prominent as muscles do not develop and the fat layer beneath the skin seems to be absent.
3. The skin becomes dry and wrinkled. The child becomes so thin that loose folds of skin can be seen all over the body.
4. It leads to retarded physical as well as mental growth.
5. The child suffers from repeated diarrhoea, digestive disorders due to atrophy of digestive glands, but there is no oedema or swelling of body parts like in Kwashiorkor.

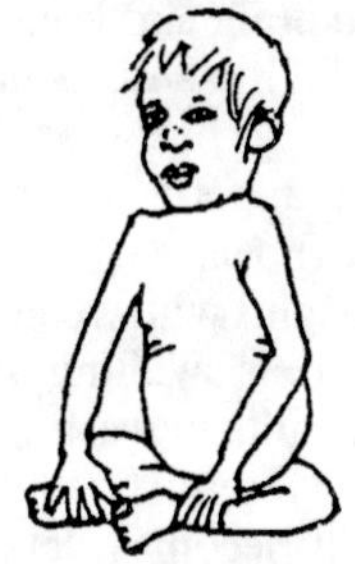

Fig. 14.1: A Child Suffering from Marasmus

Prevention/Control

Marasmus can be controlled by giving the child a rich protein diet in sufficient amount. The diet should have a combination of wheat, gram, peanuts, soyabean and gur jaggery to give proteins as well as sufficient calories. The diet may also contain animal proteins like mutton, chicken and fish. It is important to educate mothers about the significance of spacing the birth of children and importance of breast-feeding the baby as long as possible.

2. Kwashiorkor

Kwashiorkor is a serious protein deficiency disease and prevalent among babies and very young children aged 1-8 years in parts of Africa, Asia, southern Europe and South America.

"Kwashiorkor is an African word meaning *the rejected one*."

This disease affects the children who are fed on low protein diet and get no milk. They get less than 1 gm protein per kg of body weight. If not treated early, more than half of the

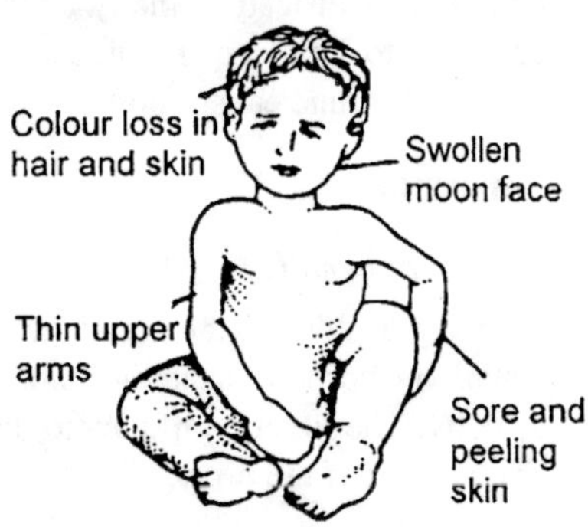

Fig. 14.2: A Child Suffering from Kwashiorkar

children suffering from Kwashiorkor may die.

Symptoms (Fig. 14.2)

1. The child shows emaciated appearance, retarded growth of the body and brain and is emotionally depressed.
2. Child has a distended belly *i.e.* stomach protrudes out.
3. The legs become thin and show curvature-called as 'matchstick legs'.
4. The appetite is poor and the child is troubled with vomiting and diarrhoea.
5. It begins with weight loss and later leads to oedema *i.e.* water retention. There is swelling of hands feet, and face. Face shows bulging eyes.
6. It results in wasting of muscles-thin upper arms.
7. Hair lose lustre and become brown.
8. Skin becomes dark and irregularly pigmented and may peal of at places. Likely to develop skin rash, inflammation about the mouth and eyes.

Prevention/Control

The child needs to be treated early and properly. The disease can be cured by giving protein rich diet.

For babies and young children, the most important dietary treatment is to give lots of milk and eggs. The diet should have a combination of wheat, gram, peanut, soyabean and jaggery.

Soyabean is the best vegetable source of complete protein. Diet can have animal proteins (which are generally complete proteins) like egg, chicken and meat.

14.4 MINERAL DEFICIENCY DISEASES

Minerals are inorganic molecules which must be present in the diet in the required amount. They are required in small amount but are extremely important as they regulate various metabolic functions of the body. Deficiency of minerals can lead to many abnormalities. Given below are the diseases caused due to deficiencies of iron and iodine. Deficiency of iron causes anaemia and that of iodine causes goitre.

1. Anaemia

Cause of Anaemia

Anaemia is due to the deficiency of iron in the diet. Iron is required in the formation of protein haemoglobin, which is present in the red blood cells of our body. The function of haemoglobin is to transport oxygen from lungs to various parts of the body.

Symptoms of Anaemia

1. The total red blood cell (RBC) count of the person falls below normal.

2. As there is not enough haemoglobin, the person suffering from anaemia gets tired easily.
3. The person loses weight and becomes pale.

Prevention/Control of Anaemia

Anaemia can be cured by taking iron rich diet. The daily requirement of iron for a person is 25mg. It can be taken from animal as well plant sources. Liver, eggs, molasses, cereals, pulses, green leafy vegetables like spinach, apple, banana and guava are rich sources of iron.

2. Goitre

Cause: Goitre is due to the deficiency of iodine in the diet. Iodine is an important component of hormone thyroxine which is secreted from the thyroid gland. Deficiency of iodine leads to deficiency of thyroxine in the body.

Symptoms

1. Goitre is abnormal enlargement of the thyroid gland which gets visible as a lump outside in the neck region (Fig. 14.3).
2. Deficiency of iodine, induces more and larger cells to grow in the thyroid, hence thyroid gland keeps enlarging and goitre is formed.
3. In children, it is noticed in the retarded physical and mental growth.
4. In adults, it shows symptoms of hypothyroidism like low respiration rate and low heart beat rate. Blood pressure becomes low and person feels cold, tired and sluggish.

Fig. 14.3: A Man Suffering from Goitre

Prevention

Goitre can be prevented by taking iodine rich food. Iodine comes into the food through iodine rich water and soil. Goitre is prevalent in the iodine-poor regions of the world. In India whole of sub-Himalayan region of Kashmir to Arunachal Pradesh is prone to it since the soil in which vegetables are grown is iodine deficient (due to removal of top soil containing iodine over the centuries).

The deficiency of iodine can be prevented by adding iodised salts like potassium iodate (KIO3) to cooking salt or to the drinking water supply. Goitre is a rare disease along the sea coast because the sea food contains a large amount of iodine.

The sources of iodine are sea food, leafy vegetables grown in iodine rich soil, water and iodised salt. "One of the successful ways to prevent goitre is to add one part of iodine to 10-20 thousand parts of common salt."

Control

- Goitre is generally controlled by injecting controlled doses of radioactive iodine. This is taken up by the thyroid cells killing those where it accumulates above a certain level.

Other ways found effective against goitre are:

- The intramuscular injections of iodised oil (mostly poppy-seed oil).
- Sodium iodate tablets to be taken orally. These tablets are developed by ICMR (Indian Council of Medical Research).
- ICMR is on its way to develop common salt fortified with iron and iodine *i.e.* 'two-in one' salt to check anaemia as well as iodine deficiency.

14.5 VITAMIN DEFICIENCY DISEASES

Vitamins are organic substances required in very small amount or in 'trace amounts' (ug or mg/day) in the diet, for e.g. we need only about 0001 gm. of Vitamin A dose per day. They are important for certain metabolic activities and some act as co-enzymes. They need to be present in our diet. Absence of these in our diet for a long period may cause deficiency diseases or a vitaminosis.

Depending on their solubility vitamins are of two types:

Types of Vitamins

Fat soluble Vitamins Diseases

Vitamin A.........Xerophthalmia; Night-blindness
Vitamin A.........Rickets; Osteomalacia
Vitamin E.........Reproductive failure
Vitamin K.........Prolonged bleeding

Water soluble vitamins

Vitamin B Complex Diseases
Vitamin B1.........Beriberi
Vitamin B5.........Pellagra
Vitamin C.........Scurvy

Diseases caused by deficiencies of vitamins A, D, B_1, B_5 and C are given in Table 14.1.

Table 14.1: Diseases caused by Deficiency of Vitamins

Deficiency	*Deficient*	*Symptoms*	*Prevention/Control*
1. Xerophthalmia	Vitamin A	— Non-functioning of lacrymal gland. — Dryness of cornea and conjunctiva as mucous membrane degenerates. — Thickened, keratinised corniea. — May lead to permanent blindness if Vitamin A is not added in diet.	Vitamin A rich diet. Animal sources–Fish, cod liver oil, milk, butter, dairy products Plant sources–carrots, tomato, green leaf vegetables, papaya, guava, yellow fruits and vegetables like pumpkin
2. Night-blindness	Vitamin A	— Formation of less rhodopsin, the visual pigment. — Difficulty to see in dim light or poor vision at night. — May lead to total blindness in dim light if not cured.	
3. Rickets (in children) 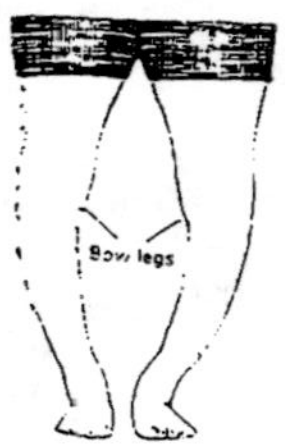 **Fig. 14.4:** A child with bow legs (Rickets) due to deficiency of vitamin D,	Vitamin D	— Increased loss of calcium (Ca^{++}) in urine, hence no calcium deposition in bone. — Soft, thin weak bones due to failure of the growing bones to calcify. — Bow legs (Fig. 14.4) in younger, children and knock knees in older. — Deformed ribs makes the child pigeon chested. — Painful bones, difficulty in movement.	Diet rich in Vitamin D like cold liver oil, fish, milk, and yok. "Vitamin D is also synthesised in the skin in the presence of light."

(Contd.)

(*Contd.*)

Deficiency	*Deficient*	*Symptoms*	*Prevention/Control*
4. Osteomalacia (in adults)	Vitamin D	— Weak bones of vertebral column — Pelvic bones get bent and deformed by body weight. — Painful bones, may result in spontaneous fractures.	Same as above
5. Vitamin B_1 (Thiamine) also called anti beri-beri or anti neuritic factor.	Beriberi	— Muscular dystrophy *i.e.* muscles become weak and painful. Many result in paralysis. — Heart enlargement — Affects nervous system, nervous disorder — Poly neuritics (Inflammation of peripheral nerves causing pain and numbness) — Oedema *i.e.* swelling of hands and legs due to fluid accumulation.	Occurs most frequently among people whose diet consists mostly of polished rice *i.e.* dehusked rice. Also affects people highly refined starchy or sugary foods. Diet should contain plenty of Vitamin B1 Plant sources-Cereals (rice, wheat) pulses, nuts and green leafy vegetables. Animal sources-Liver kidney, milk, egg yolk. Whole wheat bread and 'Dalia' are the richest sources, because Vitamin B1 is present in the outer layers of rice and wheat gains.
6. Vitamin B5 (Niacin or Nicotinik	Pellagra	People suffering from pellagra show	Diet should consist of plenty of Vitamin

(*Contd.*)

(*Contd.*)

Deficiency	*Deficient*	*Symptoms*	*Prevention/Control*
6. Vitamin B5 (Niacin or Nicotinik acid or Pellagra preventing factor) 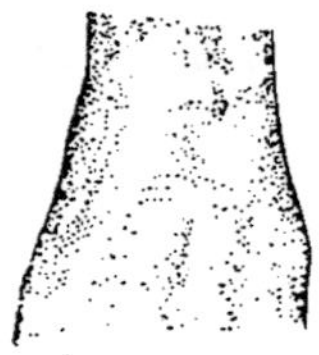 **Fig. 14.5:** Dermatitis (Pellagra) due to deficiency of Vitamin B_5	Pellagra	People suffering from pellagra show following four symptoms hence it is also called 4 D-syndrome. (i) Dermatitis-Fig. (14.5) inflammation of skin, skin lesions, thick pigmented, cracking skin at the back of hands, wrists, face and neck. Skin eczema on the arms and back of legs. (ii) Dementia-memory disorder, memory loss and forgetfulness, may lead to insanity. (iii) Diarrhoea-repeated loose motions. (iv) Death-if not cured properly (i) Dermatitis-Fig. (14.5) inflammation of skin, skin lesions, thick pigmented, cracking skin at the back of hands, wrists, face and neck. Skin eczema on the arms and back of legs. (ii) Dementia-memory disorder, memory loss and forgetfulness, may lead to insanity. (iii) Diarrhoea-repeated loose motions. (iv) Death-if not cured properly	Diet should consist of plenty of Vitamin B5 **Plant sources**-Cereals husk, peas, beans, green leafy vegetables, yeast. Animal sources-Liver fish, milk, egg yolk and meat. *"Pellagra is common in the areas when maize is the staple food item. This is because maize interferes with the absorption of Vitamin B5 (niacin) in the body."* **Plant sources**-Cereals husk, peas, beans, green leafy vegetables, yeast. Animal sources-Liver fish, milk, egg yolk and meat. *"Pellagra is common in the areas when maize is the staple food item. This is because maize interferes with the absorption of Vitamin B5 (niacin) in the body."*
7. Vitamin C (Ascorbic acid or Anti scorbiutic acid) 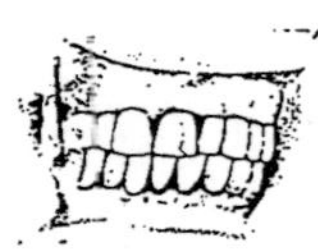 **Fig. 14.6:** Bleeding gums (Scurvy) due to deficiency of Vitamin C	Scurvy	-Bleeding gums (Fig. 14.6)	Citrus fruits (like lemon and orange), pineapple, grapes, green leaf vegetables like spinach green peper. Tomatoes like spinach green pepper, Tomatoes "*Correction of diet brings miraculous improvement and symptoms disappear within a few days.*"

14.6 HEALTHY EATING HABITS

It is important to observe good and proper dietary habits for a healthy living. Proper habits include good personal and domestic hygiene also. Given below are some important habits one should take care of:

1. Food eaten should be fresh.
2. Food should by kept always covered and away from dust, flies, insects and microbes to avoid infection and spoilage.
3. Utensils for cooking as well as in which food is eaten be kept clean.
4. Hands should be washed with soap before eating or handling the food.
5. Food should be cooked with good feelings and cheerful state. There is a saying that, food cooked with happy feelings brings cheerfulness to the person who eats it.
6. Bad habits like smoking, chewing tobacco, drinking alcohol, taking addictive drugs should be avoided. They can have serious damaging effects on the body and mind. Smoking affects the lungs and tobacco chewing can lead to oral cancer. Alcohol reduces alertness of mind and in extreme cases causes liver damage. Narcotic addictive drugs lead to mental and physical ailments.
7. Food should be chewed properly.
8. Food should be taken in a cheerful mood.
9. Food should be taken at regular hours.
10. Over-eating should be avoided.
11. Food should be eaten hurriedly.
12. Green vegetable should be eaten daily.
13. Food should be eaten slowly and not hurriedly.
14. Boiled water should be taken when pure water is not available.
15. Contaminated food by house flies and cockroaches should not be taken.
16. Undereating should not be done.

15

Communicable Diseases

15.1 MEANING AND TYPES OF DISEASES

A disease is a disturbed state of body or mind. The term 'disease' itself means without ease or discomfort. The disease can be in any part of the body and due to malfunctioning of the body organ for some or the other reason. For time immemorial, man has tried to understand the nature and cause of diseases and has tried to cure them.

Types of Diseases

The diseases can be categorised into two basic types: (i) Congenital, present at birth and (ii) acquired, that are contracted after birth.

(i) *Congenital diseases:* These diseases are present at the time of birth. They could be due to genetic defect or due to malfunctioning of any organ or system. They are permanent, generally not curable and may be inherited by the children.

(ii) *Acquired diseases:* The acquired diseases develop after birth and can be broadly classified into two types.
Communicable diseases and non-communicable diseases.

15.2 COMMUNICABLE DISEASES AND THEIR CLASSIFICATION

Communicable diseases are those diseases that can be spread from diseased persons to healthy person. They are transmitted from one person to another by means of air, water, food, physical contact and insects (insects act agents). Diseases are caused by germs which are organism that are either invisible or visible only under a very powerful microscope. They invade the body and multiply rapidly.

The poisons manufactured by the germs circulate in the blood and give rise to symptoms of particular diseases. Germs are carried from one person to another and the diseases spread. Germs can be carried by flies and other insects, human beings, articles used by the infected person and public conveniences.

Classification of Communicable Diseases

(1) Diseases caused by bacteria	(2) Diseases caused by viruses	(3) Disease caused by protozoa
(i) Cholera	(i) AIDS	Malaria
(ii) Typhoid	(ii) Hepatitis	
(iii) Tuberculosis	(iii) Influenza	
	(iv) Jaundice	
	(v). Rabies	

15.3 MEASURES FOR THE PREVENTION AND CONTROL OF COMMUNICABLE DISEASES

The following steps should be taken to prevent and control the communicable diseases.

1. Notification

As soon as any case is noticed, the concerned department should be informed. The department takes the following suitable steps for preventing the disease to spread.

1. Patients are isolated.
2. Necessary disinfection is done.
3. Inoculation is done on a large scale.
4. Main sources of information can be found out.
5. Necessary instructions are issued to schools and other educational institutions to isolate affected students.
6. Sources of water supply and milk depots are checked to find out any factor which can cause such diseases.
7. Doubtful cases are detected and necessary steps taken in this regard.

Notifiable Diseases: Information of the following diseases should be provided to health officers:

Cholera, small pox, plague, enteric fever, dysentery dyphtheria, mumps, tuberculosis, influenza, whooping cough, measles, yellow fever, typhoid, typhus etc. diseases.

Who should notify? When a doctor comes to know by examining a person that he is affected by infectious diseases, then it becomes his prime duty to inform health officer about. If he does not act is such manner, action can be taken against him under Municipal Act. Guardian or caretaker of patient should inform about infectious disease. Any person living in the house of the patient may inform about it. Manager of a hotel or other institution should also inform about it.

2. Isolation

For controlling extension of the communicable diseases, isolation is the best method. By isolation, the patient is separated from other persons so that, through direct or indirect sources, his infection may not be communicated to other persons. The patient suffering from a communicable disease may be isolated by putting in separate hospital and by providing separate place in home. In hospital, there should be separate wards for various infectious diseases.

At the time of isolating the patient in the house, the following points should be kept in mind.

1. The ideal situation is that the room of patient is at the upper floor.
2. All unnecessary furniture of the room should be removed.
3. Cloth wetted in solution carbolic acid (1 : 20) should be used as curtain on the door.
4. For fresh air, as far as possible, windows should be kept open.
5. Clothes of patient should be dipped in disinfectant solution later on and should be boiled for disinfection.
6. Excrement of the patient should be collected in a vessel. Strong disinfectant solution should be kept in the vessel. The excrement should be burnt or buried in the ground.
7. After taking out the vessels from the room of patient, they should be disinfected completely.
8. Appropriate steps should be taken for removing flies and mosquitoes from the room of the patient.
9. The visitors should not be allowed to enter the room of patient to see him.
10. Affected children and others affected in the house should not be sent to their respective institutions.
11. Caretaker or nurse only should be allowed to go inside the room of the patient.
12. After recovery, the patient should be given a bath and his clothes should be changed. Thereafter, he should be allowed to meet others.
13. In the case of the death of the patient, his dead body should be covered with cloth wetted in the carbolic lotion and should be burnt as far as possible.
14. The room of the patient should be disinfected completely after it is vacated by the patient.

3. Disinfection and Disinfectant

Disinfection: Disinfection implies the use of disinfectant (chemical liquid or powder) by which specific bacteria of infectious diseases are destroyed. Disinfection should be done during disease period and at the end of disease. When person is affected, then his excrements should be disinfected immediately. Such disinfections are called concurrent disinfection. When the patient recovers from disease, then his room and other articles should be disinfected necessarily. Such disinfection is called terminal disinfection.

Disinfectants: Disinfectants are those elements which destroy microbe. Disinfectants may be divided in three categories:

Classification of Disinfectants

(1) Natural Disinfectants | 2 Physical Disinfectants | 3 Chemical Disinfectants

1. **Natural Disinfectants**: In natural disinfectants, fresh air and sunlight are very important. Both provide a good deal of help in preventing infectious diseases. Increase of micro-organisms can be checked by drying. Oxygen of air helps in killing microbes. The light of sun in powerful germicide because Actinic Rays are available in it. This is mainly done by Ultraviolet Rays. In atmosphere, Actinic Rays, through their action make oxide ozone and hydrogen. These two work as a main source for making oxygen. Microbes of dyphtheria die out in an hour in direct sunlight. Likewise tubercle microbes also die out in sunlight very soon.

2. **Physical Disinfectants**: These disinfectants may be divided in two categories: (1) Dry Heat, and (2) Moist Heat.

(1) *Dry Heat*: Under this come two disinfectants (i) Burning, and (ii) Hot Dry Air.

(i) *Burning:* This is the best method of disinfection. Act of burning should be done in hearth but this hearth should be in open place. *Juggi Jhopris* affected by infectious disease like plague should be burnt. Spittle, phlegm and other excrements of the patient should be burnt completely.

(ii) *Hot Dry Air:* This method is not so effective in destroying microbes as burning. On account of this limitation, this method is not so common. It is a useful method for disinfecting articles of leather, books, rubber articles etc. This is also quite effective for killing lice and other insects.

(2) *Moist Heat*: This includes two disinfectants:

(i) Boiling, and

(ii) Steam.

(i) *Boiling*: For destroying germs, boiling for 10 minutes is enough. But for destroying spore, boiling is needed at least for half an hour. Clothes smeared in blood or excrement should be washed first with soap, then they should be boiled. Woolen clothes should not be boiled for disinfecting. The method may be used for disinfecting bed sheets, bedpan, urine pot and utensils of cooking etc.

(ii) *Steam*: This can be used in three forms:

(a) *Current Steam:* It is also called "Low pressure steam". To start with, this disinfectant is cheap. But, in the long run it becomes costly, because more fuel is used in it.

(b) *Saturated Steam:* When the steam is prepared in closed vessel, its pressure increases. Steam prepared in this way is called saturated steam.

(c) *Superheated Steam:* This can be prepared by two methods:
   (i) When the steam is heated without increasing pressure, its temperature increases.
   (ii) It can also be made by boiling solution of salt, because salt solution boils at high rate of temperature than ordinary water. In this steam, the qualities of dry gas are found.

3. **Chemical Disinfectants**: These disinfectants can be divided as under:
(a) Solids, (b) Liquids, (c) Gases, (d) Aerosols.

Main Chemical disinfectants are:

(i) *Bichloride of Mercury:* It is also called perchloride of mercury. It is a very powerful disinfectant for destroying microbes, and spores.
(ii) *Carbolic Acid or Phenol:* It is obtained from distilling of coal tar (char coal). It is a cheap and useful disinfectant. But it cannot destroy spores.
(iii) *Potassium Permanganate:* It is done for disinfecting water during break of cholera. It functions only in the form of deodorant.
(iv) *Lime:* It is the cheapest powerful disinfectant. It should be used only after extinction. It is used for disinfecting water, excrements and floor etc.
(v) *Chlorinated Lime or Bleaching Powder:* It functions in both the forms as deodorant and disinfectant. 5% solution of bleaching powder is sufficient for disinfecting filth. For disinfecting rooms, solution of 1 : 30 is enough. For disinfecting wells, ½ ounce powder is sufficient for 1000 gallon water.
(vi) *Soap:* Soap is less useful is the form of disinfecant. Coconut soap is helpful in disinfecting microbes of typhoid.
(vii) *Sulphur Dioxide:* It is mainly used for disinfecting ships, cars and stables etc. It is a poisonous gas. Its germicidal action depends upon presence of humidity.
(viii) *Formaldehyde gas:* It is a powerful disinfectant and is used as steam. It does not leave any bad effect on metal. Its powerful solution is very harmful to eyes and lungs. Its smell can be removed from the room by spraying ammonia. It can be used in the following ways:
   (a) Using permanganate
   (b) Using bleeching powder
   (c) Using paraform
(ix) *Chlorine Gas:* It is both disinfectant and deodorant. For disinfecting per thousand cubic feet of place, one pound sulphuric acid or hydrochloric and 2 pounds of Bleaching powder are enough. By mixing these two, chlorine gas is formed. It is harmful for eyes.
(x) *Hydrocyanic Acid Gas:* Bacteria is not affected by this gas. Its use is done mainly for destroying rats. It is chemically inactive. For disinfecting per thousand cubic feet of place, 5 ounce potassium cyanide; 7.5 ounce sulphuric acid and 10 ounce water mixture form this gas.

(xi) *Aerosols:* Following are the qualities of good aerosols:
   (i) Rapid Germicidal Action.
   (ii) High Dispersibility

   Aerosols do not leave any bad effect on the human beings and/or animals. In these sodium hypochloride, ethylene, glycol, and propylene glycol are the main elements.

4. **Public Education**-Public should be suitably educated regarding various aspects of communicable diseases-how these diseases are spread, how to prevent them and what steps they should take to control their spread.

15.4 CHOLERA

Cholera is a highly infectious disease. It is commonly called as '*Haiza*'. It was once a dreaded and a fatal disease. Since it spreads through water, it is more common during fairs and after floods. If proper sanitary and hygienic conditions are not maintained, it spreads over a large population i.e. takes an epidemic form.

Causes and Mode of Infection/Spread

Cholera is caused by the bacterium vibrio cholerae Fig. 15.1. It is mainly a water-borne disease. It also spreads through contaminated food and drinks or touching by contaminated hands. It is transmitted by flies and spreads rapidly when sanitation is poor. It takes an epidemic form (spreads in a large population) during fairs and after floods. It is communicated from one person to another.

Symptoms of Cholera

(i) In the beginning an individual suffers from loose motions. The motions become water-like.
(ii) Along with dysentery the patient vomits.
(iii) The patient feels too much thirsty.
(iv) The urine of the patient tends to stop.
(v) The patient feels sharp twisting in hands and legs.
(vi) Temperature continuously goes down.
(vii) The patient becomes physically very weak and becomes unconscious. If timely treatment is not given to the patient, his heart may fail.

Prevention of Cholera

(1) Boiled water should be used for drinking purposes.
(2) Eating outside the house during epidemic should be avoided.
(3) Chat from the vendors should not be taken.
(4) Vegetables and fruit should be used in a dilute solution of potassium permanganate.
(5) Water should be chlorinated.
(6) Drains should be kept neat and clean by disinfactants.

(7) Eatables should not be kept open for flies.
(8) Cut-fruit like water-melon should be avoided.
(9) Anticholeral or oil mixture may be used.
(10) Special care should be taken to store water in the school.
(11) The toilets of the school should be cleaned at least three to four times a day by using disinfectants.

Oral rehydration therapy should be given immediately at short intervals. For this oral rehydration, mixture is available in small packets at primary health centres/hospitals/dispensaries medical shops. The oral rehydration solution (ORS) is prepared by mixing one packet of oral rehydration mixture in one litre of water. Small sips of this solution at short intervals prevents dehydration. The contents of this mixture are:

Sodium chloride 3.5g
Sodium bicarbonate 2.5g
Potassium chloride 1.5g
Glucose .... 20.0 g
Sucrose .... 40.0 g

It is advisable to prepare the solution in cooled water which has earlier been boiled.

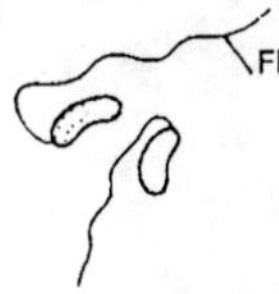

Fig. 15.1: Bacteria Vibrio cholerae

Control

Cholera can be fatal if not treated in time. Immediate medical advice should be taken.

Treatment

1. *Notification:* Information regarding cholera case should be immediately given to concerned health department.

2. *Segregation:* (i) Contact with other persons of the family should be severed. The patient should be segregated from others, (ii) The patient may be sent to hospital.

3. *Local measures:*

1. The excrements of the patient should be collected in a pot with lime in its base inside. These excrements should be buried or burnt.
2. The patient should be kept warm.
3. The patient should be given small quantities of water with glucose repeatedly.
4. The patient should be given ice pieces for quenching thirst by sucking.

15.5 TUBERCULOSIS (T.B.)

Tuberculosis commonly known as TB affects millions of people every year. It was first discovered by Robert Koch in 1822. It is a highly infectious disease that spreads from one human being to another directly or indirectly. Every year more than 10 million people get affected by it in our country.

Causes and Mode of Spread

TB is caused by bacterium Mycobacterium tuberculosis (Fig. 15.2).

It is a highly infectious disease that spreads from one human being to another directly or indirectly. It may also be contracted from the animals. TB spreads by:

(i) Droplet infection i.e. by inhaling the droplets thrown out into the air by the infected person while coughing, sneezing, talking or spitting.

(ii) On contact with sputum or through contaminated food, water or clothes.

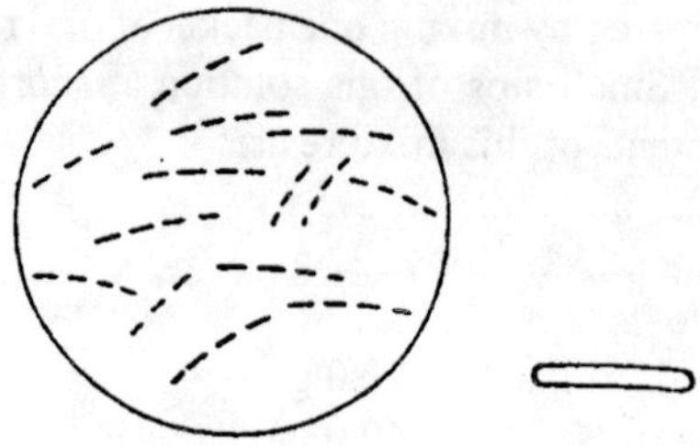

(a) Mycobacterium Tuberculosis (b) Rod-shaped Tuberculosis bacteria (highly magnified)

Fig. 15.2: Mycobacterium Tuberculosis (bacteria causing tuberculosis)

Part of the Body Infected

Tuberculosis bacteria can infect any part of the body; it could be bones, lymph glands, brains or lungs. Lung TB is most common. The bacteria releases a toxin tuberculin which destroys the tissues it infects.

Symptoms

The symptoms vary depending on the site of infection. Some of the common symptoms are:

(i) Loss of appetite.

(ii) Gradual weakening of the body. Patient feels sick.

(iii) A typical fever pattern. (Fig. 15.3)

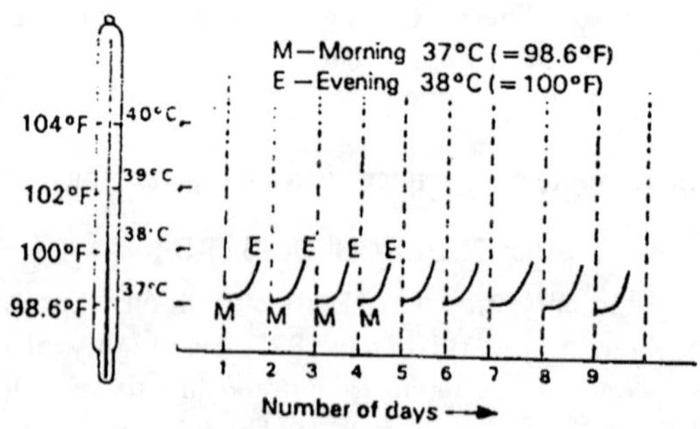

Fig. 15.3: Typical Fever Pattern in T.B. Normal Temperature is 37°C or 98.6°F.

The fever rises in the afternoon to about 38°C (100°F) and falls back to normal in the morning to 37°C (=98.6°F). This pattern may go on for days, even months continuously.

(iv) Loss of body weight
(v) Coughing and phlegm, sometimes blood coming with phlegm.
(vi) Perspiring in the night.
(vii) Ligh palpitation.
(viii) Fast pulse.
(ix) Pain in chest and throat.
(x) Breath hastily. Swelling of breath in moving.
(xi) Ribs and bones begin to peep on drying flesh of body.
(xii) In women, blood stops to come in menses.

Incubation Period: It is regarded 4-6 weeks. It may take several years also to develop since primary infection.

Prevention: For controlling this disease, the following common measures may be used:

(i) General cleanliness should be observed.
(ii) Persons should live in an open air and light.
(iii) Roads should be wide. There should be enough space between houses. In the area, there should be park, garden and open space.
(iv) Improvement should be brought in daily routine.
(v) People should be educated through a variety of media-speeches, pamphlets, slides and filmstrips.
(vi) Edible and drinkable things (food and drinks) should be looked after properly.
(vii) *Unhealthy avocations*: Coal mines, and Bidi making-factories should be suitably equipped and inhalation of dust should be prevented by proper arrangements.

Notification

For controlling this disease, the following specific measures may be used:

(i) Notification should be made compulsory. Patients should be enlisted and declared by doctors. Family members should not be kept in the dark about this disease.
(ii) Children should be isolated from parents affected with this disease.
(iii) All the phlegm producing patients of tuberculosis should be sent to sanitorium till the phlegm is stopped.

Technical and Medical Arrangements

(1) *Clinic System:* Clinic should be completely equipped:

(i) to diagnose Tuberculosis disease.
(ii) to give counsel regarding treatment to patients.
(iii) to advise the patients to keep their things separate viz. cup, spoon, glasses, and other things.
(iv) to work as an information centre. Along with, it should work as publicity-centre.

(v) to work as curative centre.

2. Hospital and Sanitorium
3. *Domiciliary Treatment:* It may not be possible to admit all the patients of the community in the hospital on account of the non-availability of beds for all the patients. Therefore, it becomes necessary to arrange domiciliary treatment. In domicialiary treatment, there must be adequate arrangement of health visitors for visiting the patients. These patients, need open houses, so that they may get fresh air and light in day time.
4. *Tuberculosis Colonies:* For the patients of tuberculosis, separate colonies should be arranged near sanitorium or dispensaries or clinics, so that they may be looked after properly. In these colonies, provision should be made for crafts like binding, carpentry, painting, mating and basket making. For doing these jobs, the patients may use most of their time. Here they may also enjoy fresh air and light.
5. *Coordination:* The Health Officers of the hospitals, the doctors doing private practice and dispensaries of tuberculosis should be brought together to coordinate the work of eradicating tuberculosis.
6. *Care and After Care Committees:* For providing proper service in sanitoriums, clinics, hospitals and colonies, Care and Aftercare Committees should be constituted.
7. B.C.G. Inoculation

General Guidelines: For the treatment of this disease, the following points should be kept in mind:

(i) The patient should have complete rest.
(ii) The patient should be made available fresh air and light.
(iii) The patient should be given balanced and nutritious diet. In his food, there must be sufficient milk, fruit, and eggs etc.
(iv) For leading a healthy life, good habits should be built up.
(v) It is very important that medicines must be taken regularly as advised by the doctor. The treatment may last for about six to nine months.

With the advancement in medical science, persons suffering from this disease can carry on their normal work if the disease is diagnosed well in time. Now this disease is not considered as dreadful as it was the case in earlier times.

Symptoms of Lung (Pulmonary) TB

1. Constant cough and in severe cases blood-stained sputum.
2. Pain in the chest or upper back while coughing.
3. Breathlessness, chronic cough especially just after waking up.
4. Weight loss and weakness.

Symptoms of Lymph Gland TB

1. Swelling and tenderness of lymph glands, often in the legs and neck.
2. These glands may discharge secretions through the skin.

Prevention

1. Good sanitary and healthy hygienic conditions in the community.
2. BCG vaccination (Bacillus-Calmette-Guerin) given in childhood gives protection against tuberculosis. The vaccine contains weakened bacteria Tuberculosis bacillus.

Control

Tuberculosis can be cured fully if discovered early on time.

1. Use of specific anti tubercular therapy (ATT). The medication usually continues for a minimum of one year. Usually three drugs are used-streptomycin, paraminosalicylic acid and isoniazid. Each is used according to the need and relative response of each patient.
2. Rest and balanced diet is a must for a TB patient.

15.6 WHOOPING COUGH

Whooping cough is an acute respiratory infection. This disease occurs due to microbes namely bacillus pertusis or hemophilus pertusis.

Symptoms: Main symptoms of this disease are the following:

(i) Fever 100-102°F with coughing.
(ii) Dry coughing at high rate.
(iii) Eye pupils becoming red by coughing repeatedly.
(iv) Vomiting by coughing again and again.
(v) Coming out pasting phlegm by coughing repeatedly.

Incubation Period: Generally, this period is of 7 days. Its maximum period is of 21 days.

Control and Treatment: For controlling this disease, the following measures may be used:

(i) Isolation of the patient.
(ii) If the child is school going, he should be kept at home at least for six weeks.
(iii) All the susceptible children should be given immunity by inoculation.

15.7 MALARIA

Meaning of the Word Malaria: The word malaria is derived from two Italian words '*Mal*' and '*Aria*'. '*Mal*' means bad and '*Aria*' means air. Thus malaria means bad air. This name remained associated with the disease till 1763. It was considered that this disease originated in marshy land by inhaling poisonous smell through respiration. Malaria has existed since immorial times. Hippocrates, in 442 BC, mentioned about this disease.

Though malaria has been controlled to a great extent, still more than two million people die every year and about 300 million get infected.

Cause and Mode of Spread of Malaria

Malaria is caused by a parasite called Plasmodium. Plasmodium is a single celled organism from the group protozoa. (Fig. 15.4) It is spread by the bite of female Anopheles mosquito (Fig. 15.4) which feeds on human blood. The male Anopheles mosquito feeds on plant juices and so is harmless. Female Anopheles mosquito transmits the malarial parasite from an infected person to a healthy person and acts as-carrier or vector of the disease. "Plasmodium- the malarial parasite spends a part of its life cycle in female Anopheles mosquito and survives in its salivary glands".

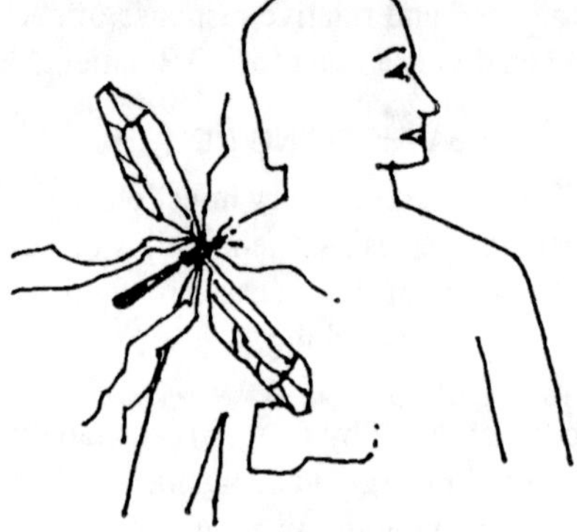

Fig. 15.4: Carrier and Cause of Malaria

Symptoms

A person suffering from malaria shows following symptoms. If malaria is not treated, these symptoms appear again after a specific gap of 24 hours, 48 hours or 72 hours.

(i) Each malarial attack lasts for about 6-10 hours and the patient goes through three stages-cold stage, hot stage and sweating stage.
   (a) Cold stage: Malaria begins with feeling very cold and recurrent shivering chills. There is a gradual rise in temperature.
   (b) Hot stage: Next is high temperature up to 104°F accompanied by headache and severe body ache. It also leads to faster respiration and heart beat.
   (c) Sweating stage: The fever may subside on its own after about 3-4 hours and come to normal. It is followed by sweating so profuse that clothes are wet.

(ii) If malaria is not treated, the above symptoms appear again. The fever may come after a gap of 24, 48 or 72 hours at the same time.

(iii) Malaria leaves the patient weak and anemic. After the patient is cured, it takes some time for the person to come back to normal health.

(iv) Malaria may also lead to enlargement of liver and spleen if not cured properly.

Prevention

Malaria is a communicable disease and spreads from an infected to healthy person by the bite of female anopheles mosquitoes. The only way to prevent malaria is to prevent the mosquitoes from biting and by destroying their breeding places.

(i) A fine net or wire gauze should be used on doors and windows to prevent the entry of mosquitoes.
(ii) Insect-repellent creams (like odomos) also help in keeping mosquitoes away.
(iii) Sleeping under fine-mesh mosquito nets helps to prevent mosquito bites.
(iv) Adult mosquitoes can be killed by spraying insecticides like DDT.
(v) Mosquito larvae can be destroyed by spraying kerosene oil in open drains, water-stagnant bodies, and ponds. A few drops of kerosene oil should be put in the water of water cooler as well.
(vi) Another effective mean to kill mosquito larvae is to introduce fishes like Gambusia, minnows and trouts that feed on mosquito larvae (larvivorus fishes) in large water bodies.
(vii) Water should not be allowed to collect around the houses.

Control

Malaria can be controlled by taking the drug quinine in prescribed doses. Quinine is extracted from the bark of Cinchona tree. Malaria parasite has become resistant to this drug due to over prescription and over dose taken by the people. Now malaria is being treated by other medicines like sulphadoxin, fencider etc. The research is on to develop a vaccine for malaria.

15.8 TYPHOID OR ENTERIC FEVER

Nature and Causes of Typhoid: Typhoid is an infectious disease. It is caused by germs bacillus Typhus. Water is the main cause leading to this disease. Other sources of this disease are: milk, other edible things and excrements. The germs enter the body through air, water and food.

The germs or microbes of the disease come out of the body of the patient with filth. These are carried by flies to edibles and drinkable things when a healthy person uses these defiled things, these enter his body.

Incubation Period. On an average, the incubation period is 2 weeks.

Symptoms: (1) In the beginning the patient feels acute pain in head and waist. Fever increases slowly, (2) The tongue becomes dry, (3) Pulse is slow in comparison with high temperature, (4) The intestine gets weak, (5) There is loss of appetite, (6) Spleen gets swollen, (7) Sometimes red spots appear on the skin of the trunk.

Diagnosis: Its diagnosis is done by blood culture and widal reaction.

Preventive Measures: (1) Public water supply should be chlorinated.

(2) Eatable things should be protected from flies.

(3) Pure milk should be used.

Notification

When some person is suspected to be affected from this disease, its information should be given to the concerned department.

Control and Treatment: 1. The patient should be shifted to a room which is free from flies. Where such an environment is not available, the patient should be sent to a hospital.

2. Anti-typhoid injection should be given.

3. Proper arrangement should be made for concurrent disinfection.

4. Excrements (latrine, urine and phlegm) should be collected in a container and proper arrangement for its disposals should be made.

5. Pure and boiled milk should be given to the patient.

6. The patient should be given sufficient water and orange juice to drink.

7. The patient should be kept in bed and given complete bed rest.

8. In case of pain in the abdomen, formentation with hot water bottle should be provided.

9. In case of high temperature, icebag on the forehead should be used.

10. With the consultation of the physician, liquid diet should be given.

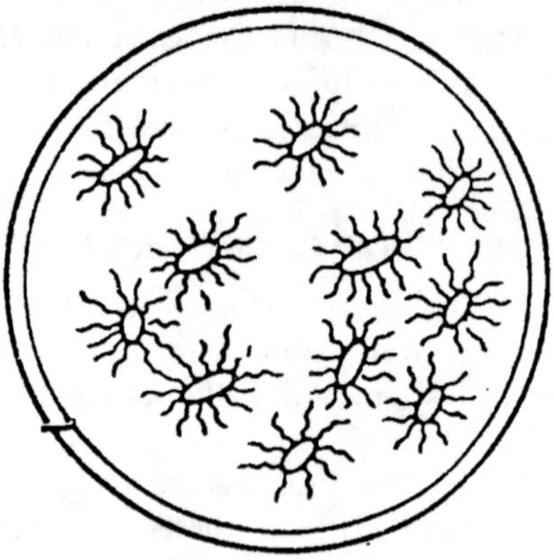

Fig. 15.5: *Salmonella typhi* (Bacteria that causes typhoid)

15.9 DIARRHOEA

Diarrahoea is a leading cause of death of children under the age of five. *Diarrhoea* can be defined as loose, watery, frequent motions several times a day. At times, there can be a few motions every hour.

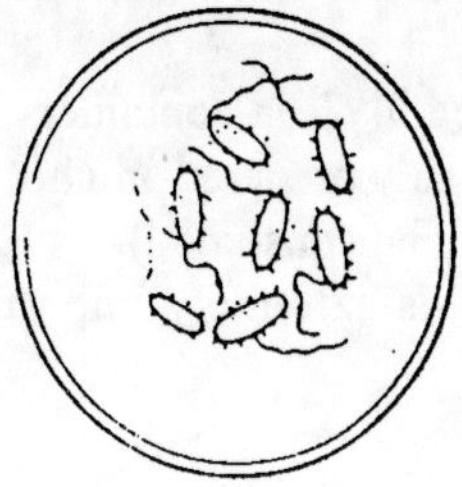

Fig. 15.6: *Escherichia coli* (Bacteria that causes diarrhoea)

Causes and Mode of Infection/spread

Diarrhoea may be caused by certain Bacteria, protozoa and viruses. It is mainly due to bacteria (such as Escherichia coli (Fig. 15.6) commonly written as E. coli, Shigella, Campylobacter and Salmonella. A protozoan Giardia and certain viruses also cause similar conditions. Diarrhoeal disease is a group of infections of the intestinal tract, including food poisoning.

Diarrhoea is a Highly Infectious Disease

- It spreads through contaiminated water, food and drinks.
- The infection also spreads through contaminated fingers, clothes, bed linen and utensils.

Symptoms

Symptoms of diarrhoea can range from mild diarrhoea to severe dehydration.

(i) Sudden onset of frequent loose, watery motions.
(ii) Abdominal pain and cramps. The pain could be at intervals or sharp and continuous.
(iii) Vomiting and loose motions may lead to dehydration i.e. excessive loss of water from body.
(iv) During dehydration, the patient becomes irritable, the eyes appear sunken, nose is pinched and the tongue and inside of cheeks appear dry.
(v) In severe cases, it leads to fever fits. There is sudden weight loss and the pulse becomes weak.

Prevention

Proper sanitation and hygienic conditions are needed for prevention of diarrhoea.

1. All food should be protected from dirt, flies, cockroaches etc. Eatables should always be covered.
2. Fruits and vegetables should be washed properly before use.
3. Water should be boiled before drinking.

4. Personal hygiene should be taken care of, for instance washing hands before eating.
5. Food should be stored in clean containers.
6. As far as possible freshly prepared and hot food should be consumed (stale food should not be consumed).
7. Community hygiene is extremely important to avoid epidemic of diarrhoea.

Control

1. The patient needs complete bed rest till the illness is fully cured.
2. To prevent dehydration, care must be taken to give enough fluids and electrolytes.
   Oral rehydration Solution (ORS) should be given by mouth at short intervals. A good ORS can be easily prepared at home by mixing the following things:
   — 1 teaspoon of sugar
   — 1/4 teaspoon of salt
   — a pinch of sodium bicarbonate (if available)
   — a few drops of lemon juice
   — 1 glass of water (200 ml).
   The above mixture should be freshly prepared each time before feeding. It is an ideal mixture to prevent dehydration.
3. Dilute soups, dals, rice water and butter milk can also help to compensate the water loss.
4. Pulp of boiled unripe banana with salt, turmeric powder and lime is also helpful in controlling diarrhoea.
5. Husk of isabgol seeds (*Plantago ovate*) mixed with water or curd taken orally helps in retaining water and reduces the intestinal irritation.
6. A complete dose of anti-microbial drugs and anti-diarrhoeal drugs should be taken.

15.10 INFLUENZA (FLU)

Influenza virus has been quite a lethal virus in human history. It killed about 21 million Americans and Europeans within 18 months in 1918 and 1919. There are generally three types of flue viruses-A, B and C. It is type A virus that causes serious flue epidemics in humans.

Cause and Mode of Infection and Spread

Influenza (Flu) is caused by an RNA virus called Myxovirus influenzae. Flue is a highly infectious viral disease. It spreads through air by droplet infection. The droplets emitted into the air from sneeze, cough or spit of the infected person are laden with the virus. By inhaling the air containing these droplets one can get the infection.

Symptoms

(i) Flu begins with bodyache, a feeling of discomfort, followed by cough and cold.

(ii) Within a few hours, the body develops fever. The fever may range from 101-104°F depending on the type of infection. (Flu can be caused by different types of viruses).

(iii) Along with high fever, the patient may suffer from running nose, cold and sneezing.

Prevention: The only effective way to prevent flue is to keep away from the flue patient.

Control

There is no effective control for influenza.

15.11 JAUNDICE (HEPATITIS)

Jaundice: It is a condition of the body when there is yellowish tint. It is caused by an abnormal amount of bilirubin (bile pigment) which is yellow in colour, in the blood. It indicates malfunctioning of liver. During jaundice not only the skin but the whites of the eye also give a yellowish-tint.

Jaundice can result from Hepatitis or blockage of bile duct.

Jaundice is commonly referred as hepatitis and hepatitis as jaundice.

Jaundice or hepatitis is a disease of liver. It causes enlargement of liver. Since liver is an important organ of digestion, its inflammation affects digestion.

Jaundice/Hepatitis is caused by viral infection. Hepatitis occurs in several forms like A, B, C, D, E and G. Here we will discuss about two common hepatitis: hepatitis A and hepatitis B only.

Hepatitis A

Hepatitis A: Hepatitis A is also called infectious hepatitis.

Cause and Mode of infection/spread

Hepatitis A spreads by food and water. It is a highly infectious disease that attacks both children and adults.

Symptoms

1. High fever, headache and pain in joints.
2. Deceased appetite, nausea and vomiting.
3. Irritating, itching rash on the body.
4. Within 3-4 days urine becomes dark yellow (due to large amount of bilirubin, the yellow pigment) and stools light coloured (pale yellow).

Prevention

1. Use chlorinated, boiled and ozonised drinking water.
2. Since it spreads from person to person by faecal-oral route, good personal hygiene is extremely important. Wash hands with soap after handling the bedding and vessels of the patient.

Control

1. Interferon injections on the advice of the doctor.
2. Adequate rest is necessary for early cure.
3. Juice of sugarcane, radish with gur (jaggery) is helpful.
4. Foods containing high protein and fats should be limited.

Hepatitis B

Cause and Mode of Infection/spread

It is caused by Hepatitis B virus (HAV). It usually spreads by sexual contact. It can also spread by blood transfusion or contaminated needles. "The hepatitis B virus is more contagious than the AIDS virus which also spreads the same way." Hepatitis B can also be passed on from the infected mother to her embryo through placenta.

Symptoms

1. Patient suffers from flue like symptoms-fatigue, fever and headache.
2. There is nausea, vomiting, muscle ache and dull pain in the upper right side of abdomen.
3. Yellow-tint in the skin and whites of eye.
4. Severe damage to liver.

Prevention

1. Hepatitis B vaccine now available is the only safe way of prevention.
2. Other ways include educating the people about use of disposable needles and bringing awareness about the disease.

Symptoms

1. There is no treatment for an HAV infection.
2. Adequate rest and proper diet recommended by the doctor (generally it is low protein and low fat diet.)

15.12 RABIES (HYDROPHOBIA)

Rabies is a serious and highly infectious disease which results due to the bite of a rabid (mad) dog or some other rabid mammal like monkey, cat or rabbit. It is a fatal disease if not treated properly and on time.

Cause and Mode of Infection/Spread

Rabies is caused by a rabies virus which is present in the saliva of infected animals. It affects the brain of the animal.

Fig. 15.7: Dog Bite by a Rabid Causes Rabies (hydrophobia)

The rabies virus enters the body through the bite of a rabid animal or through its saliva coming in contact with an open wound or a break in the skin of the person. A rabid dog (or some other rabid animals) behaves in a furious manner and bites other animals or humans without provocation. Since the dog's saliva is laden with virus, the wound becomes infected and the person who has been bitten needs to take precautions to prevent it. Once the symptoms of the disease begin, the infection invariably progresses to a fatal outcome.

In humans, symptoms of the disease may not be expressed up to 1-3 months after infection. The symptoms may develop anytime between 10 days-1 year.

1. The symptoms in man start with mental depression, severe headache, high fever and a growing restlessness.
2. The restlessness goes on increasing and then there is a feeling of choking.
3. Excessive salivation is accompanied by a painful spasms of throat, (larynx and pharynx) muscles and chest.
4. Patient develops fear of water called hydrophobia and refuses to drink.
5. Severe damage to central nervous system causes paralysis and painful death. Death occurs within about 3-5 days after the symptoms begin.

Prevention

Rabies can be prevented by following the precautions given below:

1. Clean the wound thoroughly with large amount of medicated soap and clean water. Apply antiseptic medicine and leave the wound open, without suturing.
2. Consult the doctor for anti-rabies vaccine without delay. The decision regarding the use of antirabies vaccine must rest with the physician. Earlier a course of 14 injection of anti-rabies vaccine used to be given to the patient in the stomach. It is known as Pasteur's treatment. Now

a-days a course of 5 anti-rabies vaccines is given at an interval of 0, 3, 7, 14 and 30 days of dog bite. The injection are given in the upper arm

3. The animal in question should be kept in observation for at least five days. If at any time it is clear that the animal has rabies, such an animal should be killed. A rabid animal shows excessive salivation and tries to seek isolation after the bite.
4. Pet dogs should always be vaccinated with anti-rabies vaccine. There should be compulsory immunization of other dogs and cats in the area.

Control

Uptil now there is no treatment for rabies, once the symptoms of the disease set in. It is important to prevent it by taking early and proper treatment.

16

Physical Health Education: Diverse Issues

16.1 PHYSICAL FITNESS AND ITS COMPONENTS

Meaning of Physical Fitness: Physical fitness is a relative term. Different people attach different meaning to physical fitness. For a doctor, physical fitness implies the proper functioning of the physiological systems. For a common man, it implies having a good physique. In fact physical fitness is more than proper health and physique.

Physical fitness means the possession of certain capabilities like strength and endurance that enable a person to face various stress situations effectively or it means the successful adaptation to the stresses and strains of one's life style. It implies a relation between the task to be performed and the individual's capability to perform it effectively.

Thus physical fitness varies according to the nature of the task.

Physical fitness in general terms means the capacity to do the routine work without any exertion or fatigue.

Physical fitness implies:

1. The possession of strength and endurance.
2. The capacity to do every day's work effectively.
3. The capacity to engage in recreational pursuits.

Definition of Physical Fitness

In the words of Edward Bortz, "Physical fitness implies that the body systems are capable of carrying on their activities satisfactorily."

According to Dr. K.L. Anderson, "Physical fitness is the ability for respiration and circulation to recover from a standard work load."

Bruno Balle states, "Physical fitness depends on the bio-dynamic potential of an individual which is composed of his functional and metobolic potential."

Importance of Physical Fitness

1. Physical fitness prevents disease and illness.
2. Physical fitness develops power of endurance and sustained effort.
3. Physical fitness increases efficiency in work.
4. Physical fitness develops stamina.
5. Physical fitness helps in meeting emergencies.

6. Physical fitness develops grace.
7. Physical fitness develops agility and proficiency in sports.
8. Physical fitness prevents pre-mature ageing and thereby increases longevity.

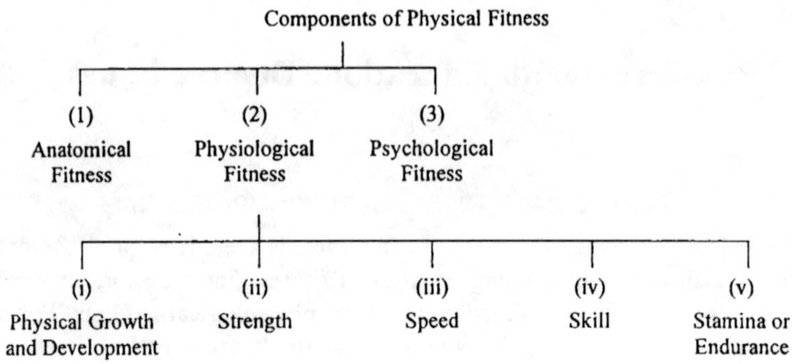

Anatomical Fitness: Anatomical fitness implies:

(a) Proper body size and shape for an activity.

(b) All essential body parts for an activity.

Physiological Fitness: It depends on the type of an activity. For instance fitness for playing tennis requires endurance, skill and strength and for marathon running, lot of endurance is required.

Psychological Fitness: Psychological fitness refers to proper awareness, interest, motivation and emotional stability to perform a task.

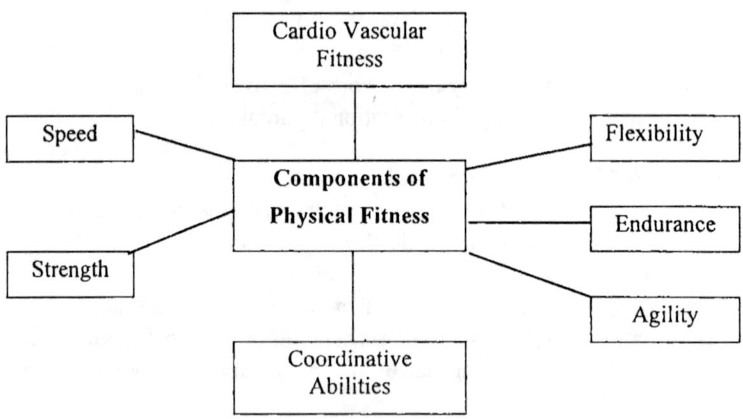

Fig. 16.1: Components of Physical Fitness

Co-ordinative Abilities: Coordinative abilities imply relatively stabilized and generalised pattern of motor control and regulatory prices. These enable the individual to do a group of movements with effect and efficiency.

Endurance: According to Harre, endurance is the ability to resist fatigue.

Agility: Agility means the ability of an individual to change position in speed.

Flexibility: Flexibility is the capacity of a muscle to extend without any damage.

Cardio Vascular Fitness: Cardio vascular fitness is the ability of an individual to strengthen muscles.

Speed: Speed implies performance pre-requisite to do motor action under given conditions in minimum time.

Strength: Strength is the ability to overcome resistance or to act against resistance.

Factors Affecting Physical Fitness

Following factors play an important role in physical fitness of an individual:

1. Heredity
2. Proper diet.
3. Regular exercise.
4. Observance of natural laws.
5. Standard of living.
6. Nature of work.
7. Scientific way of training.
8. Good postures.
9. Proper rest and sleep.
10. Freedom from stresses.
11. Humorous nature.
12. Environment.

Principles of Physical Fitness Development

1. Principle of warming up before undertaking exercises.
2. Principle of selection of right exercise.
3. Principle of regularity in exercises.
4. Principle of variety.
5. Principle of progression-exercises of low intensity to high intensity.
6. Principle of rest.
7. Principle of specificity of exercise
8. Principle of selection of exercise on the basis of age and sex.
9. Principle of medical check-up.
10. Principle of overloading, overloading is achieved through increase in intensity, frequency and duration. For instance, to achieve overload principle, distance runners gradually increase the time of exercise. As the load increases, the body acquires the capacity to bear that load and prepares for higher adaptation.

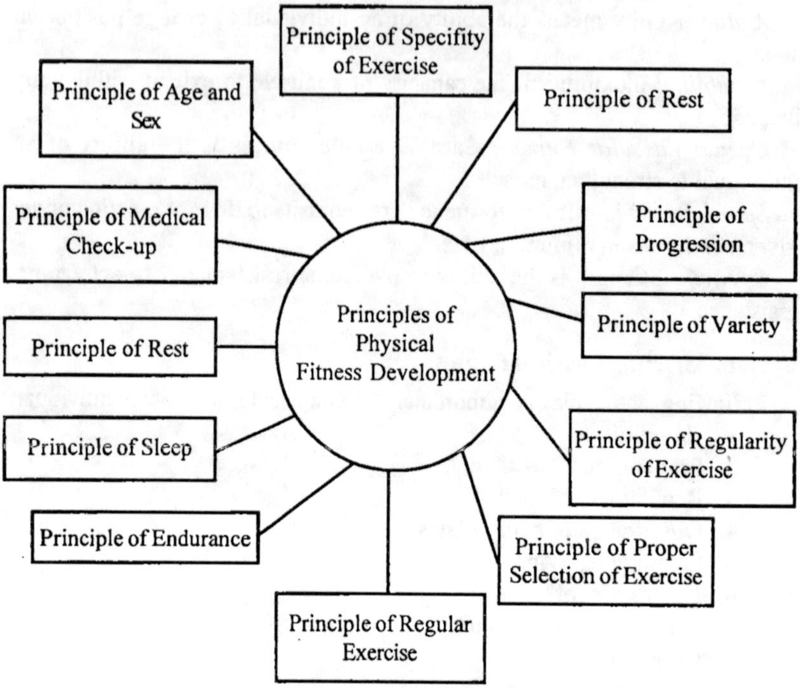

Fig. 16.2: Principles of Physical Fitness Development

Means for Physical Fitness Development

Importance means for physical fitness development are given below:

1. Aerobics.
2. Calisthenies.
3. Circuit training.
4. Cycling.
5. Games and sports.
6. Jogging.
7. Weight lifting.

16.2 INTRAMURALS AND EXTRAMURALS AND THEIR ORGANISATION

Meaning of Intramurals and Extramurals

Intramural word is a Latin word which is composed of 'Intra' and 'Mural'. 'Intra' means 'within' and 'Mural' means 'wall'. This intramural means 'within walls'. In other words intramural games or activities are those programmes which are organised within the school. 'Within the school' is also included school playground. Thus intramural games are those games which are organised within the school premises. Not only this, in these games, students of the same school take part.

The word 'Exramural' is also derived from two Latin words *i.e.* 'Extra' and 'Mural' implying thereby 'without walls'. Thus extramural games and activities are those programmes which are organised by different schools. There are known 'inter-school games' or activities.

Organisation of Intramural and Extramural Games, Play Activities and Tournaments

Benefits of Tournaments

1. They develop a sense of desire among students to excel.
2. They increase standards of games and sports.
3. They provide opportunities to learn from others.
4. They develop a spirit of cooperation.
5. They develop values of Sociability.
6. They provide opportunities for physical and health development.
7. They provide outlets for the sublimation of various instincts like aggressiveness.
8. They develop qualities of followership and leadership.
9. They develop appropriate recreational pursuits.
10. They develop team spirit.
11. They provide opportunities to organise activities and this trains the students in student self-government.
12. They prepare for a vocation.
13. They broaden outlook.

Specific Benefits of Extramurals

The extramurals develop in the students 'esprit de corps' – love for the school, "we feeling comes to the forefront."

Tournaments if properly conducted help in developing the idea of corporate like in the minds of the students. The players play for the respective schools and the other students of the respective schools cheer them up. How thrilling it is to witness the students clapping and encouraging the respective players of their sides! Love for the institution is clearly manifested in the minds of the students.

Limitations of Interschool or Extramural Programmes

Following drawbacks and limitations of the inter-school programmes are quite visible.

1. They benefit too few students.
2. They are expensive in money and time.
3. Money is spent on a few 'star players' at the cost of others.
4. They sometimes lead to interschool conflicts, resulting in physical fights also. Injuries are caused to students and players.
5. They may cause emotional disturbances.
6. They tend to foster professionalism and commercialism.
7. They may give rise to anti-social elements.

8. Victory, by fair or foul may become the motto of the institutions and players.

Principles of Organizing Intra-mural Programmes

1. Keeping in view the different needs of children, a variety of programmes should be organised.
2. Every student should be induced to take part in one or the other game/ sport.
3. Games/Sports time table should be framed. Regular time should be give to this programme.
4. Indian as well as western games/sports should find a place in the programme.
5. Supervision by the teachers is very essential.
6. Tournaments should be organized systematically.
7. Rules of the tournaments should be explained very clearly to the students.
8. School funds should not be spent on a few selected players.

Summing up: There is no rose without a thorn. It we are not quite cautious to pluck a rose, thorn is sure to prick us. Likewise if programmes of games and sports are not well planned and executed, they are likely to do more harm than good.

In the words of Aldous Huxley, "Like every other instrument that man has invented sports can be used for good or for evil purpose. Used well, it can teach endurance and courage, a sense of fair play and respect for rules, co-ordinated effort and the subordination of personal interest to those of the group used badly it can encourage personal vanity; greedy desire for victory and hatred for rivals, an intolerant 'esprit de corpse' and contempt for people who are beyond a certain arbitrarily selected pole. In either case sports inculcate responsible cooperation."

Motto of Games and Sports: "To suffer defeat cheerfully and not to burst into rowydism or even resort to discourtesy, to do one's best against odds and not to lose heart, to be fair to the opponent and not to take any mean advantage of him, to play on equal and honourable terms for the sake of play and not try to win by hook and crook, in short to love the game above the prize." This is the spirit which should prevail in these inter-school programmes.

Organisational Set-up of Tournaments and Especially Extremural or Inter-school Tournaments

For organising tournaments effectively and efficiently following committees may be formed.

1. Administrative Committee for coordinating the entire programme. In the case of inter-school tournaments, it may be headed by the chief physical supervisor of the District or the town as the case may be.

2. Programme Committee.
3. Invitation Committee.
4. Finance Committee.
5. Committee for Providing Equipments and Apparatus.
6. Board and Lodging Committee.
7. Registration Committee.
8. Disciplinary Committee.
9. Publicity Committee.
10. Reception Committee.
11. Refreshment Committee.
12. Transport Committee.
13. First Aid Committee.
14. Committee for the Arrangement of Officials-referee/umpires.
15. General Discipline Committee.

16.3 DRAW OF FIXTURES (KNOCK OUT AND LEAGUE BASIS)

Meaning of Fixture: Fixture may be defined as the procedure of declaring results of tournaments when several teams participate in a tournament. It is the procedure of deciding which team to play against the other team/teams. What would be the order of the play of teams?

Methods of Drawing Fixtures

Generally Speaking, following two methods are followed in drawing fixtures:

1. Knock out or Elimination.
2. League Basis

Knock out tournaments may be on the basis of straight single elimination or double elimination.

In straight single elimination, a team which is once defeated automatically gets eliminated.

In double elimination tournament, team must be defeated twice to be eliminated from this type of tournament.

Single Knock out: As already stated in this types of tournament, after draw, no team after its defeat is allowed to participate. This is the most simple method of organising tournament. This method is followed when the number of teams is 4, 8, 16, 32, 64 and 128.

When there are four teams, in terms of draw teams play. In the first round, two teams lose and two teams win. Thereafter, match is played between the two winner teams. The defeated two teams are out of the tournament and they are eliminated. In case of 8 teams, in the first round four teams win. In the second round two teams. In the third round, the winner and the runner teams are declared.

Following will be the blue-print when there are 8 teams in the tournament 'A' to 'H' teams

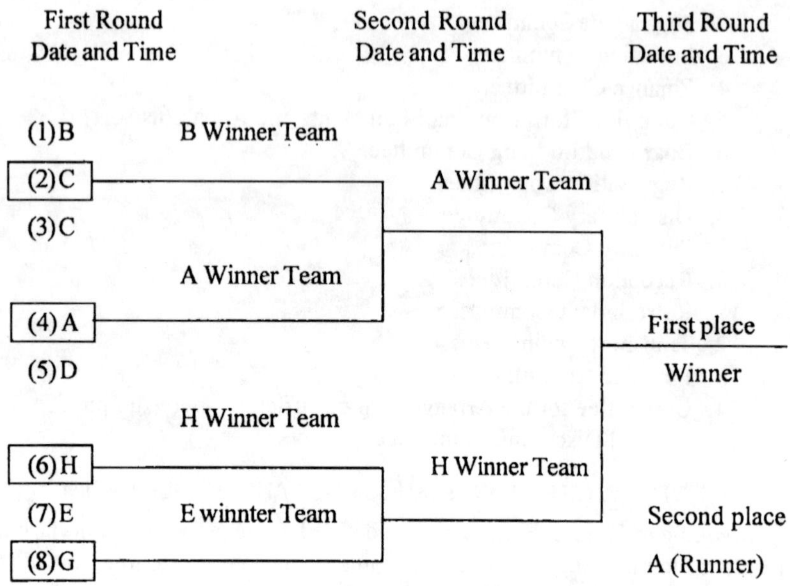

Order of Play of Team: Which team will play in the first round is determined on any of the following:

1. Teams are allotted numbers 1, 2, 3, 4 etc. in their order of registration.
2. Lottery system.
3. Which team can compete with which team.

Bye Method in the Knock Out System. A difficult situation in the simple knock-out system arises when the number of participating team is not like this 4, 8, 16, 32, 64, 128 or 2^2, 2^3, 2^4, 2^5, 2^6. In such a situation 'BYE' system is followed.

Suppose there are 9 teams instead of 8.

The number of byes in a fixture is the actual difference between the number of teams, entering a tournament and the next highest number which is the power of two. Example.

(i) Number of participating teams is 9.
(ii) The next highest number above 9 which is the power of two is 16.
(iii) The number of byes (difference) is 7.

B.R. Goel and Veena Goel have explained the procedure in '*Encyclopaedia of Games and Sports*' (Vikas Publishing House Pvt. Ltd.)

How to distribute the byes:

(i) If the number of byes is an odd number *i.e.* 7, put four dumy teams (Byes), at the bottom half and three at the upper half.

Fixture of eight teams (EVEN) in a single knock-out tournament

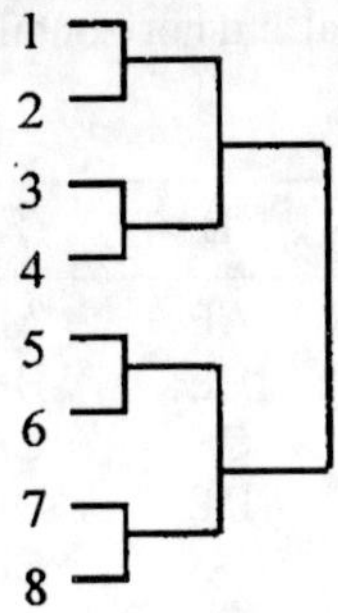

Fig. 16.3: *Fixture of eight teams*

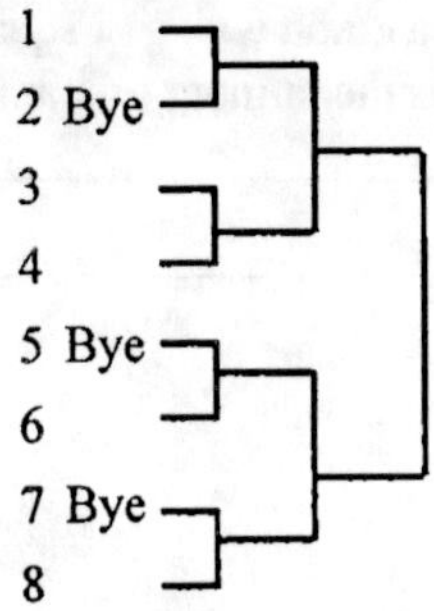

Fig. 16.4: *Fixture of five teams in a single knock out tournament*

The number of games to the played in a knock out tournament is n-1. Where n represents the number of teams entering in the tournament.

In all fixtures, the time, date and the place be mentioned in the brackets. At the bottom of the fixture, important instructions for teams may be given.

Procedure for Drawing a Knock-out Fixture: Suppose there are five teams participating in a tournament:

(i) Note the number of teams-5.
(ii) Next higher number with the power of two-8.
(iii) Number of Byes in the first round-3.
(iv) Write vertically 1 to 8 number with enough gaps in between.
(v) Take uniform sized slips of paper and write the name of one team in each slip and put them in a bowel after the proper rolling of slips.
(vi) As per principle of this type of tournament, put two byes at the bottom half at service number 5 and 7 and one bye at upper half at service no. 2.
(vii) Take out the slips one by one and with the names of each team against the vacant number in such manner that 1st draw is placed at upper round and 2nd draw at bottom round and so on.
(viii) Bracket teams as indicated in Fig. 16.4. Winners of the upper and bottom rounds shall play the final as indicated in Figs. 16.3 and 16.8.

League or Round Tournament

This is one of the very desirable tournaments where each team plays with every other team once (single league), twice (double league) irrespective of victory or defeat.

Formula $\frac{n(n-1)}{2}$, where n represents the number of teams taking part.

If 'n' is 7 we get $\frac{7(7-1)}{2} = 21$ games

or cancel the highest number and then add the rest as shown below:

$6 + 5 + 4 + 3 + 2 + 1 = 21$

after cancelling the highest number 7.

Draw a graph with n+1 squares on the vertical and horizontal lines where n represents the number of teams competing.

	A	B	C	D	E	F	G
A		AB	AC	AD	AE	AF	AG
B		-	BC	BD	BE	BF	BG
C			-	CD	CE	CF	CG
D				-	DE	DF	DG
E					-	EF	EG
F						-	FG

16.4 GRAPHIC REPRESENTATION OF ROUND ROBIN SCHEDULE FOR SEVEN TEAMS

The teams are named after the alphabets A to G. Draw a diagonal line connecting the middle square. Take the team A in the vertical column and proceed horizontally along horizontal squares of A. 'A' cannot compete with 'A' and therefore the diagonal line. Then A can meet B C D E F G in the succeeding squares. Similarly work out for other teams. When the horizontal and vertical squares meet, the competition takes place between the concerned teams.

Each square may be filled up with the date of the game, the team which won and the score when the matches are over.

If it is a single league when one team meets every other team only once, the squares above the diagonal line are to be used. If it is a double league, where each team meets every other team twice, then all the squares above.

16.5 INTRODUCTION OF OPERATION BLACK BOARD (OB): PHYSICAL EDUCATION KIT (EQUIPMENT) AND ITS UTILISATION

Meaning of O.B.: The National Policy on Education (1986) Programme recommended a number of schemes for the quantitative and qualitative improvement of primary education in India. One of these programmes was termed as Operation Blackboard which laid down the minimum essential facilities for a primary school.

The use of the word 'operation' indicates that there is an urgency to implement this programme.

Components of the Scheme: There are three components of the scheme of O.B.

1. Provision of at least two reasonably large rooms that are usable in all weathers, with a deep verandah along with separate toilet facilities for boys and girls.
2. Provision of at least two teachers, as far as possible, one of them a woman, in every primary school.

3. Provision of essential teaching and learning material.

The scheme envisages to cover all primary schools run by the government, local bodies and Panchayati Raj institutions.

The responsibility for providing facilities under O.B. is being shared by the Central and the State Governments.

List of Essentials Facilities at the Primary Stage

1. Teacher's equipment
2. Classroom teaching material including charts on Health
3. Play materials and Toys
4. Games Equipment
5. Primary Science Kit
6. Mini Tool Kit
7. Mathematics Kit
8. Books for Library
9. School Bell
10. Musical Instruments
11. Contigency Money with the Teacher
12. Chalk and Duster
13. Water facility
14. Trash Can

Games Equipment

Games equipment includes the following items:

Item	Qty
1. Skipping rope	10
2. Footballs	02
3. Volleyballs	02
4. Rubber balls	10
5. Air pump	01
6. Rings	05
7. Swing Rope with Tyre	01

Utilisation of Essentials under B.O. for Physical Education

1. Black Board should be effectively used for teaching subject matter relating to physical education. Tables, figures and graphs on physical education should be drawn on the blackboard.
2. Health Chart should be used for illustrating rules of health and keeping the body physical fit. Charts relating to 'Asans' should prove useful in yoga education.
3. Maximum use should be made of play material.
4. Skipping rope could be used in organising several types of physical activities.
5. Ring rope with tyre can be used in teaching gymnastic activities.
6. Mats can be used while teaching yoga.

16.6 PHYSIOLOGICAL EFFECTS OF EXERCISE

Meaning of Physiological System of the Body. With a view to understand the physiological effects of exercise, it is very important to understand the meaning of human physiology and physiology of exercise.

Physiology is the study of normal functions of the living organism and its parts. Physiology of exercise deals with the effects of exercise on these parts, i.e. the changes taking place in the structure and functions of various systems and organs of the human body.

Human body is a unique gift of nature to man. Systems of the body have several functions and these are effected by exercise.

There are nine systems as shown in the Table 16.1.

A system, generally consists of cells, tissues and organs.

Cell are considered to be the smallest living units of structure. A cell is a mass of colourless semifluid substance which forms the essence of life. It consists of water, protein, fatty acids, carbohydrates, organic and inorganic salts, Different groups of cells perform different functions.

A tissue is an organisation of many similar cells that act together to perform a common function.

Organs are formed by groups of tissues: The special work of organs is known as 'function'. Eye is an organ of sight while tongue is an organ of taste. All the organs function together for the whole body.

Table 16.1: Main Physiological Systems and Their functions

Organ System	*Names of Organs*	*Functions*
1. Circulatory System	Heart, Arteries, Arterioles, Capillaries, Venules, Veins, Lymph and blood	Transport of nutrients, respiratory gases, hormones and minerals in the body. Transport of waste products to excretory organs for removal.
2. Digestive System	Mouth, Tongue, Pharynx, Oesophagus, Stomach, Small intestine, Large intestine. Salivary glands, liver and pancreas are the associated glands.	Ingestion, digestion and absorption of food. Egestion of undigested food.
3. Endocrine System	Pituitary, Thyroid, Pancreas, Adrenal etc.	Secretion of hormones. Coordination and regulation of various processes.
4. Excretory System	Kidneys, Ureters, Urinary bladder, Urethra.	Removal of metabolic wastes to maintain homeostasis.
5. Muscular System	Striated, unstriated and cardiac muscles.	Movement and locomotion of the body.
6. Nervous System	Brain, Spinal cord, Sympathetic and Parasympathetic nerves, Sensory organs.	Response to stimuli. Coordination and regulation of activities by transmitting information.

(Contd.)

(*Contd.*)

Organ System	*Names of Organs*	*Functions*
7. Reproductive System	Testes, Epididymis, Vas deferens, Ovaries, Fallopian tubes, Uterus etc.	Production of gametes and multiplication of species.
8. Respiratory System	Nostrils, Nasal passage, Nasopharynx, Larynx, Trachea, Bronchi, Bronchioles, Lungs.	Exchange of gases between the organism and environment. Release of energy by oxidation of food.
9. Skeletal System	Bones, Cartilage	Support and protection of soft tissues from external injury.

1. Effects of Exercise on Circulatory System

1. Exercise makes the heart muscle fibres thicker and stronger.
2. Exercise improves the stroke volume. Stroke volume is the amount of blood ejected by the left ventricle during a systole.
3. Exercise improves heart rate.
4. Exercise improves oxygen exchange capacity.
5. Heart minute volume improves.
6. Exercise results in reducing level of cholesterol.

2. Effects of Exercise on Digestive System

1. Exercise improves digestion.
2. Exercise helps to lose fat in the body.
3. Exercise helps in regular bowel movement.
4. Exercise improves appetite.
5. Exercise results in increase in lean body mass.

3. Effects of Exercise on the Muscular System

The following are the important effects of exercise on the muscular system.

1. *Muscle hypertrophy*: When there is prolonged inactivity, muscles usually shrink in mass a condition called 'disuse atrophy'. Exercise helps in increasing muscle size called 'hypertrophy'.
2. *Supply of energy to muscles*: Exercise helps in increasing the size of mytochondria leading to improvement in energy supply to the muscles.
3. *Reduction in fats*: Proper training reduces the fat surrounding the muscles.
4. *Improvement in postures:* Regular exercise improves postures.
5. *Improvement in the reaction time:* Proper exercise increases the muscle tone which helps to reduce the contraction time as well as to improve the reaction time.
6. *Increase in capillarisation:* Training increases the number of

capillaries in the muscles and thus the muscles get more dark red colour.

7. *Withstanding fatigue:* Training increases the power of muscles to withstand fatigue. This is on account of the increased ability in lactic acid tolerance capacity.
8. *Increase in speed and strength:* Regular exercise helps to increase the speed and strength of the muscles. This is partially due to the hypertrophy of the muscles and partially on account of increase in the capacity of giving and receiving stimulus.

4. Effects of Exercise on Respiratory System

1. Exercise brings about an increase in the tidal volume.
2. Exercise improves vital capacity.
3. Breathing becomes more rhythmic and regular
4. Gas exchange capacity increases.
5. There is improvement in the oxygen uptake.
6. Recovery after strenuous exercise is faster.
7. Heroic capacity improves.

16.7 EXERCISE, RELAXATION, RECREATION AND REGULAR SLEEP

Exercise and Relaxation

Exercise is necessary to keep the body and mind fit. It is essential for sedantary people who do most of their work in sitting position. Exercises vary with age, physical condition and nature of work of the individual. Exercise not only helps in maintaining the normal weight but also keeps the body in good shape.

Relaxation and regular sleep are also equally essential for good health.

— Relaxation may be defined as an activity or recreation which provides relief or diversion from work or effort. It is important to have a hobby that absorbs a person in free time or off hours-one into which a person can throw himself completely and with pleasure, forgetting all about his work.

— There are various ways of relaxation. Yoga, meditation, listening to music, reading can relax body and mind. For some, an outdoor activity like gardening or walking could be relaxing.

Recreation

Meaning of recreation: By recreation we mean a pursuit generally taken up for the sake of pleasure and the joy which it provides. Profit motive is completely absent in such a pursuit. Enjoyability is its chief characteristic. Of course, creativity may also be considered as its other important characteristic.

Value of recreation: For the all round development of the child's personality, the element of recreation is an important one. 7R's i.e. Reading, Writing, Arithmetic (traditional concept of education in terms of 3 R's), Rights, Responsibilities, Relationships and Recreation are the elements which constitute the concept of all round development. The last 'R' of Recreation is also an integral part of complete education. Harmonious development of the student cannot be considered complete without the development of the element of recreation in one's life.

The present machine age has placed enough time at the disposal of man. Every prudent person would like to make the best use of this opportunity. Hobbies provide a good opportunity to make use of leisure time. School time is the best time to train children to develop suitable habits of recreation. For this purpose, a variety of co-curricular activities may be introduced.

There should be enough scope for games and sports which provide a lot of recreation to the students.

Cycling, mountaineering, skating, swimming, etc. are useful recreational pursuits.

Different types of handwork such as paper-mache, card board, clay modelling, toy making, flower making etc. provide recreation.

Stamp collecting, coin collecting and photography etc. are also good means of recreation.

Dramatics, folk dance and music are the other means of recreation.

Radio and T.V. programmes are also very useful media of recreation of students and they need to be properly guided and supervised while participating in such programmes in the school.

Regular sleep is also necessary for good health. it depends on age, health and nature of one's work. For example:

- Infants (young children of 0-6 months) sleep for long hours may be up to 16-18 hrs. a day is necessary for them.
- For children, an average of 7-8 hours of sound sleep is sufficient.
- For adults, 6-7 hours of sleep is sufficient.

16.8 PHYSICAL IMPAIRMENTS OF THE STUDENTS AND THE ROLE OF THE SCHOOL

Identification

Following are the usually observable impairments:

1. Deformity in fingers, hands, legs, neck and waist.
2. Difficulty in sitting, standing and walking.
3. Difficulty in handling objects, picking up and putting down at appropriate places.
4. Frequent complaints of pains.
5. Difficulty in holding pen to write.

6. Walking with jerks.
7. Involuntary movements of jerks.
8. Ampulated legs.
9. Difficulty in seeing the writing on the blackboard.
10. Difficulty in hearing.

Role of the Teacher

1. Parents should be informed as soon as some defect is noticed.
2. Medical inspection should be arranged whenever any physical impairment is noticed.
3. Front seats may be provided to students having low vision.
4. Front seats may be given to students with crutches and wheel chairs.
5. Recreational needs of such children should be attended to.
6. Students free from such impairments may be motivated to show due regard to students with impairments.
7. Special attention should be paid to the postures of students.
8. Peers may be encouraged to assist such students.
9. Special cases may be referred to appropriate authorities dealing with impairments, with parents' consent.

Education of Children with Visual Impairments (Other than Blindness)

Several children do not have sufficient vision. They find it difficult to read the writing on the blackboard clearly. There are partially sighted children also. Some can read only large print. Visual impairment results in several learning problems. Children with visual impairments may have enormous capacity to work. However, this depends upon the nature of the impairment.

Identification of Children with Visual Impairments.

It is very necessary to identify each category of children with visual impairments. Medical treatment may become necessary in some cases. Parents also need to be informed.

Children with visual impairment may be identified from the following symptoms:

1. Having watery eyes.
2. Rubbing eyes frequently.
3. Reddening of eyes frequently.
4. Covering one eye and titling the head forward.
5. Holding objects and books close to the eyes.
6. Asking help from others when taking notes from the blackboard.
7. Blinking frequently-squinting eyelids together.
8. Complaining about headache following close eye work.
9. Bumpening into people or objects.
10. Skipping words or lines while reading.
11. Having poor eye-hand coordination.
12. Moving head forward and backward while looking at distant objects.

Role of the School and the Teacher in the Education of Students with Visual Impairment

1. Children with visual impairment may be seated in the front rows so that they can read the writing on the blackboard without any difficulty or pressure.
2. Such children may be given training in listening with comprehension.
3. Books with bold letters may be provided to such children.
4. Radio and T.V. broadcasts may be arranged for such children.
5. Efforts may be made to procure cassettes in different curricular areas. State Institutes of Education or State Councils of Educational Research and Training or District Institutes of Education and Training or Centres or Institutes of Educational Technology may be approached for this purpose.
6. Blind children need Braille script books.
7. School doctor may be consulted from time to time.
8. Co-operation of the parents be sought in the follow-up work.

Education and Identification of Children with Hearing and Speech Impairment

Listening plays an important role in academic learning. Hearing problems interfere with the achievement of the students. It is, therefore, desirable to identify such children and take steps to meet their educational needs. Such children may be identified as under:

- — Some observable deformity of the ear or ears.
- — Frequent complaints of pain in ears.
- — Frequent scratching of ears.
- — Frequent discharge from ears.
- — Turning head on one side to hear better.
- — Frequent requests to teachers to repeat questions and directions etc.
- — Making errors in taking dictation or notes.
- — Displaying speech difficulty.

Guidelines for Education of Children with Hearing and Speech Impairment

1. Children with hearing problems may be given front seats.
2. While speaking, the teacher may use a reasonable level of pitch.
3. The teacher should avoid mumbling.
4. The teacher should avoid speaking too fast.
5. Students should be encouraged to speak gradually and steadily.
6. Other students of the class may be asked to give due consideration to such students.
7. A lot of visual aids may be used in the classroom.
8. Some of the hearing problems can be corrected through drill and practice.

9. Medical help may be needed if speech disorder is due to an organic defect in speech mechanism.

Education of Children with Orthopaedic and Locomotor Impairment/Disability

Identification: Such children can be easily identified as their impairment is usually observable.

1. Deformity may be observable in fingers, hands, legs, neck or waist etc.
2. Showing difficulty in sitting, standing and walking.
3. Showing difficulty in picking up and holding objects and putting them on the ground.
4. Frequently complaining of pains in the joints.
5. Experiencing difficulty in holding the pen to write.
6. Walking with jerks.
7. Experiencing difficulty in the movement of limbs.
8. Amputated limbs.

Guidelines for Education of Children with Orthopaedic and Locomotor Impairment

1. The teacher should accept such children in the meaner he accepts other children.
2. The teacher should avoid sarcasm for the disability of the child.
3. Other children should be advised to appreciate the disability and show due regard to such children. They should be made to understand the disability.
4. Seating arrangement in the class may be adjusted to the specific needs of such students.
5. Reasonable opportunities for participation in recreational activities, sports and games should be provided to these children.
6. Remedial teaching may also be arranged for them.

16.9 COMMON AILMENTS NOT COVERED EARLIER

Common Cold or Nasal Catarrh

Common cold is a common ailment and when uncared for, it may become very serious. The child suffering from common cold loses health slowly.

This ailment is caused by virus.

Symptoms of Common Cold: There are: (i) Heaviness in the nose, (ii) Sneezing, (iii) Shivering, (iv) Swelling of the nose and eyes.

Treatment: (i) Isolate the child, (ii) Let him take rest, (iii) Give hot tea, (iv) Refer to the doctor.

Precaution: (i) Nasal catarrh is a communicable disease. Hence other students should not come into direct contact with the student who suffers from cold.

(ii) Child should be asked to use a clean handkerchief when coughing or sneezing.

(iii) The clothes such as handkerchief, pillows and bedsheets used by the patient should be disinfected with boiling water.

Sore Throat

Meaning: It is the inflammation of the throat and like common cold it is also a communicable disease and spreads like fire. Some children get sore throat with a slight change in humidity and temperature.

Symptoms: (i) Slight fever, (ii) Headache, (iii) Pain in the body, (iv) Shivering, (v) Pain in swallowing food, (vi) Redness in the throat, (vii) Dried up mucous membrane and discharge, (viii) Change in voice, (ix) Restlessness, (x) Rapid pulse, (xi) Fast breathing.

Treatment. (a) Giving rest to the patient, (b) Letting the patient lie down in warm bed in a ventilated sunlit room, (c) Applying hot dry heat or hot compress from outside, (d) Letting the patient gargle with fresh warm water in which potassium permanganate is mixed, (e) Giving nutrious food.

Constipation

Constipation is related to the digestive system. The symptoms of constipation are: headache, loss of appetite, loss of vitality and vomiting sensation. It is retention of forces, the excretion though the bowel and is usually caused by rotten food, irregular meals, lack of exercise and fresh vegetables in the food.

Constipation, if not checked may result is appendicitis and ulcer: Constipation can be cured by taking green vegetables, taking a proper amount of water, taking meals at regular hours and doing regular exercises and especially morning walk.

Dyspepsia

Dyspepsia means indigestion. It occurs when the digestive system fails to dissolve solids and make food capable of assimilation by tissues. It implies that either the food has been bolted and has not been converted into sugar in the mouth. In such a situation, additional work has to be done by other organs which increases risk of indigestion. Indigestion also occurs when food is taken in an excess quantity and an undue strain is caused to organs of digestion and excretion.

In the event of indigestion, these steps are recommended: (i) Taking light food, (ii) Administering hot water to produce vomiting, (iii) Administering some purgative to empty the bowels.

16.10 SUMMERY: DESCRIPTION OF VARIOUS DISEASES

Disease	*Incubation Period*	*Symptoms*	*Affected Age*	*Precaution to be Taken in the School*
1. Chicken Pox	11 to 19 days	Rashes consisting of red spots, blisters, scabs	All ages	1. Student to be sent home 2. Student not to be allowed to attend school for about three weeks
2. Cholera	A few hours to a few days	Severe pain in the abdomen vomiting, diarrhoea	All ages	Cleanliness of urinals and lavatories
3. Diphtheria	2 to 10 days	White patches on the soft palate, tonsils and throat	Before 2 or 3 years of age	Child should not be allowed to attend the school
4. Influenza	A few hours to a few days	Pain in the head, back, and limbs, shivering, rise in temperature, running of eyes and nose, sneezing and coughing	Children and Adults	1. Students to be advised not to visit crowdy places 2. Use of handkerchief 3. Students to be separated from the school.
5. Malaria	7 to 21 days	High fever, shivering	All ages	1. Boiled water to be arranged 2. Less eating
6. Measles	One or two weeks	Cold, rise in temperature, reddish rash on the body.	Usually before 10 years of age	1. Consultation of the doctor 2. Sending the child home 3. The child to be kept away from school for at least 3 weeks
7. Mumps	14 to 28 days	Swelling from ear to ear, painful eating		Child to be separated from the school for about 20 days
8. Small Pox	10 to 15 days	Severe headache, backache, high fever	All ages	1. Vaccination2. Students to be sent home
9. Typhoid	12 to 15 days	Severe headache and vomiting, high temperature.	All ages	1. Inoculation.2. Cleanliness and disinfection
10. Whooping Cough	6 to 18 days	Common cold, Running of nose, continuous coughing for sometimes along with vomiting	Childhood before 5	Child to be kept at home for nearly 2 months

16.11 EVALUATION IN HEALTH AND PHYSICAL EDUCATION

The NCERT Guidelines and Syllabi (2001) suggests the following programme of action regarding evaluation in health and physical education.

Evaluation in health and Physical Education should be based upon the student's individual capacity, performance and progress. Assessment should, therefore, be continuous and comprehensive using rating scale, checklist and observation and should be such as to measure the multi-dimensional progress of the student. At this stage, the five-point absolute grading should be used for indicating student's achievement level. Self-evaluation by students and peer evaluation may also form part of the total evaluation procedure and it should be reported quarterly. It should be done for the purpose of diagnosis, remedy and feedback. If a student's assessement is regular and objective, it can also serve as motivation as it will give the student the result of his/her efforts and performance.

However, the following guidelines ought to govern the evaluation-plan in Health and Physical Education:

- The evaluation is based on the objectives of the comprehensive syllabus.
- The process of evaluation of pupil's progress is continuous and comprehensive.
- The evaluation is based on the day-to-day observation by the teacher during the process of learning the activitics as well as the final performance through knowledge and skill-tests.
- The result of evaluation should form a part of the scheme of examination at all levels.
- The evaluation should provide scope for the improvement of syllabus.

17

Yoga Education and Health: Needs of a Child

17.1 MEANING OF YOGA

Sage Patanjali, the author of an ancient book '*yoga sastra*' (circa second B.C.), explains yoga as a method of controlling the mind. Some scholars regard yoga as an attempt of uniting oneself with the Supreme Spirit i.e. '*Parmatma*' or God. Yoga is also described as a way of life for the harmonious development of the body, mind and soul.

What yoga is Not! Very often, yoga is misunderstood and thought of in term of certain exercises or *asans* (postures) for training the body. This is a very narrow concept or meaning of Yoga. It is certainly not a physical act or exercise only. It is much more.

17.2 MAIN FEATURES OF YOGA

The most important feature of Yoga is that it deals with the entire person, not a part of him like other types of exercises. Yoga helps the practitioner to gradually progress at the intellectual, physical, moral and spiritual levels.

Yoga is a system of physical, mental and spiritual culture to develop every human faculty so that every individual can lead a healthy, happy and long life. It provides eternal bliss.

Yoga can be practised by all, irrespective of Faith, age group, sex and wealth etc.

Yoga is based on ethical and moral codes which are common to humanity.

Yoga 'asans' ideally do not involve any investment.

Yoga *ideals* helps in self-improvement process.

Yoga consists not only of physical postures ('Asanas')-Control of the internal organs through '*Kriyas*' and '*bandas*' and breath control (*pranayama*') but also mental, intellectual and spiritual discipline.

17.3 STAGES OF YOGA

According to sage Patanjali, following are the eight stages of yoga:

1. '*Yama*': This refers to the moral discipline for the individual and it includes the practices of '*brahamcharya*' (celibacy), non-stealing, non-receiving of gifts and observance of the creed of non-violence.

2. '*Niyama*': It means self-purification by practising cleanliness, contentment, studying scriptures and surrendering oneself to God.

3. '*Asana*': This implies practising certain body-postures for acquiring health and developing steadfastness of mind. '*Asanas*' (exercises or postures) have been developed over the centuries and they help in strengthening every muscle, nerve and gland of the body.

4. '*Pranayama*': It is the practice of controlling breath for strengthening the respiratory system, purifying blood and soothing the mind.

5. *Pratyahara*': This is an attempt to free the mind from the domination or control of senses.

6. '*Dharana*': This is concentration on a single object or point.

7. '*Dhyana*': It refers to the concentration on the all-pervading 'Divinity' through practice.

8. *Samadhi*: This is the last stage of yoga. In this stage, the yogi merges himself with the Divine Spirit, although he is alert and conscious.

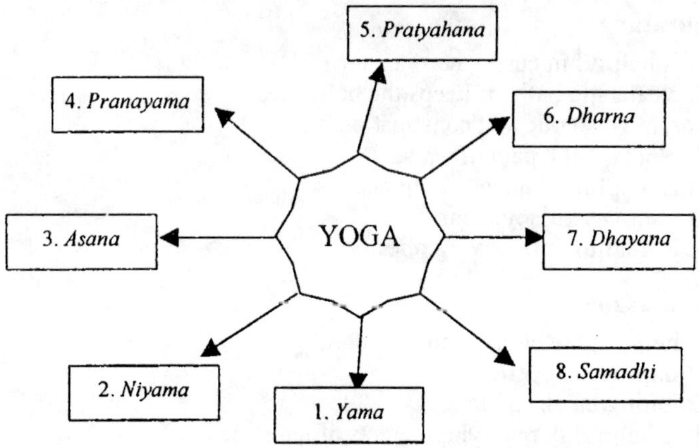

Fig. 17.1: Stages of Yoga

17.4 GENERAL GUIDELINES FOR PRACTISING YOGA ASANAS

1. Consult an expert before practicing yoga, if you suffer from severe back, head or stomach aches, eye or ear trouble, hernia or if you have undergone any major surgery.
2. Always breathe through the nose, keeping the mouth closed.
3. Breathe out when bending, especially forward and breathe in when in normal position.
4. Never do other physical exercises and yoga simultaneously. Give a gap of at least two hours.
5. A bath should follow after an hour of yoga. During yoga practice, the bodily system hots up and this state is not conducive to bath. Take bath when the body has cooled down.
6. Never stand on your head from day one. Move forward gradually.

7. Never overdo any posture.
8. It is advisable to learn yoga postures under the guidance of an expert so as to avoid mistakes.

17.5 BRIEF DESCRIPTION OF EACH ASAN WITH ITS BENEFITS

I. Ardhamatsyendrasana

1. It keeps gall bladder and prostrate healthy.
2. It enhances the stretchability of back muscles.

II. Bhujangasana

1. It removes constipation.
2. It increases digestion.
3. It improves the postures.
4. It stimulates thyroid gland.
5. It makes muscles and vertibral column strong.

III. Chakrasana

1. It is helpful in curing hernia.
2. It cleans the bally or keeps the bally clean.
3. It removes colic and constipation.
4. It removes the pain of waist.
5. It is helpful to diabetic patients.
6. It removes kidney pain.
7. It is helpful in removing obesity.

IV. Dhanurasana

1. It helps in the circulation of blood.
2. It improves appetite.
3. It improves digestion.
4. It is helpful in removing defects of intestines.
5. It makes backbone flexible and strong.
6. It removes fat of stomach.
7. It makes arms and shoulders strong.

V. Gomukhasana

1. It improves the functions of lungs.
2. It makes the leg muscles elastic and strong.
3. It is helpful in keeping the shoulder joints flexible, healthy and strong.

VI. Halasana

1. It keeps the abdominal organs healthy.
2. It keeps the spine supple.
3. It is helpful in removing slumber region pain.
4. It prevents gas trouble.
5. It relieves stomach pain.

VII. Matsyasana

1. It removes eye defects.
2. It is helpful in removing skin diseases.
3. It is helpful in removing back pain, and knee pain.
4. It is helpful in the treatment of diabetes.

VIII. Mayurasana

1. It removes constipation.
2. It improves digestive system.
3. It is helpful in removing the diseases of stomach.

IX. Padmasana

1. It helps to reduce abdominal fat.
2. It helps to remove backache.
3. It is helpful in the concentration of mind.
4. It removes unitary disorders.
5. It helps to solve sciatica problem.

X. Pschimotanasana

1. It provides relief in asthma, backache and sciatica.
2. It removes gas trouble.
3. It helps in removing constipation.
4. It prevents the early ossification of bones.
5. It helps in overcoming several menstrual disorders.

XI. Sarvangasana

1. It improves eye-sight.
2. It relieves headache.
3. It prevents the untimely wrinkling of the face.
4. It helps in controlling the body weight.
5. It provides strength to vertibral column and increases flexibility.
6. It improves digestion.
7. It enhances the power of self-control.
8. It is helpful in the treatment of leprosy.
9. It helps in the better functioning of kidneys and liver.

XII. Savasana

1. It controls high blood pressure.
2. It relieves mental tension.
3. It strengthens the nervous system.
4. It helps to cure several cardiac problems.
5. It gives vigour to both mind and body simultaneously.
6. It regulates blood circulation.
7. It provides relief in various aches and pains.
8. It removes many psychosomatic problems.

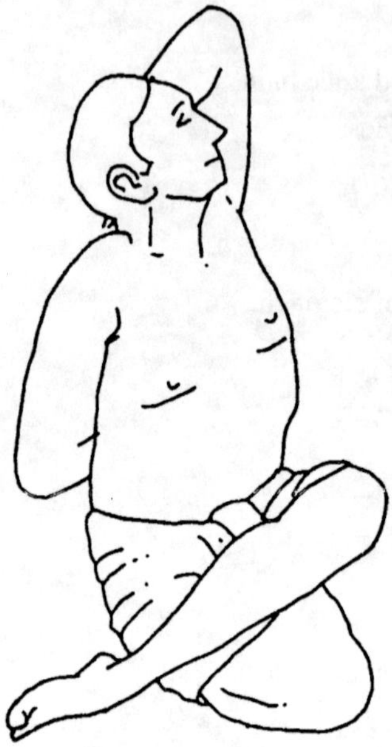

Gomuh-Asana

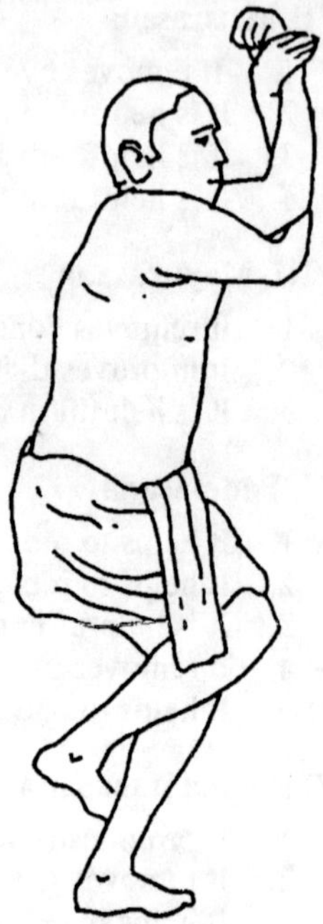

Garuora-Asana

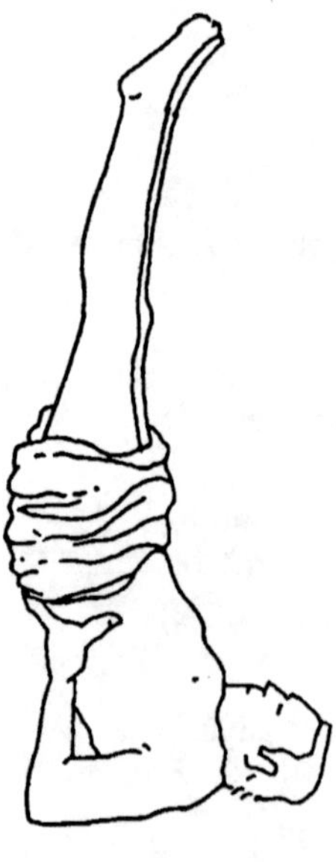

Sarvang-Asana

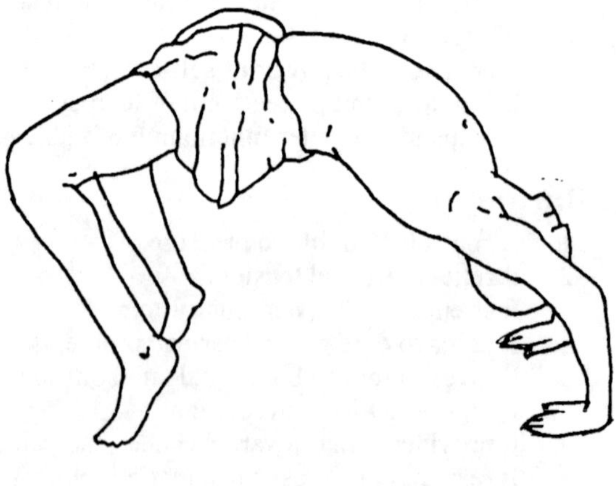

Chakra-Asana

Ardhmatsya-Asana

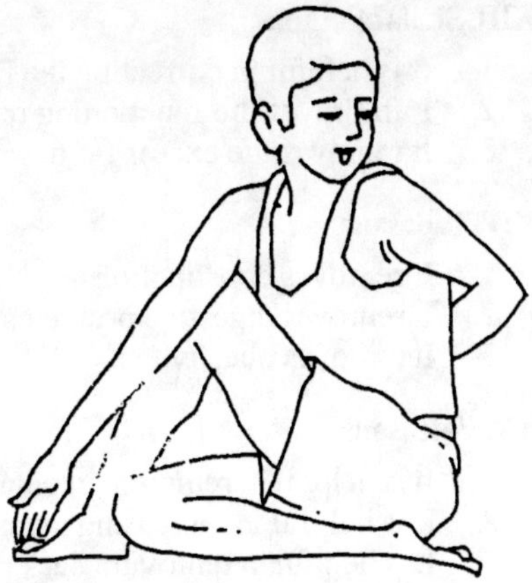

Padma-Asana

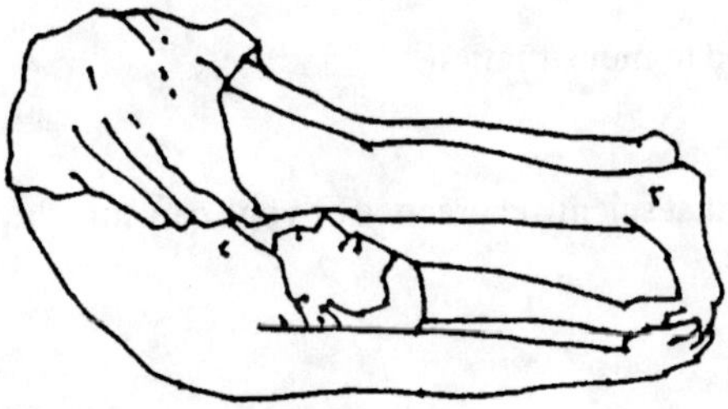

Hal-Asana

Garma-Asana

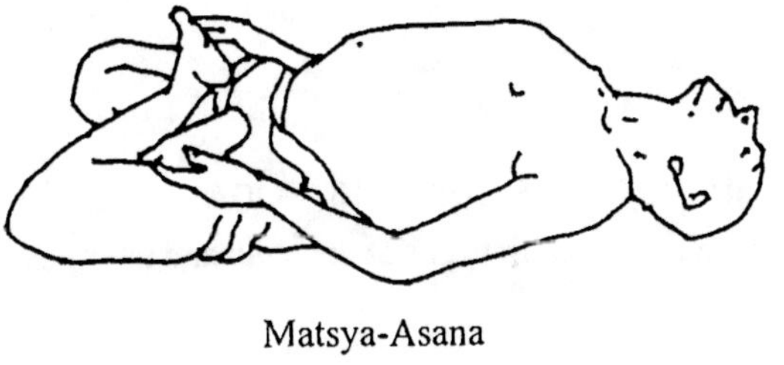

Matsya-Asana

XIII. Shalabhasana

1. It is helpful in correcting the faulty curvature of spine.
2. It improves the functioning of intestines.
3. It removes the excess fat from the abdomen, hips, thighs and waist.

XIV. Tadasana

1. It removes constipation.
2. It removes digestive problems.
3. It removes obesity.

XV. Vajrasana

1. It is helpful in removing mental disappointment.
2. It is helpful in increasing concentration.
3. It is helpful in removing back pain.
4. It is helpful in curing dysentery.
5. It removes back pain.
6. It increases memory.
7. It removes problems related to menstruation.

Curative Effects of Yoga

The protagonists of yoga claim that scientific practice of yoga can cure the following deformities and diseases.

1. Acidity
2. Arthritis/Joint Inflamation
3. Ashtma
4. Backache
5. Blood pressure
6. Bronochitis.
7. Constipation.
8. Deformities of bones and defects of postures.
9. Diabetes
10. Dysentery
11. Flatulence
12. Heart ailments.
13. Hernia
14. Indigestion
15. Migraine
16. Piles
17. Sciatica
18. Ulcers.

17.6 HEALTH NEEDS OF THE CHILD AND YOGA

The following description gives the health needs of the child and the role of yoga in this regard.

1. *Needs for concentration on studies:* Yoga improves the power of concentration of the students in studies.
2. *Need for improvement in memory:* Yoga contributes to the improvement in memory.
3. *Need for improving grasping power:* Yoga in very helpful in the improvement of the grasping power of the child.
4. *Need for sharp brain:* Yoga helping in sharpening the brain power of the child.
5. *Need for keeping the body trim and attractive:* Yoga helps in removing fat. It keeps the weight normal.
6. *Need for keeping the body in proper proportion:* Yoga enables the child to develop the body in a balanced way.
7. *Need for upkeep of the ductless glands:* Yoga makes the ductless glands secrete their vital juices in proper quantities.
8. *Need for cleanliness of the body and mind:* Yoga renders great help in developing purity of the body and mind of the child.
9. *Need for nourishment:* Yoga supplies nourishment and oxygen through proper blood circulation.
10. *Need for keeping body organs healthy:* Yoga keeps body organs healthy.

17.7 CHART SHOWING SPECIFIC NEED OF THE CHILD AND THE ASANA MOST SUITED FOR THE SATISFACTION OF THE NEED

Need of the Child	*Name of the Asana*
1. Need for concentration on studies	Padmasana
2. Need for proper digestion of food	Bhujangasana
3. Need for keeping the curvature of spine in order	Shalabhasana
4. Need for free movement of bowels	Paschimotanasana
5. Need for relaxation	Makarasana
6. Need for correct postures	Bhujangasana, Dhanurasana
7. Need for meditation	Shidhasana
8. Need for having good eye sight	Sarvangasana
9. Need for controlling the weight of the body	Sarvangasana
10. Need for relief from headache	Sarvangasana
11. Need for keeping good stomach	Mayurasana
12. Need for removing back pain	Chakrasana
13. Need for having vigour in mind and body simultaneously	Savasana
14. Need for increasing memory	Vajrasana
15. Need for removing skin diseases	Matsyasana
16. Need for preventing gas trouble	Halasana
17. Need for enhancing the stretchability of back muscles	Ardhamat-syendrasana
18. Need for keeping muscles strong	Gomukhasana
19. Need for developing sense of balance	Vriksana

18

Physical Education Programme

18.1 MEANING OF PHYSICAL EDUCATION PROGRAMME

We have already emphasised that physical education is an integral programme of school education. It is therefore very important that it should be organised scientifically. Physical education programme may be defined as a programme which is conceived with to-day's latest knowledge, planned and implemented by persons aware of the many sided potentialities of these activities and aimed at serving the physical, mental and well-being of the participants.

18.2 PRINCIPLES OF SELECTION OF ACTIVITIES AND PROGRAMMES

Principles of Selection of Activities and Programmes

(1) Physiological Principles

(2) Psychological Principles

(3) Sociological Principles

A. Physiological Principles

1. Principle of development of the movement of large muscles.
2. Principles of growth and development of the child.
3. Principle of meeting the physical fitness needs of the students.

B. Psychological Principles

1. Principle of natural activities
2. Principle of construction of curriculum according to 3 A's-age, abilities and aptitudes
3. Principle of sublimation of various instincts of the child
4. Principle of gradation and integration.
5. Principle of learning skills.

C. Sociological Principles

1. Principle of training for citizenship.
2. Principle of cooperation and team work.

3. Principle of social adjustment.
4. Principle of utilisation of leisure time profitably.

18.3 COMPONENTS OF PHYSICAL EDUCATION PROGRAMME

Physical education programme should include a variety of activities. Following are the major types of activities to be included in a comprehensive physical education programme.

1. Developmental Activities
2. Rhythmics
3. Games, Sports and Athletics
4. Formal Activities
5. Gymnastics
6. Combatives
7. Aquatics
8. Self Testing Activities
9. Camping and Outdoor Activities
10. Special Activities
11. Classroom Activities
12. Free Play

1. *Developmental Activities:*
   (i) Exercise tables, '*dands*', '*baithaks*' and yogic exercises.
   (ii) Fundamental movements such as climbing, jumping, running throwing and walking.
   (iii) Mimetics and story plays.
   (iv) Stunts, pyramids, weight training and conditioning exercises.
2. *Rhythmics*: Rhythm fundamentals, rhythm games, folk dances, social dances, singing games, community singing, Indian rhythmics, '*garha*', '*phugdi*', 'himma', '*tipri*', etc.
3. *Games, Sports and Athletics:*
   (A) *Games:*
   (i) Major games, such as '*Kabaddi*', '*kho-kho*', Volleyball, basketball, hokey, cricket etc.
   (ii) Dual games such as tennis, table tennis, badminton, ring-tennis, etc.
   (iii) Recreative games, minor games, relays, social games, group games, lead-up games, etc.
   (B) *Sports*: Cycling, canoeing, shooting, riding, skating etc.
   (C) *Athletics*: Running, jumping, throwing, walking and relays.
4. *Formal Activities*: Drill and marching, light apparatus, calisthenics, mass P.T. exercises aerobics.
5. *Gymnastics:* Parallel bars, vaulting, beam, roman rings, ropes, pommel horse, single bar, 'malkhamb', etc.
6. *Combatives:* Wrestling, boxing, judo, '*lathi*' fight, dagger fight, *farigadga*, sword fight, simple contests and mass combatives based on 'attack and defence'.
7. *Aquatics:* Swimming, diving and life saving.
8. *Self-Testing Activities:* All types of tests.

9. *Camping and Outdoor Activities:* Hiking, cross country, camping and mountaineering, picnics, excursions etc.
10. *Special Activities:* Demonstrations, ceremonial parades, singing the National Anthem, Flag salutations, practical projects, citizenship training etc.
11. *Classroom Activities:* Physical education is not merely to be confined to the playground but should pervade the classroom. Physical education in the classroom may take the following forms:
    (a) Direct instruction emphasisting the necessity of having a good physique.
    (b) Suggestions regarding the maintenance of good health.
    (c) Emphasis on right postures.
    (d) Provision of good seating and lighting arrangements in the classroom, thereby impressing upon the students the importance of studying under healthy surroundings.
    (e) Providing ample opportunities to the children for physical activity *i.e.* asking and answering questions, use of audio-visual aids etc.

It should be borne in mind that physical development and mental development are inseparably allied to each other. Classroom should not be devoid of physical activity. Instruction in a play-way manner affords ample opportunities to the students to be physically active and a wise teacher would always bring this spirit of play-way in classroom work. The students should play an active role in the teaching-learning process. They should not remain merely as passive listeners. For pre-primary classes, Kindergarten and Montessori methods afford opportunities for the physical development of the children. Basic system of education is based on the principle of learning by doing. This involves many physical activities. Project Method and the Dalton Plan are the other examples which require many activities on the part of children. Paper cutting and folding may be associated with Elementary Geometry and Arithmetic. Students may learn Nature Study and Geography with he help of clay modelling. A variety of programmes may be introduced in the classroom. Reading, writing, figuring, drawing, etc., should be profitably attempted to provide practical activities. A few minutes drill or music after every lesson of the class may introduce bodily activity among the children. Display of maps and charts etc. bring clarity and vividness in the lesson. Technology of teaching provides ample opportunities for various kinds of student involvement in the lesson.

Gymnastics and Athletics

Gymnastics and athletics are two important forms of physical education. The effect of gymnastic exercises is internal and primary. They are based on sound principles. Each exercise has its own value for a specific purpose. Gymnastic exercises are very helpful in teaching correct postures. Gymnastic exercises with apparatus (Bars, Horse, Ladder etc.) are greatly liked by the boys as these involved a great degree of skill and difficulties. Gymnastic exercises like marching, easy exercises in jumping and skipping, aesthetic dancing and folk dancing appeal to the girls.

Athletic activities include running, jumping, disc throwing, hammer throwing and weight throwing, etc.

In carrying out gymnastics, the following points should be taken into consideration:

1. Lessons and exercises should be purposive and not at random.
2. One shirt and shorts are sufficient.
3. The postures should be good.
4. The body should not be held in a straight position for a long time.
5. The gymnastic exercises should be correlated with material and play.
6. All material should be kept in order.

Physical Drill

Physical drill should be organized regularly and properly graded. 'Simple to complex' and 'easy to difficult' should form the basis of physical drill. The duration of the physical drill period should depend on the age and the number of pupils in the group or class. A good system of physical exercises would provide exercise to all parts of the body, *e.g.*, hands, legs, muscles, neck and trunk etc.

Following types of exercises will make the programme effective:

(i) Preparing or warming up exercises, running in a circle, marching etc.
(ii) Corrective exercises
(iii) Recreative exercises
(iv) Psychological exercises

Free Play

Modern educationists believe in freedom of children. They dislike every sort of compulsion as they think that the element of compulsion robs the child of the enjoyment which he would otherwise derive.

A child derives immense pleasure in free play. He wants to choose games and other kinds of activities according to his interest. He does not like that any time limit should be imposed on him while he is at play. Free play has direct appeal to his natural urges and it satisfies his psychological needs. "Play is a biological and social necessity for children. It is the most fundamental things about a child-play for the child is one of the most serious facts of life; it is a form of work for the young, and the basis for all natural education," writes Davie.

It is in the nature of the child to play. He is interested in it from the very birth. Stern defines play as "voluntary self-constrained activity". The values of play may be classified as under:

(a) Educational
(b) Intellectual.
(c) Physical.
(d) Social.
(e) Emotional.
(f) Developmental.

18.4 PLAYGROUND AS THE CRADLE OF DEMOCRACY: THE BATTLE OF WATERLOO WAS WON ON THE PLAYGROUNDS OF ETON

The phrase 'The Battle of Warterloo was won on the playgrounds of Eton' points but that the generals of England who fought the Battle of Waterloo with the foreign enemies had received valuable taining in leadership qualities at Eton, which enabled them to win the battle. It may be mentioned that Eton is one of the most prestigious public schools in England. It has produced several eminent personalities of England who have played a leading role in all walks of life and made their mark.

The playground has been rightly called the 'cradle of democrcy' as games and sports properly organized and supervised can contribute a lot for the development of ideals and values needed in an enlightened citizen.

Following are the important values of games and sports:

1. *Teach Cooperation*: Team work is the pivot round which the wheel of games revolves. If the members of the team do not work for the team but for their individual distinctions, the team is sure to go to the walls. Games and sports bring home this fact to the students that loyalty and cooperation are the important contributory factors for the honour of the team. They serve to eliminate selfishness and teach the students to subordinate their own interests for the sake of a broader aim of winning the game. This lesson is very important and every citizen is expected to follow it.

2. *Prepare for Life Situations*: The players have to play some times against heavy odds. Courage, patience, steadfastness and perseverance are needed to play well and effecively. The players get accustomed to face very critical situations and this stands in good stead when they enter life. We cannot think of an ideal citizen without posessing these qualities.

3. *Provide Opportunities for Leadership*: Games and sports provide opportunities for leadership of a very high order. The captain of the team has to put right players at their right plces and has to bring about harmony among the different members of the team. Only a man of self-confidence, imagination and enterprise can lead others.

4. *Development of Various Senses*: The games and sports call for a variety of movement-physical and mental. "School games involve a wide range of activity. Most of the senses are called into action, "Comparison and judgment are needed", says William Gowers. The mind has to by kept alert to meet the changing situation of the ball. Body and mind work in harmony.

5. *Physical Development*: Games and sports promote good health, which is perhaps more important than wealth. Good health is also a sign of a good citizen.

6. *Emphasis on Struggle*: They teach the lesson that struggle is more important than success. Baron de Conbertin states, "The important thing in sports is not to win but to take part. The important thing in life is not the triumph but the struggle. The essential thing is not to have conquered but to have fought well. To spread these precepts is to build up a stronger and more scrupulous and more generous humanity."

7. *Satisfaction of Various Urges of Children*: Play is the most important urge of the children. In fact it is a natural urge. It is a biological and social necessity for children. Similarly various other urges of children are satisfied.

8. *Development of 'Esprit de Corps'*: Tournaments are very helpful in developing 'we feeling' among the students. Team spirit is developed through games and sports.

9. *Profitable Use of Leisure Time*: Games and sports provide recreational avenues.

10. *Character Training*: For promoting qualities of courage, obedience, perseverance, self-control and steadfastness etc., games and sports are very effective.

Concluding Observations

A perusal of the educative value of games and sports leads us to state that playground is an other school.

There is no rose without a thorn. It we do not take precaution to pluck a rose, the thorn is sure to prick us. Likewise it games and sports are not rationally and scientifically organized and supervised, they are likely to do more harm than good.

We may sum up the merits and limitations of games and sports with a quote from Aldous Huxley, "Like every other instrument that man has invented, sports can be used either for good or for evil, purpose. Used well, it can teach endurance and courage, a sense of fair play and a respect for rules, coordinated efforts and the subordination of pesonal interest to those of the group. Used badly it can encourage personal vanity and group vanity, greedy desire for victory and hatred for rivals, an intolerant 'esprit de corps' and contempt for people who are beyond arbitrarily selected pole. In either case sports inculcate cooperation."

18.5 PRINCIPLES OF ORGANIZING GAMES AND SPORTS

1. A variety of games and sports should be provided to the students to meet their specific needs.
2. Every child should be motivated to take part in one or the other game or sport.

3. Games and sports time-table should be framed and regularly followed.
4. Indian as well as western games and sports should be duly mentioned.
5. The attainments of the students in games and sports should be duly mentioned in important records.
6. Indoor as well as outdoor games should find place in the programme of the school.
7. In case no playgrounds are available to some schools, a cluster of schools may share common playground. A sports complex at suitable place be set up for this purpose.
8. Games and sports should be properly supervised by teachers.
9. Games' fund should be spent for games only.
10. Games' fund should not be utilised on a few selected players.
11. Tournaments should be organized systematically.

18.6 PRINCIPLES AND SUGGESTIONS FOR THE PROMOTION OF PHYSICAL EDUCATION

1. The programme of physical education should become an integral part of school education.
2. Physical education should be treated at par with other subjects.
3. Every class/section should be provided with one period daily for physical education in the time-table.
4. Greater facilities should be provided in educational institutions in the form of equipment, playgrounds and funds.
5. Incentives in the form of credit for achievements in sports should be provided.
6. Health, power of endurance, physical well-being of young people should be developed by improvement in nutrition.
7. Planned coaching at all stages in essential. There is a vast talent potential in the country which should be exploited by intensive and planned coaching.
8. Sports and games should be organised in rural areas through Vyayamshalas, Vyayam Mandals, Akharas, etc. and in co-operation with the community.
9. Sports festival should be organised and sports events encouraged on the occasion of fairs. Indigenous sports like Kabaddi and indigenous style of wrestling should be encouraged.
10. Where separate playgrounds cannot be made available for each educational institution, a common pool for a group of institutions should be created.
11. Standard equipment should be manufactured in the country so as to be available at cheap rates and facilities for its manufacture should be provided.

12. For the development of sports and games in the country, it is essential that umpiring and refereeing should be of a high standard.
13. All teachers below the age of 40 should actively participate in many of the physical activities of students and thus make them a lively part of the school programme.
14. Full records of physical activities of the students must be maintained.
15. The training in physical education should be comprehensive enough to include all aspects of health education.
16. The teachers of physical education should be associated with the teaching of subjects like Physiology and Hygiene and given the same status as other teachers of similar qualifications.
17. The existing facilities for training of teachers of physical education should be expanded by increasing the seats in the existing colleges, by opening new colleges where necessary and by reorganising some of the institutions as All India Training Centres to which aid may be given both by the Centre and the States.
18. Leadership in the field of physical education should consist of:
    (a) qualified staff.
    (b) specialist coaches, and
    (c) student leaders
19. In primary schools, classroom teachers should teach physical education. They should be given in-service training in physical education.
20. Periodical refresher courses should be organised for in-service physical education teachers.
21. Special coaching camps should be conducted for school physical education teachers.
22. Playgrounds should be provided to schools as laid down in the National Plan of Physical Education and Recreation. Schools may, however, have playgrounds with the following minimum limits:

Category	*Boys*	*Girls*
(a) High Schools	5 acres	3 acres
(b) Middle Schools	3 acres	2 acres
(c) Primary Schools	½ to 1 acre	½ to 1 acre

23. Schools having excess open space may be required to permit the use of such open space by the neighbouring schools.
24. Each cluster of schools or big schools should have an indoor gymnasium with the dimensions of 60' × 15'.

18.7 RECOMMENDATIONS OF COMMITTEES AND COMMISSIONS ON THE DEVELOPMENT OF PHYSICAL EDUCATION PROGRAMME

I. Recommendations of the Secondary Education Commission 1952-53

1. Physical activities should be made to suit the individual and his capacity for physical endurance.

2. All teachers below the age of 40 should actively participate in many of the physical activities of students and thus make them a lively part of the school programme.
3. Full records of physical activities of the students must be maintained.
4. The training in physical education should be comprehensive enough to include all aspects of health education.
5. The teachers of physical education should be associated with the teaching of subjects like Physiology and Hygiene and given the same status as other teachers of similar qualifications.
6. The existing facilities for training of teachers of physical education should be expanded by increasing the seats in the existing colleges, by opening new colleges where necessary and by recognising some of the institutions as All India Training Centres to which aid may be given both by the Centre and the States.

II. Recommendations of the All India Seminar on Physical Education for State Inspectors and University Directors (1958)

The All India Seminar was held at Mahabaleshwar from 16th to 30th May, 1958 under the chairmanship of Shri D.G. Wakharkar. Inter alia, the seminar made certain recommendations regarding physical education at the school level. Among the important recommendations are:

1. Physical education should be a curricular subject in the schools at all levels and should be on par with other subjects.
2. The programme of physical education and recreation should cater to the needs, interests and capacities of the pupils, and should have 'carry over' value. It should promote normal growth and development, maintenance of health, acquisition of skills and desirable social attitudes and behaviour.
3. Leadership in the field of physical education should consist of (a) qualified staff, (b) specialist coaches, and (c) student leaders.
4. Any of the following qualifications should be considered as approved qualification for a person to work as a physical education teacher in a secondary school: (a) A Degree in Physical Education; (b) A University Degree with a Diploma in Physical Education; (c) A pass in Intermediate or its equivalent with a Certificate in Physical Education; (d) A pass in Matric or S.S.L.C. or S.S.C. or S.F. Examination with a Certificate in Physical Education.
5. In primary schools, classroom teachers should teach physical education.
6. Periodical refresher courses should be organised for in-service physical education teachers.
7. Special coaching camps should be conducted for school physical education teachers at Government cost.
8. Playgrounds should be provided by schools as laid down in the National Plan of Physical Education and Recreation. Schools may, however, have playgrounds with the following minimum limits:

Category	*Boys*	*Girls*
(a) High Schools	5 acres	3 acres
(b) Middle Schools	3 acres	2 acres
(c) Primary Schools	½ to 1 acre	½ to 1 acre

9. Schools having excess open space may be required to permit the use of such open space by the neighbouring schools.
10. Each school should have an indoor gymnasium with the dimensions of 60' × 15'.
11. Schools should provide daily one period for physical education in the time table.
12. The syllabus given in the National Plan of Physical Education and Recreation should be followed in all schools with suitable modifications wherever necessary.
13. Medical inspection should be compulsory for all pupils.

Supervision of Health: Physical Education and Recreation in Schools: In order to make supervision serve its purpose fully, the following staff may be provided in each state:

(i) Deputy Director of Education for Physical Education and Recreation.
(ii) Two State Physical Education Officers for men's branch and women's branch separately;
(iii) Regional or Divisional Physical Education Officers (Men's and Women's branches separately), each in charge of a unit of about four District Physical Education Officers;
(iv) District Physical Education Officers (Men's and Women's branches separately), each in charge of about 50 high schools.

III. Report of the Ad Hoc Enquiry Committee on Games and Sports (1958)

The Government of India, appointed a Committee in 1958 to investigate the persistence of low standard in sports in India and the performance of the Indian teams in international contests, such as Olympic and Asian Games, and to recommend measures for improvement. Its major recommendations are as under:

1. More facilities and better opportunities for training and competition should be provided and greater administrative efficiency achieved.
2. Greater facilities should be provided in educational institutions in the form of equipment, playgrounds and funds.
3. Incentives in the form of credit for achievements in sports and games should be provided.
4. Health, power of endurance, physical well-being of young people should be developed by improvement in nutrition.
5. Sports and games should be organised in rural areas through Vyayamshalas, Vyayam Mandals, Akharas, etc. and in cooperation with the Community Projects. Sports festivals should be organised and sports events encouraged on the occasion of fairs. Indigenous

sports like Kabaddi and indigenous style of wrestling should be encouraged.

6. If schools and colleges and universities have to play their part in the development of sports and games in the country, they must have the minimum requirements in respect of playgrounds and equipment. The following standards have been recommended:

A College (with a student population of 1000 to 1500):	10 acres for playground
A High School (with a student population of 500 to 1000):	5-6 acres
A Middle School (with a student population of 200 to 500):	3-5 acres
A Primary School:	1 acre

7. Where separate playgrounds cannot be made available for each educational institution, a common pool for a group of institutions should be created.

IV. Recommendations of the Education Commission 1964-66

Writing about the concept of physical education, the Education Commission 1964-66 felt, "It must be emphasized that such education contributes not only to physical fitness but also to physical efficiency, mental alertness and the development of certain qualities like perseverance, team spirit, leadership, obedience to rules, moderation in victory and balance in defeat."

Five Forms of Physical Activities according to the Commission: According to the Education Commission 1964-66, physical education should include:

(i) Development exercises.
(ii) Rhythmic activities.
(iii) Sports and games.
(iv) Outing activities.
(v) Group handling activities.

Simple and Advanced Forms. The Commission further observed that all these have simple and advanced forms. The simpler activities should be introduced in the early classes, the more advanced ones should be gradually provided as boys and girls become more and more mature.

Principles of Developing a Programme of Physical Education. The Education Commission (1964-66) suggested the following eight principles for developing a satisfactory programme of physical education:

1. The physical education programme should be planned for desirable outcomes keeping in mind the interests and capacity of the participants.
2. The traditional forms of play and physical activities that have developed in our country should receive due emphasis in the programme.
3. The activities promoted should develop in each child a sense of personal worth and pride.

4. A sense of sharing responsibility in a spirit of democratic cooperation should grow from experience on playground and also in the gymnasium.
5. The programme offered should supplement other programmes of education and not duplicate them.
6. The programme should be within financial means.
7. The programme should reach all rather than a selected few.
8. Special instruction and coaching should be provided for students with talent and special aptitude.

V. National Policy on Education 1986 and Sports and Physical Education

Sports and physical education are an integral part of the learning process, and will be included in the evaluation of performance. A nationwide infrastructure for physical education, sports and games will be built into the educational edifice.

The infrastructure will consist of playfields, equipment, coaches and teachers of physical education as part of the School Improvement Programme. Available open spaces in urban areas will be reserved for playgrounds, if necessary by legislation. Efforts will be made to establish sports institutions and hostels where specialised attention will be given to sports activities and sports related studies, along with normal education. Appropriate encouragement will be given to those talented in sports and games. Due stress will be laid in indigenous traditional games. As a system which promotes an integrated development of body and mind, yoga will receive special attention. Efforts will be made to introduce yoga in all schools, to this end it will be introduced in teacher training courses.

VI. NPE Programme of Action (1992)

1. Allocation of sufficient time to sports and physical education.
2. Introduction of physical education and yoga for at least 45 minutes per day.
3. Inclusion of approved games in the school time-table for at least two periods a week.
4. Provision of special attention to students who perform well in sports and games.
5. Special incentives for subject teachers who perform extra duty in conducting classes in physical education, sports and games.
6. Provision of basic equipment.
7. Provision of contingent found.
8. Improvement of playgrounds on a phased basis.
9. Organisation of an extensive programme of teachers training to equip all subject teachers with the necessary skills to impart training in physical education, games and yoga.

10. Introduction of a comprehensive system of inter-school tournaments and competitions in select disciplines.
11. Introduction of a scheme of special cash awards to winning schools and incentives to outstanding players and athletes.

VII. NCERT Guidelines and Syllabi on Physical Education at Various School Stages (2001)

1. Calisthenics

— Two exercise tables consisting of six to eight exercises in each, of four counts, are to be arranged in a sequence-rhythm involving arms and shoulders, leg balance, trunk bending and twisting for agility as well as co-ordination.

2. Atheletics

— General physical fitness exercise in circle/open order/scattered order.
— Short sprints/skipping/relays (50m, 100m, 200m, 4x50 m), obstacle race.
— Techniques of start and finish jumping for distance-approach, run, take off, mid-air action and landing. Jumping for height-approach run, take-off, body action over the bar and landing.
— Throwing cricket ball.
— Rhythmic and aesthetic exercises, 2-3 to be selected by the teacher.

3. Games

— Lead-up games-Circle Kho-Kho, game of five passes, cant-kabaddi, round race.
— Relays: Over and under relay, human obstacle, crab relay, sedan-chair relay, Siamese twins relay.

Major Games

— Basic fundamental skills of kabaddi, kho-kho, basket-ball, hand-ball, cricket and hockey.

Note: All major games on miniature courts and with small size equipment.

4. Aquatics

— Gliding (floating), crawling, free-style, back stroke, breast strokes (50 M) cover distance using leg kick only.

5. Rhythmic Activities

— Dance-legs stepping to rhythm, flat heel and toe, clap and step with legs on the spot, alternative cross stepping, moving sideways. Toe-stepping forward, sidewards, backward positions. Cross stepping with hands on waist, behind the neck, sideways stretched.
— Lezium-Fundamentals-lezium aram lezium skandh, lezium hushiar,

pavtra, Exercises: Char awaz, ek jaghe, adhi lagao, pavitra do rukh.
— Hoops drill-selected movements to be done to rhythm.

6. Gymnastics

A. General Development Exercises:
— Different kinds of walking, running and jumping exercises.
— Free hand exercises for different parts of the body.

B. Skill Part (Floor Exercises)
— Different kinds of rolling movements like front roll, back roll, side roll, etc.
— Cartwheel
— Front turn over and back turn over with both legs folded.

7. Yogic Exercises

— Padmasana
— Sukhasana
— Vajrasana
— Ardhachakrasana
— Bhujangasana
— Halasana
— Pawanmuktasana
— Shavasana
— Fundamentals in drill and marching Quick march, turning in, mark time, turning while marching, right and left wheel.

Class VII

1. Calisthenics

— Two exercise-tables consisting of six to eight exercises in each, of four counts arranged in a sequence-rhythm involving arm and shoulder, leg balance, trunk bending and twisting for agility and coordination.

2. Athletics

— General physical fitness exercises in open order/circle/scattered form.
— Techniques of start, sprint, finish (50 m, 100m, 200m, 400m, 4x100m, relay).
— Techniques of running, high-jump approach run, take off, crossing the bars, landing; techniques of running, broad jump, approach run, take-off, mid-air action, landing, putting the shot-initial stance, glide, delivery, follow through games.

3. Games

— Lead-up games, dodge and mark, touch and run, pin basketball, captain call.

- — Relays-Involving fundamentals of major games such as horse and the rider, all-up relay, jump the stick, chariot relay, lateral ball pass relay.
- — Major games-cricket, football, hockey, basketball, hand-ball, volley-ball, soft-ball, Kabaddi, kho-kho, badminton, table-tennis.

Note: Opportunities of practising the skills and playing the games with suitable modification with regard to the size of the field and the number of players should be provided. Participation of all may be ensured.

4 Aquatics

- — Crawling, back stroke, breast stroke, butterfly (50m, 100m), Spring board diving, surface diving, preliminary fundamental diving skills.

5. Rhythmic activities

- — Dance-movement exploration to the rhythm go down as low as we can, go up as high as we can: jumping and pushing, galloping, skipping, shaking, bend and stretch swinging; run and leap, combination of stepping and bending with arm movements, square walking, circle walking.
- — Lezium-Repetition of the previous class work, ghum jao; aage phalang, peeche phalang.

6. Gymnastics

- — Repetition of skills learnt in previous class.
- — Other skills: knee deep, dive and roll, monkey roll, cartwheel; handstand to forward roll; backward roll to handstand; take off from the spring board; parallel bars-grip, mounting, dismounting, dips, swings; vaulting box-jump on-off, astride vault, between vault; conditioning exercises-rope climbing, rope climbing with the help of feet.

7. Yogic Exercises

- — Ardhpadmasan
- — Tadasan
- — Utkatasana
- — Shalabhasan
- — Padhastasana
- — Pavanmuktasana
- — Shavasana

8. Judo

- — What is Judo?
- — specifications of Judo-gear and its uses.
- — Etiquette and hygiene in Judo.
- — Skills: relevant postures-natural posture, self-defensive posture; disturbing balance or posture-kuzushi (left, right, back, front);

techniques of advance and retreat movement; techniques of break fall (ukerni); methods of taking hold (kummi kata).

Class VIII

1. Calisthenics

— Exercise tables of Class VII to be repeated.

2. Athletics

— Events Races (100m, 200m, 400m, 800m, 1500m, 4x100m, Relay)
— Principles of sprints (100m, 200m, 400m)
— Fixing of starting clocks, getting off the block, stride-length, body position and finish.
— Principles of jumps: Broad jump-approach run, take-off, flight and landing, High-jump approach run, take-off, bar clearance and landing.
— Principles of Throws: Short-put: hold, placement, initial stance, glide, delivery stance, delivery action and reverse.
— Javelin: Hold, placement, carry, pegging, withdrawal of javelin, delivery stance, delivery action and reverse.

3. Major Games

Any two of the following:

(a) *Cricket*: History and development of the game; rules of the game; skill; (a) batting: front foot drive, back foot drive, hook, shot; (b) bowling: off spin, leg spin, fast bowling; (c) fielding straight ball, running and stopping, catching high and low balls and throwing; (d) pitch practice and regular game.

(b) *Football*: History and development of the game; rules of the game; skills: kicking: inside of the foot, in-step of the foot, volley land the half-volley; trapping trap: sole of the foot, drooping ball, with in-step, waist height ball with inside of the foot; dribbling: inside of the foot; and game practice in miniature field.

(c) *Hokey*: History and development of the game; rules of the game; skills: sticking, grip, back swing, forward swing, strike and follow through, co-ordination of stick and body, correct position of feet, head, eyes; stopping, dribbling, scooping, pushing, taking push; and small field games-5v/s5, 6v/s6, etc.

(d) *Basketball*: History and development of the game; rules of the game; skills: passing (overhead, chest, bounces one hand, two hands, dribbling (low and high), shooting lay up, set shot one hand; two hands; individual and team practice.

(e) *Handball*: History and development of the game; rules of the game; skills: throwing (low and high), catching (one hand, two hands) passing (long, short), shooting, goal-keeping, offence and defence; regular game.

(f) *Volleyball*: History and development of the game; rules of the game; skills: passing (under pass, two hand pass, over head pass), smashing/spiking; service (under hand, side arm, tennis); regular game.

(g) *Softball*: History and development of the game; rules of the game; skills: batting stance, batting, bunting, running the base, stealing the bases, sliding catching and throwing catching with and without gloves, pitching, fielding, covering, backing up, relay through; and regular game.

(h) *Kabaddi*: History and development of the game; rules of the game; skills: raid-cant, side kick, back kick, round kick, front kick, mule kick, leg thrust kick, jumping over and breaking the chain touching with toe and hand; catching leg catch, hand catch, wrist catch; trunk catch, thigh (single and both) catch, ankle catch and pull, dive catch cross hold, covering with chain; and regular game.

(i) Kho-*kho*: History and development of the game; rules of the game; skills: chasing (sitting, rising up, taking direction, diving, pole-dive, early kho, simple kho, late kho, fake kho, judgement kho, taping and trapping together); running (single chain, double chain, oval or ring play, mix play, turning the pole, front and back dodging, avoiding trapping); regular game.

(j) *Badminton Shuttle*: History and development of the game; rules of the game; skills: grip, service, returning, tossing, smash, regular game.

4. Aquantics

— Events: 100m, 200m
— Relays: 4 × 50m
— Diving: 1m Spring board diving.

5. Gymnastics

Repetition of the previously learnt skills: dive role (dive role from standing position, with two-three running steps, and also with take-off from the spring board), hand spring, hand stand; hand spring (through various stages of teaching); vaulting horse (board horse): jump on, jump off, squat vault, astride vault; parallel bars (for boys only) walking (single and double steps walking, straddle walking), front roll and side roll, straddle, sitting on the bars; balancing beam (for girls only) mount and dismount (simple), walking on toes, on the beam (with arms on the waist, sideways, upward, forward, and backward etc.); conditioning exercises; and tuck jumps and other jumps and other jumping exercises, abdominal exercises; combination of dance movement and matwork-series of floor exercises, swings.

Note: Special emphasis on flexibility exercises.

6. Yogic Exercises

— Trikonasana
— Vrikshasana
— Paschimottanasana

- — Parvatasana
- — Dhanurasana
- — Janusirsasana
- — Shavasana

Wrestling

- — Stance: (a) diagonal (b) square.
- — Simple holds for "Go behind": (a) wrist or palm and arm drag; (b) neck, dragging and elbow push sidewards; (c) elbow lift, head under arm.
- — Counters for the above holds: (a) blocking with forearm across the chest; (b) simple leg pick-up
- — Primary Holds: (Grand wrestling): (a) position; (b) simple nelson and counter.
- — Exercises for developing strength, stamina and agility.

8. Judo

- — Brief History and growth of Judo.
- — Safety in Judo.
- — Principles of Judo.
- — Skills: (a) techniques of break fall (Ukerni) forward, backward, right, left, forward, somersault fall; (b) methods of taking hold (Kummi-Kata): Grips: normal, reverse, under side, outer.

9. Dance and Rhythmic (for girls)

Dance; repeat skills learnt in previous class; on the spot stepping movements in rhythm; on-the-spot stopping combined with hand movements; on-the-spot stepping, hand movements and handling sidewards shifting weight; stepping and moving to right and left; on-the-spot stepping combined with hand movements; on-the-spot stepping hand movements and bending; stepping and moving to right and left; stepping forward, backward, sideways with hand movements; movements and turns bending body with grace and pose; balance shifting weight and with head movements; stepping and moving in diagonal directions; moving with shoulders, neck, eyes, hands, and fingers' gestures; skipping and jumping, turning; movements and gestures leading to express characteristics of birds/animals; balance, bending, twisting; movements and imitations of historical and mythological characters; combination of various movements to form a group dance or dance drama to be evolved by the teacher; and local dance, folk dance or tribal dance.

10. Lezium

- — Ghati Lezium, Deccan Lezium:
  Eight Strokes (atha awaj); kadam tal; age daur; kadam pavitra; pavitra baithak phirki or ardh chakra; pav chakra; pur chakra; hool

— N.F.C. Series
  Hath Ki Harkat; Paun Ki Harkat; Jhukana Harkat; Dahine Harkat; Bai Harkat; Bharat Mata Ki Jai; Mayur Chal.

Secondary Stage Class IX: Physical Education

1. Athletics

— Track Events; 100m, 200m, 400m, 1500m, 3000m
— 100m Flat Running
— 200m, 400m, sprints
  Starting from the Curves-Finding the Blocks
  Curve Running
  Body Position; start and finish
— Distance Running-800m, 1500m, 3000m for boys, 800m for girls
  Leg Action
  Foot Placement
  Stride Length
  Arm and Shoulder action
  Body Angle
— Training with various methods
— Triple Jump
  Approach run, take off and landing for hop-step and jump, mid-air action, landing.
— Discuss Throw
  Holds, spinning, initial stand and preliminary swing turn, delivery stance, delivery and reverse.

2. Major games (any two)

Badminton (Shuttle): Repetition of skills: skills-serving, spin, underhand receiving, back hand, forehand, spin service, flat service, smash, push/chapping, tossing, returning smash, pushing/chapping, float; practice of the game.

Basketball: Repetition of the skills; skills-passing one hand pass, book pass, baseball pass; shooting-two handed shot, set shot, lay up shot, jump shot; dribbling; pivoting; rebound taking; screening; training; various type of drills to develop the techniques.

Cricket: Repetition of skills; skills-batting-square cut/drives, late cut; bowling-off spin, leg spin, fast yorker; wicket keeping, field placement; development training for endurance, power, strength and speed; techniques and pitch practice.

Football: Repetition of skills; skills kicking and trapping, individual and dual practice; heading downwards, sidewards, forward, backward; tackling-side tackle, direct tackle; goal keeping-high ball, ground ball, deflecting, punching, positioning, diving and slips; training-to develop power, strength, ability, endurance and skills.

Handball: Repetition of skills; skills-passing; shootings; blocking; carrying;

catch and turn, taking penalty; positional play.

Hockey: Repetition of skills; skills-passing-for development of speed, direction and timing pass-back bass and cross pass: goal keeping-kicking, padding, positioning, pushing and palming: dribbling; positional play.

Kabaddi: Repetition of skills; skills-cant; fast raiding; back kick; sqant leg thrust; toe-touching; jumping; movement of arm and shoulder; catching, trapping; chair, formation; game practice.

Kho-Kho: Repetition of skills; skills-pole dive; playing around the pole; single chain, mix play-oval/ring; coverin training; regulation game.

Volleyball: Repetition of skills; skills-passing-underhand pass, both hands, jump and pass; pass for smashing back pass, jump pass; smashing-round arm smashing and twist smashing; placing; service-underhand round arm; over arm; defense blocking; positional play; regulation game.

3. Gymnastics (Boys)

Repetition of previously learnt skills; skills floor exercises-head spring, round off (cartwheel cut), pyramids; vaulting horse-straddle vault on broad-hourse, hand spring on broad-horse, take-off and sitting on the long-horse, straddle from the standing position on long-horse; parallel bars-different kinds of mounts and dismounts, one bar roll, shoulder stand; 'L' position hold; horizontal bar-different types of grips, back turn over, one leg circle forward, simple swing; conditioning exercise-same as in the previous class with emphasis on more repetitions.

4. Gymnastics (Girls)

Repetition of skills learnt in the previous class; skills (floor exercise)-one hand cartwheel, round off (cartwheel), pyramids; balancing beam-dancing movements, turning movements, front roll and back roll, different balances; vaulting horse-straddle vault on broad horse, wolf vault, side vault, cat spring and jump horse on long horse; conditioning exercises-same as in the previous class.

5. Yogic Exercises

Surya-namaskar; Tadasaria;
Trikonasana; Vrikshasana;
Padahastasana; Vajrasana; Ardha
Padmasana; Ardhachakrasana;
Dhanurasana; Pawan Muktasana;
Shavasana.

6. Combatives (Wrestling)

Repetition of skills learnt in previous classes; simple holds: take towns-single leg dive; double leg dive; counter for the above; head push and sit through; pinning holds; three quarters nelson; double arm role; chicken wing nelson; hip throw; breakdowns and counter for the above; exercises for developing quickness, strength, power and endurance.

7. Dagger Fight (Jambia)

Repetition of the strokes and defense skills learnt in the previous class; side stroke; chest stroke; defence hip throw; arm drag, holding wrist and pull; actual fight practice.

8. Judo

History and development; rules of the game; warming up and its importance; knowledge of grading (evaluation); skills-floating drop (uki toshi), shoulder throw seanase), body drop (taiotoshi), shoulder drop (seaiotoshi), shoulder wheel (kataguruma), belt drop (obiotoshi), outer winding throw (sotomakikomi).

9. Swimming (Optional)

Repeat the skills learnt earlier; treading water; horizontal and vertical floating; underwater swimming; board diving.

Class X: Physical Education

1. Athletics

- Repetition of skills and techniques of the events learnt in the previous class.
- Hurdles-100m, Low (3′ height), warming up exercise, running, over the sticks.
- Conditioning lead by action (with or without hurdles)
- Specializing, sprints; endurance run; jumps, throws.

2. Major Games (any two)

Badminton: Repetition of skills learnt in the previous class; drills to develop techniques of spin service, flat service; floating; pushing; drop; game practice.

Basketball: Repetition of skills learnt in the previous class; practising drills and techniques; offensive and defensive techniques; positional play; training for endurance and speed.

Cricket: Repetition of skills learnt in the previous class; specific drills to develop technique-batting, bowling, fielding, offensive and defensive tactics; training-endurance; practice matches.

Football: Repetition of skills learnt in the previous class; specific drills to develop techniques; kicking; trapping; shooting into goal; dribbling; goalkeeping; positional play; offensive and defensive tactics; training for endurance and speed; regular game.

Hockey: Repetition of skills learnt in the previous class; specific drills to develop techniques; passing; hitting; pushing; kicking; dribbling; scooping; goalkeeping; goal shooting; positional play; offensive and defensive tactics—training endurance, speed and moves; regular game.

Kabaddi: Repetition of skills learnt in the previous class; specific drills to develop techniques; offensive and defensive tactics; regular game practice.

Kho-Kho: Repetition of skills learnt in the previous class; skills-single and double-chain. dodging; practice of skills; regular game practice.

Volleyball: Repetition of skills learnt in the previous class; skills-passing: upper hand pass and turn; upper head pass with back and side roll; blocking; positional play; offensive and defensive tactics; regular game.

Gymnastic (Boys): Repetition of skills learnt in the previous class; skills (floor exercises); combination of previously learnt exercises, flic-flac through teaching stages with the help of a teacher; forward salto with take off from the spring board; parallel bars-upper arm swing, back uprise, up start swing in support position; vaulting horse-mastery over the teaching stages of straddle vault on long horse, complete straddle vault on long hourse; horizontal bar-one leg up start, one leg circle backward; conditioning exercises-these would include various exercises to develop strength, endurance, speed, agility, flexibility and coordination.

Note: Skills with asterisks should only be taught keeping in view the capability of an individual.

3. Gymnastic (Girls)

Repetition of skills learnt in the previous classes; skills part (floor exercises) mastery over the previously learnt skills with emphasis on dancing movement incorporating with music, flic-flac through various teaching stages keeping in view the capability of an individual; balance beam-combination of various movements, various kinds of jumps on balancing beam, straddle legs sitting on balancing beam; vaulting horse-mastery over the various stages of handspring, complete handsrping, keeping in view the capability of an individual; conditioning exercises-these would include various exercises to develop strength, endurance, speed, flexibility, agility, rhythm and coordination.

4. Yogic Exercises

Surya-namaskar; Sukhasana; Utkatasana; Parvatasana;
Janusirsasana; Pashchimottanasana;
Halasana; Bhujangasana; Shalabhasana; Shashankasana; Padmasana; Shavasana.

5. Combatives (Wrestling)

Repetition of skills learnt in the previous class; pinning holds; single arm roll; single arm roll one leg; double arm roll from underneath; cradle; rough lift; breakdown and counter for above holds; regular bouts.

6. Dagger Fight (Jambia)

Repetition of the strokes and defence skills learnt in the previous class; stroke to any of the body and defence; fight after dagger release; demonstration fight.

7. Judo

History and its development; rules of judo; conditioning; purpose and methods of Rehdori/Yakhoku Rensho; skills-eiani goshi (spring hip/throw), taio otoshi (body drop), koshi gurma (hip wheel), sotomaki korni (outside drop), ouchigari (major inside reap), ko uchigari (minor inside reap), escape to newaza, hadaka jime (bare handed chock), akutierijime (sliding lapel check), ude garrami and gatami (armlock), hand spring, counter techniques and contest.

8. Swimming (optional)

Repeat the skills learnt earlier; develop the skills of all the four strokes; simple ways of entry in the water (life saving); release from the victim; methods of resuscitation; simple methods of carry-head, cross-chest.

Note: Life saving methods should be taught only to highly skilled students.

School should develop special Physical Education programmes for children with special needs.

19

AIDS, HIV, STD, Drug Abuse and Smoking: Prevention/Treatment and Control

19.1 MEANING AND CAUSES OF AIDS, HIV, AND STD

Meaning of AIDS

- AIDS stands for Acquired (not inborn, passed from person to person, including from mother to baby); Immune (relating to the body's immune system, which provides protection from disease-causing germs); Deficiency (lack of response by the immune system to germs); Syndrome (a number of signs and symptoms indicating a particular disease or condition).
- AIDS is caused by a virus, called HIV (human immunodeficiency virus) which attacks and, over time, destroys the body's immune system (Fig. 19.1).
- A person has AIDS when the virus has done enough damage to the immune system to allow infections and cancers to develop.
- These infections, cancers etc. make the person ill and lead to his/her death. At present, there is no vaccine or cure for AIDS.
  AIDS was first detected in USA in 1987.

Meaning of HIV

- HIV, like other viruses, is very small, too small to be seen with an ordinary microscope. Viruses cause all sorts of diseases from flu (influenza) to herpes to some kinds of cancer.
- To reproduce, HIV must enter a body cell which in this case is an immune cell. By interfering with the cells that protect us against infection, HIV leaves the body poorly protected against the particular types of diseases which these cells normally deal with.
- Infections that develop because HIV has weakened the immune system are called "opportunistic infections". These include: respiratory infections e.g. tuberculosis: Pneumocystis carinii pneumonia; gastro-intestinal infections e.g. candidiasis in the mouth or diarrhoea; and brain infections e.g. toxoplasmosis or cryptococcal meningitis.
- Some people may also develop cancers, e.g. Kaposi sarcoma, a cancer which often causes red skin lesions.

Meaning of STD

— STD stands for sexually transmitted disease or diseases. Many different STD have been identified. The most common STD include: gonorrhoea, chlamydia, syphilis, trichomonas, genital warts, chancroid, genital herpes, hepatitis B and HIV infection.

— STD are caused by viruses, bacteria, and parasites. Viruses cause a number of STD, including genital warts, hepatitis B and genital herpes. Bacteria cause STD such as gonorrhoea and syphilis. Scabies, trichomonas and pubic lice are parasite STD.

— Most STD can be cured.

— Certain STD infections, if not treated soon enough, can lead to long-lasting health problems in both males and females, e.g. damage to the reproductive organs so that a woman is no/longer able to have children, cancer of the cervix, heart and brain damage, and possibly death.

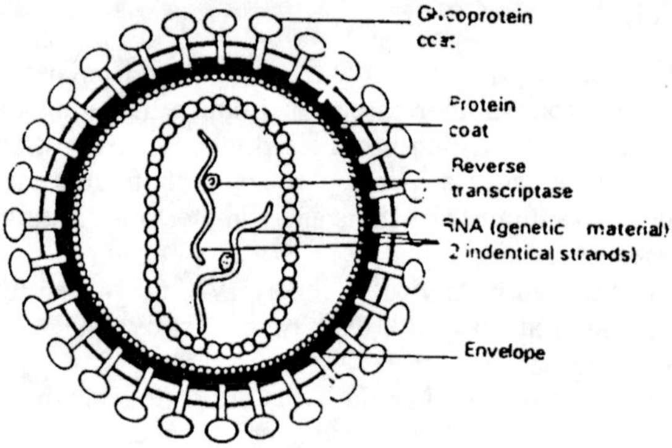

Fig. 19.1: Structural Model of AIDS Virus-HIV

19.2 MODE OF INFECTION/SPREAD

The infection from the AIDS virus occurs only:

- When a person has sexual contact with an infected person.
- By using contaminated needles and blades or razors. Even the smallest amount of infected blood left in the used needle or on blade can contain live AIDS virus which can be passed on to the next user.
- By blood to blood contact as in blood transfusion.
- From an infected mother to foetus (if a women is infected with the AIDS virus and becomes pregnant, she can pass the AIDS virus to her unborn child).

19.3 SYMPTOMS

People infected with AIDS virus remain apparently well even after infection. They may not show any physical symptoms of illness for a long time. When the AIDS virus enters the blood stream, it begins to attack certain white blood cells and destroys the protective immune system of the body. Once an individual is infected, the body may respond in many ways.

1. Swollen lymph nodes and fever. Some early signs may be persistent cough and fever associated with difficulty in breathing.
2. Decreased count of blood platelets. It leads to haemorrhage and fever. "Blood platelets help in blood clotting, hence decrease in the blood platelets count affects stool clotting."
3. Sweating at night and tiredness.
4. Weight loss and loss of appetite.
5. AIDS virus may attack nervous system causing damage to brain. It may lead to memory loss, loss of coordination, partial paralysis, mental disorder, and loss of ability to speak and think.
6. Since AIDS virus destroys the protective immune system of the body, the person becomes susceptible to other infections and diseases like pneumonia, tuberculosis and certain cancers.

19.4 HOW DOES ONE GET AIDS

— HIV can be found in body fluids like blood, semen, vaginal fluids, and breast milk.

— Any practice which allows the penetration of the virus from these fluids through the skin or mucous membranes and into the bloodstream of another person can cause HIV infection.

— The skin normally is a barrier to this type of penetration, but this barrier can be broken. Breaks in the skin include such minor things as cuts, abrasions, sores and ulcers.

HIV is transmitted from person to person in 3 major ways:

(i) When semen or vaginal fluid from an infected person comes in contact with the mucous lining (membranes) of the vagina, penis or rectum and the virus moves into the bloodstream.

(ii) When the skin is penetrated by a needle, or other skin-piercing instruments (e.g. razor or tattooing instrument), and that instrument has blood on it from an HIV-infected person. Sharing the same syringe and needle among infecting drug users is particularly risky for transmission. Any unsterile syringes and needles can transmit infection.

(iii) HIV may also be transmitted from on infected mother to her baby, either through the placenta before birth, during birth, or, in some cases, through breast milk after birth.

19.5 PREVENTION

So far there is no vaccine to prevent AIDS. However, it is preventable. It can be prevented by bringing changes in personal behavior. People can be educated on following points so as to help ignorant people from becoming victims.

1. Insist on the use of fresh new blade at the barbers shop. Common razor should not be used.
2. Only disposable needles and syringes should be used (whether it is for injection or testing of blood).
3. Sexual contact with unknown people should be avoided.
4. During any blood transfusion, blood transfused should be tested for HIV negative. (Currently in many countries as in USA all blood donors are initially screened for AIDS virus and proper precautions are taken before blood transfusion.)

19.6 FOCUS ON THE CONTROL OF STIGMA AND DISCRIMINATION: ROLE OF EDUCATION

Stigma and discrimination associated with AIDS/HIV are among the greatest barriers to prevent further infections. Stigma and discrimination occur worldwide. In India, a study conducted by ILO 'Socio-economic Impact of HIV/AIDS on People Living with HIV/AIDS and their families, (2003) revealed that as many as 70 percent of the respondents faced discrimination. Discrimination was more in the case of women than men. Education can play an important role in reducing stigma and discrimination-Twin pillars that support the continued spread of the disease. Education enhances the ability of individuals to keep themselves HIV free.

19.7 WHY AIDS EDUCATION OFTEN DENIED TO CHILDREN AND YOUNG PEOPLE

- The subject is considered too sensitive or controversial to be taught.
- It is difficult to find a place for AIDS education in an already overcrowded curriculum
- There may be only partial coverage in a country.
- Education may be limited to certain age groups
- Information on AIDS is taught, but not the behavioural skills needed for prevention and support.
- The curriculum is of poor quality.

19.8 WAYS TO OVERCOME THESE PROBLEMS.

- Creating a partnership between policy-makers, religious and community leaders, parents and teachers.
- Using this partnership to set sound policies on AIDS education
- Designing a good curriculum and/or a good exracurricular programme, adapted to local culture and circumstances.

19.9 SIGNIFICANT STATEMENTS ON HIV

A. True Statements

1. Once you are infected with HIV, you are infected for life.
2. It is not dangerous to hug a person with AIDS.
3. HIV may be passed from a mother to her new unborn or new born baby.

4. The time from getting HIV until a person becomes sick with AIDS can be as short as 6 months to as long as 10 years or more.
5. A person who has AIDS usually will die in 6 months to 2 years.
6. Delaying sex and not using infecting drugs are very good ways for teenagers to avoid getting HIV.
7. Condoms used properly and every time one has sexual intercourse protect from HIV and STD and prevent pregnancy.
8. A person with HIV who is not allowed to attend school is an example of discrimination.

B. Negative Statements (False) Statements about HIV

1. People infected with HIV are usually very thin.
2. You may get HIV from a mosquito bite.
3. HIV may be spread by wearing clothes from a person with AIDS.
4. A person may get HIV by donating blood.
5. A vaccine is available to protect people from the HIV virus.
6. A person who has tested positive for HIV is said to have AIDS.
7. You can tell if a person has HIV by how he looks.
8. Married people don't become infected with HIV.
9. If you only have sex with people who look healthy, you won't become infected by HIV.
10. There is no way to protect oneself from HIV/AIDS.
11. If you stick to one partner, you won't become infected with HIV.
12. You can't get HIV if you only have sex once or twice without a condom.
13. A condom can be safely reused.
14. People with AIDS should stay in hospitals, all the time, not at home.

(*Sources*: *School Health Education to prevent AIDS and STD*, UNAIDS, WHO and UNESCO, 1999).

19.10 DRUG ABUSE: HARMFUL EFFECTS AND PLAN FOR ACHIEVING SCHOOLS WITHOUT DRUGS

Meaning of Drug Abuse: Drug abuse may be defined as self-administration of a drug for non-medical reasons in quantities and frequencies which are most likely to impair an individual's ability to function effectively and which may cause emotional, physical and social harm.

Drug may be defined as any substance that when taken into the living organism may modify one or more of its functions.

Commonly used drugs are as follows:

1. Alcohol
2. Amphetamines and Cocaine
3. Babiturates
4. Cannabis ('hashish' and 'charas')
5. Heroin
6. Lysergic acid diethylamide (LSD)

Harmful Effects of Drugs

1. Erosion of Self Discipline and Motivation in Learning

Drugs erode the self-discipline and motivation necessary for learning. Pervasive drug use among students creates a climate in the schools that is destructive to learning.

Research shows that drug use can cause a decline in academic performance. This has been found to be true for students who excelled in school prior to drug use as well as for those with academic or behavioural problems prior to use. According to one study, students using marijuana were twice as likely to average D's and F's as other students. The decline in grades often reverses when drug use is stopped.

2. Truancy and Dropping Out of School

Drug use is closely tied to being truant and dropping out of school. High school senior who are heavy drug users are more than three times as likely to skip school as nonusers. About one-fifth of heavy users skip three or more school days a month, more than six times the truancy rate of nonusers. In a Philadelphia study, dropouts were almost twice as likely to be frequent drug users as were high school graduates; four in five dropouts used drugs regularly.

3. Victation of School Environment

Drug use is associated with crime and misconduct that disrupt the maintenance of an orderly and safe school atmosphere conducive to learning. Drugs not only transform schools into marketplaces for dope deals, they also lead to the destruction of property and to classroom disorder. Among high school seniors, heavy drug users are more than three times as likely to vandalize school property and twice as likely to have been involved in a fight at school or at work as nonusers. Students on drugs create a climate of apathy, disruption, and disrespect for others. For example, among tennage callers to a national cocaine hotline, 32 percent reported that they sold drugs, and 64 percent said that they stole from family, friends, or employers to buy drugs. A drug-ridden environment is a strong deterrent to learning not only for drug users but for other students as well.

4. Loss of Memory

Drugs can interfere with memory, sensation, and perception. They distort experiences and cause a loss of self-control that can lead users to harm themselves and others.

5. Interference in Brain's Ability

Drugs interfere with the brain's ability to take in, sort, and synthesize information. As a result, sensory information runs together, providing new sensations while blocking normal ability to understand the information received.

6. False Perception

Drugs can have an insidious effect on perception; for example, cocaine and amphetamines often give users a false sense of functioning at their best while on the drug.

7. Blurring Judgement and Vision

Drinking has acute effects on the body. The heavy, fast-paced drinking that young people commonly engage in quickly alters judgment, vision, coordination, and speech and often leads to dangerous risk-taking behaviour. Because young people have lower body weight than adults, youth absorb alcohol into their blood system faster than adults and exhibit greater impairment for longer periods of time.

8. Accidents and Injuries

Alcohol use not only increases the likelihood of being involved in an accident, it increases also the risk of serious injury in an accident because of its harmful effects on numerous parts of the body.

9. Dependency Element and Other Harmful Effects

Early alcohol use is associated with subsequent alcohol dependence and related health problems. Youth who use alcohol at a younger age are more likely to use alcohol heavily and to experience alcohol-related problems affecting their relationships with family and friends by late adolescence. Their school performance is likely to suffer, and they are more likely to be truant. They are also more likely to abuse other drugs and to get in trouble with the law, or, if they are girls.

A Plan for Achieving Schools Without Drugs

Parents

1. Teach standards of right and wrong, and demonstrate these standards through personal example.
2. Help children to resist peer pressure to use alcohol and other drugs by supervising their activities, knowing who their friends are, and talking with them about their interests and problems.
3. Be knowledgeable about drugs and signs of drug use. When symptoms are observed, respond promptly.

Schools

4. Determine the extent and character of alcohol and other drug use and monitor that use regularly.
5. Establish clear and specific rules regarding alcohol and other drug use that include strong corrective actions.
6. Enforce established policies against drug use fairly and consistently. Ensure adequate security measures to eliminate drugs from school premises and school functions.
7. Implement to comprehensive drug prevention curriculum for

kindergarten through grade 12, teaching that drug use is wrong and harmful, and supporting and strengthening resistance to drugs.

8. Reach out to the community for support and assistance in making the school's anti-drug policy and programme work. Develop collaborative arrangements in which school personnel, parents, school boards, law enforcement officers, treatment organizations, and private groups can work together to provide necessary resources.

Students

9. Learn about the effects of alcohol and other drug use, the reasons why drugs are harmful, and ways to resist pressures to try drugs.
10. Use an understanding of the danger posed by alcohol and other drugs to help other students avoid them. Encourage other students to resist drugs, persuade those using drugs to seek help, and report those selling drugs to parents and the school principal.

Communities

11. Help schools fight drugs by providing them with the expertise and financial resources of community groups and agencies.
12. Involve local law enforcement agencies in all aspects of drug prevention: assessment, enforcement, and education. The police and courts should have well-established relationships with the schools.

(Adapted from '*Schools without Drugs*' United States Department of Education.)

19.11 SMOKING, PREVENTION AND CONTROL

Smoking Trends among Adults

Smoking trends in Asia

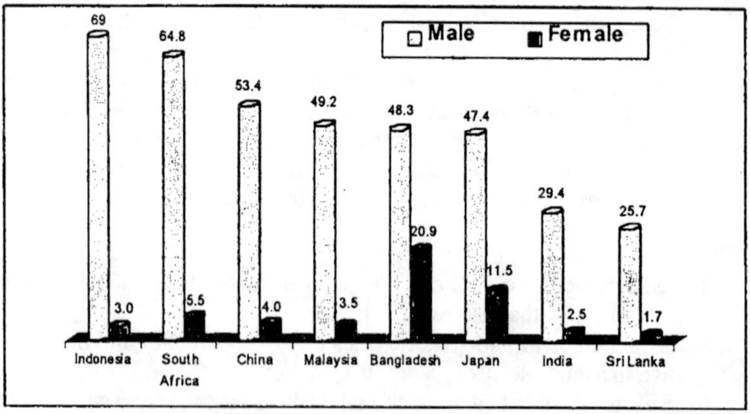

Anti-smoking campaigns are having meagre results in the continent's poorer countries

In India

Tobacco kills 8,00,000 persons each year, which means 2,200 deaths a day and 90 deaths per hour. And by the year 2020, 13.3% of all deaths in India will be solely due to tobacco.

Cigarette contains 10 mg of nicotine and one tenth of it is inhaled by smokers. An intake of 48-60 mg can even cause nicotine poisoning. In fact cigarette smoke contains more than 4,000 substances including nicotine, carbon monoxide, carcinogens, irritants and traces of other gases.

Source: WHO: *Hindustan Times*, May 24, 2004

Harmful Effects of Smoking

1. Sore throat. Coughing.
2. Increase in heart palpitation.
3. Burning sensation in eyes.
4. Prone to disease of cancer.
5. Decease in digestive power.
6. Loss of appetite.
7. Weakening brain and nervous system.
8. Skin diseases like allergy.
9. Weaking of will power.
10. Harmful effects during pregnancy.
11. Loss of Stamina.
12. Financial loss.

Prevention and Control of Smoking

Similar Plan of Action as in the case of Drug Addiction.

20

Mental Health and Sex Education

20.1 IMPORTANCE OF MENTAL HEALTH

It is of paramount importance to give due attention to the development of mental health of children. There are mental laws, principles and situations which help in the development of healthy minds of children. Any disregard to these may lead to mental disorders and conflict which ultimately may bring frustration, misery and unhappiness. Teachers in the school can play a major role in providing such an environment in which children develop healthy mental attitudes.

20.2 WHAT CONSTITUTES A HEALTHY MIND?

Following are the Characteristics of a Healthy Mind

(i) Appetite-normal
(ii) Calmness
(iii) Cheerful outlook
(iv) Good temper
(v) Habits-socially acceptable
(vi) Instincts well regulated
(vii) Philosophy of life-healthy
(viii) Physical vitality-normal
(ix) Receptivity to new ideas
(x) Sex consciousness-normal
(xi) Temper-good
(xii) Will-energetic and strong

Mental Disorders

(a) Undue anxiety
(b) Easily embarrassed in the presence of others
(c) Lack of courage
(d) Undeveloped habits and will
(e) Low intelligence
(f) Irritability
(g) Moodiness
(h) Depressed and pessimistic outlook

(i) Full of prejudice
(j) Abnormal interest in sex
(k) Bad temper

It is a matter of great relief that our educationists have begun to realise the importance of mental health. 'Feeling of insecurity' and the 'feeling of inferiority' are the two great enemies of mental health. A knowledge of mental hygiene helps us to kill these two demons. A psychological approach is needed. Our attempts should be to provide suitable emotional, physical and intellectual environment in which a child may have the 'feeling of security' and the 'feeling of equality'. He should feel that his personality is respected and given a suitable place.

Measures to Secure Mental Health

1. *Close Pupil-teacher Contacts*: The teacher should carefully observe the child in and outside the school and should know the child and his home conditions. This will development the feeling of 'oneness' in the mind of the child who feel that the teacher is interested in his welfare.

2. *Favourable Home and School Environment*: Unfavourable home and school environment leads to mental disorders. Parents should be guided to adopt good methods of upbringing. The child should be free from unsatisfactory relationships and strict discipline. Treatment by the parents should be just and impartial. Too much fondling may also lead to emotional maladjustment. The treatment of the teachers should be just and fair.

3. *Medical Examination*: There should be provision for the medical examination in schools and remedial measures be adopted to safeguard the health of the child. Defective physique becomes a contributory factor of mental disorders. Cases requiring special treatment should be sent to child guidance clinics.

4. *Intellectual Life of the School*: Sound methods of teaching suited to the individual needs of the child should be adopted. Activity Methods, e.g. Play-way, Project Method, etc. should be encouraged. Audio-visual aids develop interest in the lesson. Special time and attention must be devoted to weak students.

5. *Provision of Educational and Vocational Guidance Centres*: Schools should start such centres. It is not necessary to appoint full time psychologists in schools. Trained teachers may be asked to undergo short educational and vocational guidance course and the work of guidance be entrusted to them. For specially difficult cases, intelligence, aptitude and personality tests be conducted.

6. *Provision of Co-curricular Activities*: Properly planned activities are very helpful in providing much needed and useful training in civic sense. Sublimation of instincts is also achieved.

7. *Freedom and Self-discipline*: Unnecessary rules and regulations greatly

upset the mental equilibrium of the child. A child who breathes in an atmosphere of freedom develops initiative and courage. Severe punishments result in mental retardation. Let us be wise and remember the useful words of Hobbies, "The fool cannot be mended by flogging, and he who flogs is the greatest fool." Hence the right approach would be to give freedom to the child. A.S. Neill says, "We could abolish caning by an act of Parliament, but no act of Parliament can abolish the fear of teacher or a system."

8. *Teacher's Mental Hygiene and His Dynamic Personality*: The teachers should be mentally alert to develop mental alertness in the students. They should be painstaking, sympathetic, appreciative and trusting. They should not have any prejudice which may have an adverse effect on the emotional and intellectual conditions of children. They should have always higher ideals of life before them.

20.3 NEED AND IMPORTANCE OF SEX EDUCATION

Sex education scientifically imparted and rightly understood plays an important role in improving the quality of life. It has also a great bearing on understanding population dynamics.

There is need for soul searching why sex education, in spite of its importance has by and large remained neglected at various stages of education.

Talking about sex is ordinarily considered something secretive, sinful or not worthy of mention in sophisticated and so-called cultured society. People feel very much inhibited in talking about sex, but without sex education people cannot live a happy and well-adjusted life because it has been noted that many marital, emotional and mental problems among human beings occur as a result of the misdirection and wrong understanding of the sex urge. Alva Myrdal has observed: "In general more wholesome attitudes towards sex questions will not be created until they are discussed openly and as a matter of fact phenomena." Children ask questions about sex as the subject fascinates them and it is our answer and the way we give them that plays an important part in forming their future attitudes towards sex. Frank and honest response can help them to develop a healthy outlook. Prof. Uday Shankar is of the firm opinion, "Population education without sex education is ridiculous as the 'how' of population control cannot be answered without sex education. Sex education is no imposition, it concerns a vital matter in which children are interested. Interest in sex is instinctive and starts from early infancy. In pre-adolescent boys and girls, the sex drives further. Enlightenment on sexual matter is to be given intelligently and pleasantly but gradually and methodically. There need not be 'sex teacher' or 'sex classes' like history or geography classes. There cannot be any general rules as to the time and place or manner of imparting sex education. Through the teaching of general science, biology, physiology or hygiene, a good deal of physiological knowledge about sex differences and about animal and human reproduction, involving all the process of mating, fertilisation pregnancy or birth can be imparted."

20.4 MEANING OF SEX EDUCATION

Sex education may be defined education for the protection, preservation, improvement and development of an ideal family, enjoying quality of life with an understanding of human reproduction as its integral and inseparate part, based on accepted ethical values regarding sex.

20.5 AIMS AND OBJECTIVES OF SEX EDUCATION

In his publication '*School Health Education*' Prof. H.F. Kilander has given the following aims and objectives of Sex and Family Life Education.

1. Developing normal and wholesome attitudes and ideals in relation to sex and family.
2. Developing desirable habits, behaviour and conduct in accordance with such attitudes and ideals.
3. Acquiring knowledge and understanding of matters related to the physiology of human reproduction and related aspects of life.
4. Correcting and alleviating some of the common worries and misconceptions in the field of sex adjustment.
5. Contributing to the emotional and social growth of the individual so that he can function adequately as a member of a family, and eventually as a parent.

20.6 AGENCIES OF SEX EDUCATION

Agencies of Sex Education

(1) The home and family

(2) The church

(3) The community or the society

(4) The school

20.7 ROLE OF TEACHERS AND PARENTS IN SEX EDUCATION

An attempt is made here to suggest guidelines and measures which should be adapted to provide sex education as it plays an important role in controlling population and ensuring quality of life. Simple questions of children are sometimes difficult to answer. When a child is very young one can make up any number of stories to convince him, but young boys and girls are keen to seek answers in-depth. They may investigate, adventure or explore to find out the answers. Sometimes they find them out the wrong way.

In a growing child there is development of the body about which he is confused, there is also growth of mind and awareness. Their quest for information needs to be addressed. Nothing is better than direct communication between parents and youngsters.

Parents and teachers should not be thrown off guard by awkward questions. They should have the presence of mind and answer some questions in fun and some in utter seriousness so that the child gets a positive signal that though sex is a private thing there is nothing shameful about it. In this way children are able to confide in their teacher and parents and look upon them as friends, which in turn keeps the teachers and parents informed about children's activities.

20.8 GUIDELINES FOR IMPARTING SEX EDUCATION IN SCHOOL

D. Oberteuffer has suggested the following guidelines in his book '*School Health Education*' for imparting sex education in schools.

One. Sex education include biological, moral, psychological and social aspects of sex because sex education involves the whole person and the whole of his life style.

Two. Sex education is concerned with both facts and values.

Three. While planning sex education, individual differences and the developmental needs of children should be kept in view.

Four. Teachers who impart sex education should be carefully selected and properly prepared for this task.

Five. Instructional methods of imparting sex education should be based on sound psychological principles.

Six. Sex education should be a continuous process.

Seven. Correlation and integration approach should be followed in imparting sex education.

Eight. There should be continuous evaluation.

20.9 METHODS OF IMPARTING SEX EDUCATION

Following points in this respect deserve attention:

1. Documentaries can be shown to teenagers in schools. If made properly they can easily hold their attention.
2. Plays, seminars and workshops organised in school can also achieve this goal where the situations leading to problems can be dealt with.
3. Students can directly approach the teachers or counsellors to have their confessions cleared.
4. Students can be asked to write questions on a paper without revealing their identity so that shy students can have answers too. Teachers may be cautioned that they are likely to receive a few embarrassing, awkward and may be downright obscene questions or drawings which ought to be taken with an equanimity of mind and understanding. This may need discussion as to why some children do so. Over-suppressed, overexposed or those children who are denied recognition by their

parents of their sexual development may do these kinds of things and therefore are required to be reassured and gently pushed in the right direction.

5. Specially trained teachers, separately for girls and boys in the initial phase, or doctors can be called to give a few lectures to remove misconceptions and doubts.
6. Good books are best companions at all ages. They can serve the purpose of educating a curious mind where parents feel restricted in communicating with the child. This way parents also know that whatever a child is reading is healthy and beneficial for him.
7. Guidance from an elderly relative can also serve the very important role of a confidante to the teenager in the family.

20.10 SUGGESTIVE SYLLABUS AND ACTIVITIES FOR SEX EDUCATION

The following syllabus and activities regarding sex education cover different stages/years, content and approach.

It is obvious that in the school, elementary stage is the starting point for imparting sex education to students. Contents and approaches should be graded.

(*Source*: *Sex Education: How and Why*. Association for Social Health in India, New Delhi, 1976).

Objectives	*Content*	*Approach*
Age Group 1-3 Years		
1. To create a sense of discipline and orderliness with regard to personal cleanliness and regularity about toilet and feeds.	1. Developing love and affection for parents among children.	1. With love and affection.
2. To develop affection for parents and other family members, and obey to do small errands for them.	2. Training infant for observing regularity in feeding and for toilet.	2. Training children to observe regularity and prevent unsocial attitudes developing.
3. To develop proper behaviour towards other children and learn to be affectionate and helpful to them.	3. Prevent habit of beating and misbehaving with other children.	3. Observe non-discriminatory attitude towards all children.
	4. Ensuring that there is no discrimination in treatment between boys and girls.	4. Making the child happy and contented by careful handling, giving feeds regularly and playing with it sometime. Children must not be neglected.

(*Contd.*)

(*Contd.*)

Objectives	*Content*	*Approach*
Age Group 3-5 years		
1. To observe all stated objectives for 1-3 year group.	1. Continue as for 1-3 group.	1. Same as for 1-3 year group.
2. To encourage the child to play with other children and to develop team spirit and a sense of equality among boys and girls.	2. Prevent habit of beating or pinching weaker children.	2. Prevent children to develop aggressive attitudes towards others by strong admonition. Parents themselves should serve as a model by creating harmony and peace among all family members.
3. To show the difference between boys and girls from differences in clothing, modes of dress.	3. Prevent habit of fondling genitals by covering the parts with dress, and diverting its mind by others activities.	3. Parents should develop a habit of imparting information naturally and truthfully. They must not say anything beyond child's understanding.
	4. Inform about sex differences if the child desires to know, naturally and without emotion.	4. Picture of happy family showing father, mother, a girl and a boy.
	5. Emphasising that father and mother are necessary for a complete happy family.	
Age Group 6-8 Years		
1. To practise all mentioned objectives for earlier group.	1. Same as for earlier group.	1. Same as stated earlier to daily experience.
2. Need of both father and mother for the babies to give them food, love and to look after them till they grow up.	2. Importance of both male and female for care and growth of babies.	2. Draw child's attention to sexes in different domestic animals, and in human being.
3. To love father and mother as essential for their existence and security.	3. No discrimination in treatment between boys and girls in the family or in the school.	3. Do not give much of anatomical details at this stage and subject may be presented in the form of stories.
4. To foster proper attitudes in boys of regard and helpfulness towards girls.	4. Emphasising equality of intelligence and proficiency in various activities both in school and at home, among boys and girls.	4. Encourage boys to help mothers and sisters in household work, so that they may not consider such work to be unmanly.

(*Contd.*)

(*Contd.*)

Objectives	*Content*	*Approach*
	5. Boys being physically stronger must always help girls and weaker children whenever necessary, in day-to-day life both in the school and at home.	5. Emphasise ties of love and security between parents and children.
		6. Children should not be left alone.
9-11 Years of Age		
1. To develop a healthy attitude towards sex.	To develop comradeship and respect towards the opposite sex.	Brothers and sisters should help each other in studies, household work and play as equals.
2. To observe that all living organisms, whether of animal or vegetable kingdom, multiply for continuance of species.	Trees and plants multiplying in gardens and jungles. Dogs, cats producing litters and increasing in numbers.	Birth of a baby brother or sister in the family.
3. To inform about different modes of multiplication of a cell.	Sexual and sexual modes of cell multiplication.	Show cell multiplication of both types in pictures or diagrams as in the book.
4. To correlate male and female parts of a flower for producing a new plant.	Fertilisation of an egg-cell in a flower.	Exhibit male and female parts of a flower and mode of fertilisation as per book diagram.
5. To tell that fertilisation of the egg-cell of the female by a seed from the male.	Growth of an animal from a single fertilised cell.	Importance of both male and female in producing offspring.
6. To tell that in human beings male seed comes from the father and egg cell from the mother.	Both daddy and mummy are necessary for the birth and care of the baby.	Explain in a question-and-answer session. No anatomical details are to be shown. Exhibit diagrams of fertilisation as in the book.
7. To inform about development of a fertilised egg cell either inside or outside the mother's tummy in different animals.	Development of the fertilised egg-cell outside the female's body as in the case of birds, and inside the mother's tummy as in human female, cows, bitches, cats, etc.	Child should be shown egg of birds, as an example of development outside the body, and explained how to recognise a pregnant cow, bitch or a woman as an example of development inside the tummy of the mother.

(*Contd.*)

(*Contd.*)

Objectives	*Content*	*Approach*
Pre-Adolescent 11-13-14 Years Age Group		
1. To impart knowledge about body development.	Sudden spurt of body growth. In girls, appearance of pubic hair, breasts and enlargement of hips. Onset of menstruation. In boys appearance of pubic hair and enlargement of testicles and penis, night pollutions.	Correlating with other subjects like Nature Study, Biology and Physiology. Illustrate body growth in boys and girls with the aid of pictures, diagrams and charts, as in the book. Discussing this subject separately with boys and girls, to encourage questions and answers by each group.
2. To help in emotional and social adjustment of adolescents.	Clarifying that such body changes are natural at this age and do not produce any disease.	Reassuring the youngsters that the body changes should not cause any anxiety. These prepare them for becoming grown up men and women.
3. To develop desirable health habits.	Observing personal cleanliness and to help parents as desired by them. Develop proper regard and understanding for the opposite sex.	Should spend spare time in healthy outdoor games. Girls may like indoor pursuits such as games, sewing, knitting, etc.
4. To enable pre-adolescents to understand and control sexual tendencies.	Dangers of sex relations at this stage must be emphasised as youngsters are too immature and not in a position to undertake any responsibility. Youngsters must be warned about the adverse psychological and physical effects of the habit of masturbation.	Youngsters should be guided to make suitable friends. Show films or slides of boys and girls playing separately or in mixed groups under supervision. Discussion in question-answer session in separate groups of boys and girls about masturbation.
5. To develop correct behaviour towards members of the opposite sex.	Arrange joint programmes of boys and girls under supervision as mentioned in the book.	By arranging games, plays, dramas, debates and other cultural programmes under direct guidance.
Adult-Above 18 years of Age		
1. Recapitulate all items of 14-18 year group.		
2. To develop knowledge about population explosion.	Present rate of population growth and its impact on the life of the country and urgent need to check the same.	Charts to show the trend of birth and death rates as compared with more advanced countries.
3. To tell that planned parenthood is a means to check population growth.	Different methods. Use of contraceptive devices.	Advantages and disadvantages of the different methods of contraception.